THE CAMBRIDGE BIBLE COMMENTARY
NEW ENGLISH BIBLE

GENERAL EDITORS

P. R. ACKROYD, A. R. C. LEANEY, J. W. PACKER

GENESIS 12–50

GENESIS 12–50

COMMENTARY BY

ROBERT DAVIDSON

*Professor of Old Testament Language and Literature
University of Glasgow*

CAMBRIDGE UNIVERSITY PRESS

CAMBRIDGE

LONDON . NEW YORK . MELBOURNE

Published by the Syndics of the Cambridge University Press
The Pitt Building, Trumpington Street, Cambridge CB2 1RP
Bentley House, 200 Euston Road, London NW1 2DB
32 East 57th Street, New York, NY 10022, USA
296 Beaconsfield Parade, Middle Park, Melbourne 3206, Australia

First published 1979

Printed in Great Britain at the
University Press, Cambridge

Library of Congress cataloguing in publication data

Bible. O.T. Genesis, XII–L. English. New English.
  Genesis 12–50.
  (The Cambridge Bible commentary, New English Bible)
  Bibliography: p.
  Includes index.
  1. Bible. O.T. Genesis XII–L – Commentaries.
I. Davidson, Robert. II. Title. III. Series.
BS1235.D3   1978   222'.11'077   78-12892
ISBN 0 521 22485 3   hard covers
ISBN 0 521 29520 3   paperback

GENERAL EDITORS' PREFACE

The aim of this series is to provide the text of the New English Bible closely linked to a commentary in which the results of modern scholarship are made available to the general reader. Teachers and young people have been especially kept in mind. The commentators have been asked to assume no specialized theological knowledge, and no knowledge of Greek and Hebrew. Bare references to other literature and multiple references to other parts of the Bible have been avoided. Actual quotations have been given as often as possible.

The completion of the New Testament part of the series in 1967 provided the basis upon which the production of the much larger Old Testament and Apocrypha series could be undertaken. With the publication of this volume and its companion (*1 and 2 Esdras*), the whole series is complete. The welcome accorded to the series in its earlier stages was an encouragement to the editors to follow the same general pattern throughout, and an attempt has been made to take account of criticisms which have been offered. The Old Testament volumes have included the full footnotes provided by the translators, since these are essential for the understanding of the text.

Within the severe limits imposed by the size and scope of the series, each commentator has attempted to set out the main findings of recent biblical scholarship and to describe the historical background to the text. The main theological issues have also been critically discussed.

Much attention has been given to the form of the volumes. The aim is to produce books each of which will be read consecutively from first to last page. The introductory material leads naturally into the text, which itself leads into the alternating sections of the commentary.

The series is accompanied by three volumes of a more general character. *Understanding the Old Testament* sets out to provide the larger historical and archaeological background, to say something about the life and thought of the people of the Old Testament, and to answer the question 'Why should we study the Old Testament?' *The Making of the Old Testament* is concerned with the formation of the books of the Old Testament and Apocrypha in the context of the ancient Near Eastern world, and with the ways in which these books have come down to us in the life of the Jewish and Christian communities. *Old Testament Illustrations* contains maps, diagrams and photographs with an explanatory text. These three volumes are designed to provide material helpful to the understanding of the individual books and their commentaries, but they are also prepared so as to be of use quite independently.

With the completion of this project, there are many whom the General Editors wish to thank. The contributors who have produced their manuscripts and co-operated willingly in revisions suggested to them must clearly be mentioned first. With them we thank the succession of members of the staff of the Cambridge University Press, especially Mr Roger Coleman, but above all Mr Michael H. Black, now Publisher at the Press, who has joined so fully in the planning and development of the series and who has been present at most of the editorial meetings from the initiation of the project to its conclusion.

P.R.A.
A.R.C.L.
J.W.P.

EDITOR'S PREFACE

This companion volume to *Genesis 1–11* has for various reasons been delayed long beyond my intentions and expectations. I owe a particular debt of gratitude to the General Editors for their unfailing patience, understanding, and perseverance. They have done far more than could reasonably have been expected of them to ensure that the volume has appeared even at this late date. Their comments, always helpful and often invaluable, have added much to the commentary; for the inadequacies which remain I alone am responsible. I am grateful to my wife Elizabeth for living through the frustrations of this commentary, and for help in preparing the index, and to my student Gerritt Singgih for help with proof-reading.

R.D.

CONTENTS

THE FOOTNOTES TO THE
N.E.B. TEXT

The footnotes to the N.E.B. text are designed to help the reader either to understand particular points of detail – the meaning of a name, the presence of a play upon words – or to give information about the actual text. Where the Hebrew text appears to be erroneous, or there is doubt about its precise meaning, it may be necessary to turn to manuscripts which offer a different wording, or to ancient translations of the text which may suggest a better reading, or to offer a new explanation based upon conjecture. In such cases, the footnotes supply very briefly an indication of the evidence, and whether the solution proposed is one that is regarded as possible or as probable. Various abbreviations are used in the footnotes.

(1) Some abbreviations are simply of terms used in explaining a point: *ch(s).*, chapter(s); *cp.*, compare; *lit.*, literally; *mng.*, meaning; *MS(S).*, manuscript(s), i.e. Hebrew manuscript(s), unless otherwise stated; *om.*, omit(s); *or*, indicating an alternative interpretation; *poss.*, possible; *prob.*, probable; *rdg.*, reading; *Vs(s).*, Version(s).

(2) Other abbreviations indicate sources of information from which better interpretations or readings may be obtained.

Aq.   Aquila, a Greek translator of the Old Testament (perhaps about A.D. 130) characterized by great literalness.

Aram.   Aramaic – may refer to the text in this language (used in parts of Ezra and Daniel), or to the meaning of an Aramaic word. Aramaic belongs to the same language family as Hebrew, and is known from about 1000 B.C. over a wide area of the Middle East, including Palestine.

Heb.   Hebrew – may refer to the Hebrew text or may indicate the literal meaning of the Hebrew word.

Josephus   Flavius Josephus (A.D. 37/8–about 100), author of the *Jewish Antiquities*, a survey of the whole history of his people, directed partly at least to a non-Jewish audience, and of various other works, notably one on the *Jewish War* (that of A.D. 66–73) and a defence of Judaism (*Against Apion*).

Luc. Sept.   Lucian's recension of the Septuagint, an important edition made in Antioch in Syria about the end of the third century A.D.

Pesh.   Peshitta or Peshitto, the Syriac version of the Old Testament. Syriac is the name given chiefly to a form of Eastern Aramaic used by the Christian community. The translation varies in quality, and is at many points influenced by the Septuagint or the Targums.

Sam.   Samaritan Pentateuch – the form of the first five books of the Old Testament as used by the Samaritan community. It is written in Hebrew in a special form of the Old Hebrew script, and preserves an important form of the text, somewhat influenced by Samaritan ideas.

Scroll(s)   Scroll(s), commonly called the Dead Sea Scrolls, found at or near Qumran from 1947 onwards. These important manuscripts shed light on the state of the Hebrew text as it was developing in the last centuries B.C. and the first century A.D.

Sept.   Septuagint (meaning 'seventy'); often abbreviated as the Roman numeral (LXX), the name given to the main Greek version of the Old Testament. According to tradition, the Pentateuch was translated in Egypt in the third century B.C. by 70 (or 72) translators, six from each tribe, but the precise nature of its origin and development is not fully known. It was intended to provide Greek-speaking Jews with a convenient translation. Subsequently it came to be much revered by the Christian community.

Symm.   Symmachus, another Greek translator of the Old Testament (beginning of the third century A.D.), who tried to combine literalness with good style. Both Lucian and Jerome viewed his version with favour.

Targ.   Targum, a name given to various Aramaic versions of the Old Testament, produced over a long period and eventually standardized, for the use of Aramaic-speaking Jews.

Theod.   Theodotion, the author of a revision of the Septuagint (probably second century A.D.), very dependent on the Hebrew text.

Vulg.   Vulgate, the most important Latin version of the Old Testament, produced by Jerome about A.D. 400, and the text most used throughout the Middle Ages in western Christianity.

[...]   In the text itself square brackets are used to indicate probably late additions to the Hebrew text.

(Fuller discussion of a number of these points may be found in *The Making of the Old Testament* in this series.)

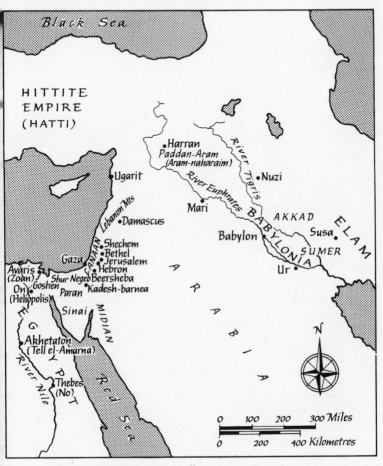

1. The ancient Near East, illustrating Genesis 12–50

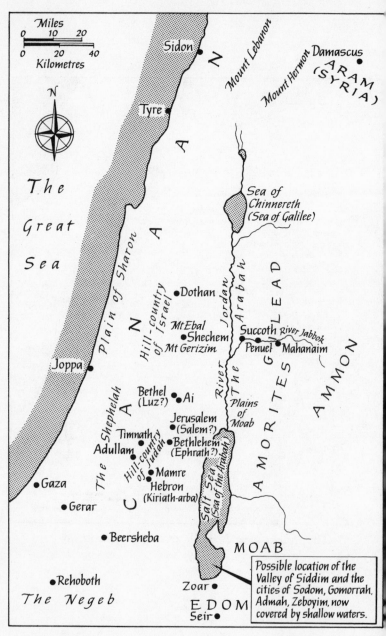

Miles
0   10   20
0   20   40
Kilometres

N

The

Great

Sea

Sidon

Tyre

Mount Lebanon

Mount Hermon Damascus

ARAM
(SYRIA)

C A N A A N

Sea of
Chinnereth
(Sea of Galilee)

Plain of Sharon

Dothan

Mt Ebal
Shechem
Mt Gerizim

Hill-country
of Israel

River Jordan

The Arabah

G I L E A D

Succoth *River Jabbok*
Penuel Mahanaim

Joppa

The Shephelah

Bethel
(Luz?)   Ai

Jerusalem
(Salem?)

Timnath
Adullam   Bethlehem
(Ephrath?)

Hill-country
of Judah

Mamre
Hebron
(Kiriath-arba)

Plains
of
Moab

A M O R I T E S

A M M O N

Gaza

Gerar

Beersheba

Salt Sea
(Sea of the Arabah)

M O A B

Possible location of the
Valley of Siddim and the
cities of Sodom, Gomorrah,
Admah, Zeboyim, now
covered by shallow waters.

Rehoboth

The Negeb

Zoar

E D O M
Seir

2. Palestine, showing places mentioned in Genesis 12–50

GENESIS

BEHIND THE BOOK

We are accustomed to think of a book as a document written
by one person. The author's name appears on the cover; the
date and place of publication are given. Often in a 'Foreword'
the author briefly explains for the benefit of his readers the
purposes of the book. To understand Genesis, and many other
books in the Old Testament, we have to think our way into a
very different world.

Writing was known and used from an early age in Israel
and the wider world of the ancient Near East. Religious
texts, letters, political treaties survive in written form from a
period before Israel as a nation ever existed. Writing, however, was a specialized skill, the possession of the few. It was
neither the only, nor the most important, way of preserving
and handing on information. Many of the traditions of a
people, their early tribal or national history, the stories and
legends about their ancestors, were handed down *orally*,
by word of mouth, from father to son, on the lips of tribal
bards and poets. Much of the material now in the book of
Genesis must have begun life in this way. Such traditions
would have a generally accepted outline and content long
before they were ever transferred into writing. Think of how
unchangeable certain well-known stories become in the
mind of a young child before ever the child can read or write.
Even after such traditions did exist in writing, for most
people they would continue, living within the community,
in oral form.

But when and why were such traditions first committed to
writing? There is good reason to believe that, as far as Israel

I

was concerned, the answer lies in the foundation and establishment of the united Hebrew kingdom under David and
Solomon in the tenth century B.C. Jerusalem then became the
political and religious capital of a people who were riding on
the crest of military success and economic growth. Just as
England in the reign of Queen Elizabeth I produced great
writers who reflect the confidence and vigour of the age,
so in Israel of the tenth century B.C. the new national self-
consciousness found an outlet in writers who recorded the
events of the day in narratives such as those now found in
2 Sam. 9 – 1 Kings 2, and gave literary form to the traditions of the past. Contemporary confidence and hopefulness
for the future drew strength from the recording of a past in
which the purposive hand of God was seen at work, from the
beginning. It has also been argued that the written record did
not really come into its own until some four centuries later
when Jerusalem was overrun by the Babylonians. The last
remnant of the once powerful Hebrew kingdom had finally
collapsed. With the breakdown of community life the continuing stream of oral tradition was in danger of disappearing.
The need for written preservation of the nation's past thus
became acute. Whenever it happened – and both periods
may have made their contribution to the book of Genesis –
no one was concerned to preserve the names of the earliest
Hebrew historical writers.

THE SOURCES OF THE BOOK

Traditionally in Jewish circles Genesis is called *Bereshith*,
'In the beginning'. This follows the common practice of
designating a book by its opening word or phrase. The title
'Genesis' comes from the Septuagint (LXX), the Greek translation of the Old Testament. Further information about the
Septuagint will be found in 'The footnotes to the N.E.B.
text', see p. xi. In Greek *genesis* means 'origin', 'beginning',
or 'creation'. *Bereshith* is the first of five books called in

2

ancient tradition 'the (five) books of Moses'. These five books, Genesis, Exodus, Leviticus, Numbers, Deuteronomy – often referred to in modern discussion as the Pentateuch (the five books) – constitute for the Jew *TORAH*, the most important part of the Old Testament. 'Law' is the conventional translation of *TORAH* but perhaps 'revelation' would be nearer the mark. *TORAH* means the instruction or teaching concerning God's purposes and demands which had been given to Israel, according to tradition, through Moses. It was early recognized that to attribute the whole of Genesis–Deuteronomy to Moses was impossible. The obituary notice of Moses in Deut. 34 is an obvious case in point. But if not Moses, then who? Is it indeed possible to think of any one author as responsible for Genesis–Deuteronomy, or even for Genesis alone?

Three examples from Genesis will illustrate the problem.

(i) Anyone who reads from the beginning of Genesis must become aware that the character of the writing changes between verses 4 and 5 of chapter 2. The N.E.B. indicates this by putting a major division of the text at this point. The opening chapter is hymn-like, formal in structure, very carefully schematized. Certain key words and phrases occur again and again, e.g. 'God said...and so it was...Evening came, and morning came.' The deliberate use of repetition is well illustrated in 1: 27: 'So God created man in his own image; in the image of God he created him; male and female he created them.' Throughout the chapter the language used to describe God is very restrained and dignified. From the words 'When the LORD God made earth and heaven', however, there is a marked difference. Here is narrative, simple yet remarkably vivid. Certain of the key words and phrases of chapter 1 have disappeared. Instead of 'created' we find 'formed' (2: 7). The language used to describe God is much more homely. He is like a potter forming man; he breathes into man's nostrils the breath of life (2: 7). He plants a garden (2: 8). He is heard 'walking in the garden at the time of the evening breeze' (3: 8). At precisely the point where such changes begin, a new name for God appears; he is now the LORD God.

(ii) Turn to the flood story in Gen. 6–8. Here again the story as it now lies before us is a curious patchwork of passages which use different divine names. In 6: 5–8; 7: 1–5 and 8: 20–2 it is the LORD; but elsewhere it is God, with the exception of 7: 16 where within one verse both God and the LORD appear. Furthermore, what the LORD says to Noah in 7: 1–5 is curiously like a repetition of what God says to Noah in 6: 9–22. Repetition is common enough in ancient narrative texts, but there also seem to be contradictions. In 6: 19 Noah is told by God to take with him into the ark living creatures of every kind, 'two of each kind, a male and a female'. In 7: 2, however, the LORD orders Noah to take with him into the ark 'seven pairs, male and female, of all beasts that are ritually clean', acceptable for use in sacrifice, 'and one pair, male and female, of all beasts that are not clean; also seven pairs, male and female, of every bird'. Again in 7: 4 the LORD warns Noah that he will send 'rain over the earth for forty days and forty nights', and this is described as happening in 7: 12. In 7: 24, however, God thinks of Noah 'when the waters had increased over the earth for a hundred and fifty days'.

(iii) Three times in Genesis a very similar story is told of how one of the patriarchs passes off his wife as his sister. Twice the narratives feature Abraham and his wife Sarah, once when they were in Egypt (12: 10–20), once when they were resident in Gerar under the jurisdiction of King Abimelech (20). The third narrative concerns Isaac and his wife Rebecca; again the third party involved is Abimelech, the Philistine king of Gerar (26: 1–11).

It is possible to lift each of these stories out of its present context in the book of Genesis and to regard each as giving us a different version of one traditional theme. There is no mistaking the basic similarity in outline of the three stories, but equally striking are the marked differences in presentation and emphasis.

For Gen. 12: 10–20 the story is the thing. It is told directly and briefly with remarkable restraint. No attempt is made either to defend or to explain Abraham's action in passing off Sarah as his sister. Indeed Sarah's entry into Pharaoh's household proves a good investment for Abraham. Pharaoh treated Abraham well because of her, and Abraham came to possess sheep and cattle and asses, male and female slaves, she-asses and camels (12: 16). Little or nothing is revealed of the inner feelings of the principal characters; no explanation is given as to how Pharaoh knew that the troubles which befell him and his household were linked to Sarah. There is but one mention of the LORD in the story (12: 17).

Gen. 20 is much more circumstantial and discursive. The characters are more sharply delineated. Religious and moral issues predominate. Much of the story revolves round two dialogues, the first between God and Abimelech (20: 3–7) – God appearing to Abimelech who claims to have acted 'with a clear conscience and in all innocence' (20: 5). God exonerates him and warns him. Abraham is described as 'a prophet' who will intercede on behalf of Abimelech (20: 7; cp. verse 17). In his confrontation with Abimelech, Abraham justifies his action on several grounds:

(i) he was living as an alien in what he believed to be a God-less community (verse 11);

(ii) he hadn't actually told a lie: 'She is in fact my sister, she is my father's daughter though not by the same mother; and she became my wife' (verse 12);

(iii) Sarah (Sarai) in true wifely obedience had long since agreed to connive at the subterfuge (verse 13).

The narrative is even concerned to vindicate Sarah's involvement in the incident (20: 16).

Gen. 26: 1–11 is in some respects the furthest removed from the story outlined in Gen. 12. Here nothing in fact happens to Rebecca. There is therefore no need for God either to exonerate or to warn. Abimelech himself discovers the true relationship between Isaac and Rebecca and after a somewhat testy interview with Isaac warns his people against laying a finger on either this man or his wife. Isaac's action in passing off Rebecca as his sister is explained but on a much more human level, 'he was afraid to say that Rebecca was his wife in case they killed him because of her: for she was very beautiful' (26: 7). In one respect, however, this version is the most explicitly integrated into the broad religious interest of the book of Genesis. Why did Isaac choose to remain in the Philistine city of Gerar during a period of famine? He was remaining faithful to a God-given promise of blessing, a promise which first appears in Gen. 12: 1–3 and echoes and re-echoes across the narrative (see commentary, pp. 97, 127, 147). In reading Genesis, therefore, we come across differences in style and vocabulary, different names for God, contradictions, overlapping yet varied stories. Such features occur at point after point throughout the first five books of the Old Testament. How do we account for them?

As traditional stories, laws and customs, were handed down orally within the Hebrew community, they would naturally tend to reflect the interests of the groups in which they circulated. Thus basically the same story told in a community in the northern part of the country and in a community in the southern part of the country would, in its detail, have a northern or southern colouring. The sanctuary at Bethel would keep alive one set of stories linking the patriarchs with the Bethel sanctuary, while the priests at Hebron would have their own traditions linking these same patriarchs with Hebron. Similarly we would expect material which circulated in priestly circles as part of the continuing theological education of the priesthood to have a rather different character from the popular stories recounted by tribal bards. There are those who believe that the books of Genesis, Exodus, Leviticus and Numbers are, in their present form, the result of a gradual, centuries-long coalescing of such traditions from many different circles. The priestly editors,

who gave final shape to the whole during the breakdown of
the nation's life in the period of the Babylonian exile, preserved the character of the different traditions, and made
little attempt to eliminate discrepancies between them.

Deuteronomy, now usually separated from the first four
books of the Old Testament, shares a common outlook and
judgement on events with the succeeding historical narratives
in Joshua, Judges, 1 and 2 Samuel and 1 and 2 Kings, and
is best considered in relationship with them. It seems likely,
however, that in the composition of Genesis, Exodus,
Leviticus and Numbers there was an intermediate stage at
which the material existed in three independent, written
sources, each with its own literary characteristics of vocabulary, style and interest. These sources may be represented by
the symbols J, E and P. J, the earliest of these written sources,
ninth or tenth century B.C., comes from Judah, in the South.
It consistently refers to God as YHWH, four Hebrew consonants, traditionally but quite erroneously rendered into
English as *Jehovah*. Most English versions translate YHWH
as 'the LORD'. *Yahweh* is probably as near as we can get to the
pronunciation of what for the Hebrews was the personal
name of their God, a name which became so sacred that the
custom grew up of not pronouncing it. When a Jew came to
the letters *YHWH* in the sacred text he substituted the word
Adonai ('my lord'). The form *Jehovah* arose through inserting
the vowels from *Adonai* into the consonants *YHWH*. J first
appears in the Genesis narrative at 2: 5. E, probably a century
later, comes from Israel (Ephraim) the northern part of the
divided Hebrew kingdom. From Genesis 15 onward it
provides a narrative parallel in many respects to J, although
it is not always easy to distinguish the two sources. It is
possible to regard E as a revision of J. The latest of the documents, P, possibly fifth-century B.C., is a priestly source which
provides the framework within which the other two sources
find their place. The character and interests of P are well
exemplified by the hymn of creation in Genesis 1: 1–2: 4.

It must be admitted that this is a hypothesis. No one has

ever seen a document labelled J or E or P; but it is a hypothesis which provides a reasonable explanation for the problems which confront us when we study in detail the material in Genesis–Numbers.

As outlined above the hypothesis is the logical outcome of over 200 years of intensive study of the Pentateuch, study which received its classical formulation in the nineteenth century in the 'Documentary hypothesis'. Fuller discussion of the sources and further information about this hypothesis will be found in the introductory volume to this series, *The Making of the Old Testament*, pp. 60–5.

Two points about this hypothesis are worth stressing:

(i) The date assigned to a source does not decide the antiquity of the material within that source, nor is it a sure guide to the religious value of that material. It is demonstrable, for example, that P, the latest source, contains very old material, particularly in its description of religious rites which tend to be tenaciously conservative. Likewise the fact that J is held to be the earliest source does not mean that it is the most primitive or naïve in outlook. No one who carefully reads the J story of the Garden in Genesis, chapters 2 and 3, should be in any doubt that it is the work of one who is not only a skilled literary artist but also a profound thinker.

(ii) J, E and P must not be thought of as free-lance authors. As we have seen, they inherit, and are the servants of, their people's religious and historical traditions. This does not mean that they have no originality. Far from it. They reshape what they inherit. They link together once independent traditions in such a way that they take on new meaning.

Let us return for a moment to Gen. 12: 10–20. Whatever the original form or meaning of this story of Abraham deceiving Pharaoh into believing that Sarah was his sister, not his wife – and there have been many attempts to peer into the dim past of the story – there is little doubt that it stands in its present context because the J narrator is using it to communicate a deep-held conviction. One of the dominant themes in the patriarchal stories is that of a promise made by God, the promise of a land, the promise of a great nation to spring from Abraham, the promise of a blessing radiating outwards from this people into the wider world. The theme is first heard in Gen. 12: 1–3; the first glimpse of its fulfilment is then given in 12: 4–9. Abraham journeys to the promised land and lays claim to it by there building an altar to the LORD. But there is to be no easy or quick fulfilment of this promise. In Gen. 12: 10–20 famine drives Abraham out of this promised land down into Egypt. Abraham has apparently so little faith in God's ability to fulfil his promise that he has to resort to deceit to save his own skin. As Sarah disappears into Pharaoh's household the reader is left wondering how the promise of a great nation sprung from Abraham can ever be fulfilled. God's promise is thus seen to be a promise under threat both from external circumstances such as famine and from the fickleness of those who ought to have believed in the promise and lived by it. This was a painful truth that men of faith had to face at many points in Israel's history. It has shaped the present form of the Genesis narrative.

Genesis preserves many of the old religious and historical traditions of Israel. In the form in which they now lie before us they have been reminted by some of Israel's greatest thinkers; no less great because they are anonymous, known to us only by the symbols J, E and P.

THE PROBLEM OF HISTORICITY

The material in Genesis falls into two main sections:

(i) chapters 1–11 which in a previous volume we have thought of as 'the Prologue' to Israel's faith;

(ii) chapters 12–50 which in general terms we may call 'the patriarchal traditions'.

The two sections are linked by the list of the descendants of Shem (11: 10–26) and the list of descendants of Terah (11: 27–32). When we come to the story of Abraham in Gen. 12

we are handling a tradition in which many Old Testament passages see the beginning of the life of the Hebrew people: 'Long ago your forefathers, Terah and his sons Abraham and Nahor, lived beside the Euphrates, and they worshipped other gods. I took your father Abraham from beside the Euphrates and led him through the length and breadth of Canaan' (Josh. 24: 2, 3). During desolate days of exile a prophet cries to his people:

> 'look to the rock from which you were hewn,
> to the quarry from which you were dug;
> look to your father Abraham
> and to Sarah who gave you birth'
> (Isa. 51: 1, 2; cp. Ps. 105: 6, 9–11).

In what sense can we claim that this tradition has firm roots in events that once happened? Was Abraham a man who one day packed his bags in north-west Mesopotamia and set off westwards to the land of Canaan? Can we accept as historical all the incidents which Genesis narrates concerning this man; and is the same to be said about Isaac, Jacob and Joseph? It must be frankly admitted that we move here into a realm where certainty is elusive and where sharply divergent views are held by scholars. If, for example, as we have argued, J, E and P are not merely free-lance authors but the servants of the religious and historical traditions of the community which nurtured them, what can we say about such traditions before they were woven into our present narratives in Genesis? Suppose a man called Abraham did travel west to Canaan some time in the first half of the second millennium B.C.: between that event and the earliest strand in the narrative as it now lies before us there lies a period of somewhere between 600 and 1000 years. Genesis itself is quite clear on this point. Gen. 36: 31–9, for example, quotes a list of the kings who ruled over Edom before there were kings in Israel, a meaningless comment except from the pen of a man who knew something of the history of the Hebrew monarchy which first emerged in the tenth century B.C. What was happening to the traditions concerning Abraham during this lengthy period? Doubtless they were being told and retold, handed down by word of mouth from generation to generation. But why were some stories about this man remembered, when much else has obviously been forgotten? Why are some incidents in his life treated at length while others are mentioned only in the passing? Presumably certain things were remembered and handed on because they were believed to be of continuing interest and importance to the community which looked back to Abraham as its pilgrim forefather. But to what extent has the tradition been modified and reshaped to reflect the beliefs and concerns of this community? The developing religious and moral sensitivity of the community would be one way of accounting for some of the differences between Gen. 12: 10–20 and Gen. 20. May not legend have so embellished and veiled historical memory that the outline of what once happened must for ever escape us? If a historical kernel becomes increasingly difficult to find, why not go further and claim that Abraham probably never existed: is he but the projection into the past of an ideal ancestor – every Hebrew as he would have wished himself to be? Would it matter if this were so? Certainly it is ludicrous to claim that the material in Gen. 12–50 would only be of value if it could be proved to be historical in a coldly factual sense. Legend and poetry may communicate a rich experience of life. Yet we must ask, 'Is there a historical basis for these narratives?' Amid many unanswered and perhaps some unanswerable questions certain broad guidelines may be suggested:

(i) The narratives as they now lie before us in Genesis do not merely reflect the social customs or religious outlook of the times in which the final editors of the stories lived. There are many features of the narrative which are difficult to reconcile with what was later accepted practice in Israel. To take one or two examples: In Gen. 28: 22 Jacob takes the stone which he had used as a pillow and sets it up as a sacred pillar, *maṣṣebah* (cp. 35: 13, 14). Because of the close associations that it came to have with Canaanite religious practices, however, the erection of such a *maṣṣebah* is rigorously prohibited in Torah (cp. Deut. 16: 22; Exod. 23: 24).

According to Gen. 20: 12 one of the reasons Abraham gives for passing Sarah off as his sister, is the fact that she is his half-sister, his father's daughter but not by the same mother. But such a marriage was forbidden in later Israel (Lev. 18: 9; 20: 17; Deut. 27: 22).

Or consider the way in which God is described or addressed. In addition to 'the LORD' and the common word for God, there is a series of titles or names which are found only in the patriarchal narratives or elsewhere in the Old Testament only in well-defined liturgical contexts which seem to reflect early tradition. Thus Melchizedek appears in Gen. 14 as a priest of *El-Elyon*, God Most High, and Abraham identifies the LORD with this *El-Elyon* (14: 22). In Gen. 17 God identifies himself to Abraham as *El-Shaddai*, God Almighty. At Beersheba, Abraham invokes the LORD as *El-'Olam*, the everlasting God (21: 33). At Shechem Jacob erects an altar and calls it *El-Elohey-Israel*, God the God of Israel (33: 20). All such names are built up from the general word for God in use among Semitic-speaking peoples, *El*, and a descriptive word or phrase. Another series of titles speaks of a relationship between God and the heads of the patriarchal families. These are 'the God of the fathers', 'the God of Abraham', 'the Fear of Isaac' (31: 42), 'the Strong One (or 'Champion') of Jacob' (49: 24).

In these and other respects the narratives reflect a tradition which was remembered and preserved across the centuries, rather than a reading back of later ideas into an earlier age.

(ii) We cannot evaluate the patriarchal traditions properly unless we draw upon the ever-increasing knowledge of the world of the ancient Near East which comes to us from extra-biblical sources. This helps to fill in the political, social and cultural background against which the patriarchal narratives must be read. The information is cumulative and comes from many different sources. Let us take a brief look at two.

(a) In northern Syria on the right bank of the Euphrates stands the modern town of Tell Hariri. Since 1933 a series of excavations have confirmed that it is the site of ancient Mari (see map, p. xiii), an important community with a Semitic-speaking population which reached its zenith under King Zimri-lim before being destroyed by the Babylonians in the eighteenth century B.C. From Zimri-lim's palace have come over 25,000 tablets belonging to the state and city archives. Some of the diplomatic correspondence in this collection throws a flood of contemporary light upon social and political events in north-west Mesopotamia. Names which appear in the patriarchal narratives are closely paralleled at Mari. Many of the personal names which appear in the list of the sons of Terah in Gen. 11: 27–32 appear as place-names in the Mari texts. Several letters refer to people called the *Beni-iamina* 'sons of the right hand' (i.e. the south), with which we may compare the biblical name Benjamin. There is mention of trouble from predatory *habiru*, a name which appears in texts from many different places in the ancient Near East, and which has been linked with biblical 'Hebrew'. It is important not to overplay such evidence. Many of the names which occur in the Mari texts are not confined to these texts nor to the period of the early second millennium B.C., but when the Genesis tradition traces Abraham back to the same area in north-west Mesopotamia from which the Mari texts come, it seems unwarranted scepticism to deny that the tradition has firm roots in history.

(b) About 9 miles (14½ km) south-west of modern Kirkuk there existed by 1500 B.C. a community known as Nuzi (see map, p. xiii). From Nuzi have come some 4000 tablets from the fifteenth and early fourteenth centuries B.C., written in Akkadian by a non-Semitic-speaking people whose mother tongue was Hurrian. In addition to administrative documents there are family and legal texts which are of great interest for the light they shed on social customs and conventions. In particular it has been claimed that these Nuzi texts provide clear parallels to certain customs found in the patriarchal narratives but not easily intelligible in the light of later Hebrew law-codes, for example:

the wife–sister relationship in Gen. 12: 10–20;

Abraham's adoption of a slave as his heir (15: 2–4);

a childless wife providing her husband with a substitute slave-wife (16: 3; 30: 3);

the tangled relationship between Jacob and Laban (29–32);

Rachel's stealing of her father's household gods (31: 19).

Again we need to exercise caution. The parallels between the Nuzi texts and patriarchal customs are not always as exact as has sometimes been claimed. But at least Nuzi does provide us with a series of datable texts from a single site which offer first-hand evidence of ancient Near Eastern family customs and legal contracts which may help us to understand similar customs in the patriarchal traditions. Further information about Mari and Nuzi will be found in *The Making of the Old Testament*, pp. 8–11 in this series. We shall have occasion at various points in the commentary to consider the relevance of information from Mari, Nuzi and other ancient Near Eastern sites. To claim that the information from such sites proves the historicity of the patriarchal narratives far outruns the evidence. The information from Mari and Nuzi, for example, comes from different centuries and from different areas of Mesopotamia.

THE CHARACTER OF THE PATRIARCHAL NARRATIVES

Although there is little reason to deny an historical kernel to the patriarchal traditions, before we attempt to use archaeological and other extra-biblical evidence to fill in the picture, we must ask, 'What kind of material is preserved in these

14

traditions?' There is no point, for example, in attempting to use archaeology to prove the historical reliability of a narrative which was never intended to be read as history.

(i) With the exception of Gen. 14, a chapter which confronts the historian with complex and perplexing problems (see commentary, pp. 32–40) the narrative is not concerned with history in the sense of the record of significant public events in the life of a community or nation. The narrative focusses on the life of a family or a group of families. It is concerned with the trivialities and with the significant events of family life, with domestic tensions, love and hatred, quarrels and reconciliation, the hopes and fears of ordinary people. It is a very human story. This is 'the Abraham saga' in much the same sense as we talk about Galsworthy's 'Forsyte saga', the story of the Forsyte family over several generations.

(ii) Although Gen. 12–50 seem to recount one connected story, a close examination reveals that this story is in fact constructed out of a series of somewhat loosely connected bits and pieces. The earliest J source has already fitted many of the pieces together, but rough edges remain and it is possible to break the pieces apart. When we do this we find that the separate bits and pieces can be classified into certain well-defined categories or types of stories which occur in the traditions and literature of many peoples. Many of these stories contain an aetiological element – from the Greek word *aitia* meaning 'cause'. They provide answers to many of the questions that people naturally ask about life and about the world in which they live. There are stories which explain the origin of well-known place-names. There are two accounts of the origin of the place-name Beersheba, one linking it with a pact between Abraham and Abimelech (21: 31), the other linking it with a pact between Isaac and Abimelech (26: 33). Incidents are recounted to explain why a particular well was called Beer-lahai-roi (16: 13–14), why another place was called Zoar (19: 22), and why a place formerly known as Luz was called Bethel (28: 19).

There are stories explaining the origin and meaning of

personal names. There are two accounts why Jacob was called Israel, one linking it with the strange nocturnal experience that befell Jacob at Peniel (32: 28), the other linking it with the sanctuary at Bethel (35: 10). Explanation is given why Abram's name was changed to Abraham (17: 5), and Sarai's to Sarah (17: 15), and why Rebecca's twins were called Esau and Jacob (25: 25–6). The explanations given in most cases have little scientific linguistic basis; they move on the level of popular story-telling.

There are cult legends which explain why God was worshipped at a particular place. This is usually linked with God's appearing to one of the patriarchs at that place. The classic illustration of this type of story is Gen. 28: 10–22 which explains why Bethel was an important centre of worship in Israel. Gen. 18 may originally have been another such cult legend accounting for the sacred site of Mamre near Hebron. It is reasonable to assume that such legends were part of a living tradition carefully cherished by the priests at these shrines.

There are stories associated with striking features in the landscape. Lot's wife turned into a pillar of salt (19: 26) may have been told in explanation of a strange rock formation. Then there was that well-known cairn of stones east of Jordan (31: 45–54) which was called by a number of names.

The fact that a story contains an aetiological element does not in itself decide the value of the story as history. I know a country churchyard which contains a large boulder called the devil's thumb stone. It is so called because a hollow in the stone is supposed to be the imprint of the devil's thumb. Several different stories are current why and how and when the devil hurled this stone. Although the stories are all obviously popular inventions, nevertheless various versions of the story are linked to events that did happen in the life of the community.

Other stories seem to reflect tribal history. This is particularly true of some of the material in the Jacob–Esau

16

stories which reflect relationships between the Israelites and Edomites. God's word to Rebecca, as she awaits the birth of twins, points to this:

> 'Two nations in your womb,
>> two peoples, going their own ways from birth!
> One shall be stronger than the other;
>> the older shall be servant to the younger' (25: 23).

We have been sampling some of the rich and varied fare now to be found in Gen. 12–50. It is as if we had wandered into the workshop of a stained-glass-window artist. Spread out before us are many pieces of glass, differing in colour and shape. Pick up one piece and it is possible to become so fascinated by its texture, shape and colour as to forget that it finds its true beauty and significance only when it is fitted into place in the window which the artist is creating. So we may study the bits and pieces that go to make up Gen. 12–50 – and a fascinating study it can be – but we must never forget that they find a new and added significance as part of the whole.

(iii) What is the design of the window into which the many-hued, varyingly shaped pieces fit? Listen to the opening words of Gen. 12: 'The LORD said to Abram, "Leave your own country, your kinsmen, and your father's house; and go to a country that I will show you"' (12: 1). And the last words, the death-bed words, of Joseph: 'I am dying; but God will not fail to come to your aid and take you from here to the land which he promised on oath to Abraham, Isaac and Jacob.'... 'When God thus comes to your aid, you must take my bones with you from here' (50: 24, 25). Here is a pattern of God's initiative. He comes to Abraham, he calls him, and at the end there is the firm conviction that this God will still come to this man's descendants to fulfil a promise once made. The whole of Gen. 12–50 is a confession of faith in *this* God, the God who comes, who calls, who promises. This has two consequences:

(a) It spells out the limitations of the help that historical and archaeological discoveries can provide in the understanding of Gen. 12–50. In the light of what we know from extra-biblical sources, it is perfectly reasonable to think of an Aramaean like Abraham moving westwards from north-west Mesopotamia towards Canaan early in the second millennium B.C. But even if by some strange chance it could be documented from extra-biblical sources that a man called Abraham made just such a journey, we would still be left asking 'Why did he make this journey?' Many reasons, political, social and personal could be suggested. What archaeological discoveries could never prove or disprove is that such a journey was made by a man who heard the LORD say to him ' "Leave..."'...And so Abram set out as the LORD had bidden him' (12:1, 4). This is no bald chronicling of an event: it is an interpretation of an event in terms of God's initiative, an interpretation which can only be a confession of faith by a man who believed in just such a living, active God. Apart from such an interpretation the event in itself would have been wholly insignificant in the eyes of those who shaped the Genesis traditions.

(b) The narratives were always to be understood in Israel as an invitation to pilgrimage. The Genesis traditions have one foot in the past – this we need not doubt. Indeed just because this is a story which deals with the ultimate mystery of faith, it is hard to see why this mystery should not have first grasped a man called Abraham. But they also have one foot in the present of each succeeding generation in Israel. Because men of faith in Israel in every generation believed in this God who comes, who calls and who promises, they identified with Abraham, Isaac and Jacob, they journeyed in faith, they cheated and lied and wrestled with God, they learned to live with promises still unfulfilled. This was their story. If we share their faith, it can still be ours.

*   *   *   *   *   *   *   *   *   *   *   *   *

Abraham and Isaac

THE CALL OF ABRAHAM

THE LORD SAID TO ABRAM, 'Leave your own coun- **12**
try, your kinsmen, and your father's house, and go to
a country that I will show you. I will make you into a great 2
nation, I will bless you and make your name so great that
it shall be used in blessings:

> Those that bless you I will bless, 3
> those that curse you, I will execrate.
> All the families on earth
> will pray to be blessed as you are blessed.'

✶ The J tradition begins by outlining the basic theme which
is to run right through Gen. 12–50. It is the story of a man,
of a nation, on pilgrimage. The LORD takes the initiative. He
calls Abram to leave the known security of his settled life,
and to go out in faith into the unknown, 'to a country that
I will show you' (verse 1). Only when Abram has made the
venture of faith and reached Canaan is he told, 'I give this
land to your descendants' (verse 7).

2. The call is backed up by a promise in which there are
several closely interwoven strands; the promise of a land, the
promise of *a great nation*, the many descendants who are to
issue from Abram, the promise of a great *name*, a reputation
which will lead to what happens to Abram being desired by
others for themselves.

This promise is to be heard again by Abram at various
crisis points in his life when events seem to cast doubt on the
possibility of its fulfilment (13: 14–15; 15: 5–7; 22: 17); it is
repeated to the other patriarchs, to Isaac (26: 24), to Jacob

(28: 3–4, 13–15; 32: 12; 35: 11–12) and to Ephraim (48: 19). The way in which the promise shapes and dominates the narrative is clearly seen in the structure of chapter 12:

1–3. the promise is given.

4–9. the promise begins to be fulfilled. Abram begins to settle in the land, the claim that this is his God-given land symbolized by the building of an altar to the LORD at Shechem and Bethel.

10–15. the promise is threatened. Abram is forced to leave the land. His childless wife Sarai passes into Pharaoh's household. What hope now is there of future greatness?

16–20. the promise is protected. The LORD shields Sarai.

it shall be used in blessings: this translation – the more traditional rendering is 'you will be a blessing' – links the phrase closely with the concluding words of the next verse.

3.   *All the families on earth*
     will pray to be blessed as you are blessed.

The form of the verb 'to bless' used here and in 18: 18 and 28: 14 should probably be rendered in the same way as the slightly different form of the word in 22: 18 and 26: 4. The appropriate meaning is best illustrated by Gen. 48: 20 where Israel blesses Ephraim and Manasseh in the following way:

> 'When a blessing is pronounced in Israel,
> men shall use your names and say,
> God make you like Ephraim and Manasseh'

The promise looks forward to the day when other peoples will say 'God make us like Abram and his descendants.' Since God controls all history, for good (blessing) and for evil (curse) the life of other peoples is bound up with what God does in and through Abram.*

ABRAM SETS OUT

And so Abram set out as the LORD had bidden him, and 4
Lot went with him. Abram was seventy-five years old
when he left Harran. He took his wife Sarai, his nephew 5
Lot, all the property they had collected, and all the
dependants they had acquired in Harran, and they started
on their journey to Canaan. When they arrived, Abram 6
passed through the country to the sanctuary at Shechem,
the terebinth-tree of Moreh. At that time the Canaanites
lived in this land. There the LORD appeared to Abram 7
and said, 'I give this land to your descendants.' So Abram
built an altar there to the LORD who had appeared to him.
Thence he went on to the hill-country east of Bethel and 8
pitched his tent between Bethel on the west and Ai on the
east. There he built an altar to the LORD and invoked the
LORD by name. Thus Abram journeyed by stages towards 9
the Negeb.

* 4. Briefly and without comment Abram's response to
God's call and promise is noted. He *set out as the LORD had
bidden him*. No attempt is made to explain or to justify this
breaking of family ties. It is an example of that obedient faith
which is one of the marks of Abram's life. *Lot went with him:*
the relation between Abram and his nephew Lot (see 11: 27),
which is to be further developed in chapters 13 and 19
probably contains material reflecting the continuing contacts
between the Hebrews and their Transjordanian neighbours
the Moabites and the Ammonites, who in 19: 30–8 are depicted
as the descendants of Lot. *seventy-five years old when he left
Harran:* this, if correct, means that Abram left Harran in
north-west Mesopotamia (see map p. xiii) sixty years before
the death of his father Terah (see 11: 26 and 32). From the

way in which chapter 11 ends, however, it would be more natural to assume that Abram's departure from Harran was subsequent to his father's death as Acts 7: 4 states. The Samaritan text solves this problem by reducing Terah's life span to 145 years (see note on 11: 32).

5. *his wife Sarai:* for this form of the name, later to become Sarah, see note on 17: 15. *dependants:* literally 'persons'; the reference is probably to slaves. *Canaan:* the name Canaan, which first appears in texts of the fifteenth century B.C., probably signified originally the Phoenician coast. It may be related to a word for 'purple', a purple dye, extracted from sea-shells, being highly valued in the ancient East, though doubts have been expressed about this interpretation.

6. *Shechem:* one of the most important Canaanite towns in the central hill country. It occupied a strategic site between Mount Ebal and Mount Gerizim at a point where north-south and east-west roads met (see map p. xiv). There is archaeological evidence of substantial settlement in Shechem by the end of the nineteenth century B.C. *the terebinth-tree of Moreh:* the terebinth is a small tree, usually between 15 and 20 feet ($4\frac{1}{2}$ to 6 m) in height. From its trunk turpentine is drawn. This particular terebinth marked a holy place which had been recognized as such centuries before Abram and which continued in use long after the Hebrews took over Shechem (see Josh. 24: 26). *Moreh* means teacher, and the teaching given at this sacred tree would be some declaration of the will of the deity, perhaps given in oracular form.

7. *There the LORD appeared to Abram:* this is the first in a series of theophanies, some of them closely associated with already existing sacred sites (see 18: 1; 28: 10–22). God appears usually to speak to Abram or his descendant a word confirming some aspect of the promise theme. Note the simple directness and reserve of the narrative. The LORD appears, but no further attempt is made to describe what exactly happened.

22

The land to which Abram comes is already in the possession of other peoples: 'At that time the Canaanites lived in this land' – a comment presupposing the standpoint of a later writer. It is also a land marked by the sacred sites of another religion. This is the land now declared to be the land the LORD gives to Abram's descendants; and in the midst of the symbols of another religion the first symbol of Abram's faith is erected. He *built an altar there to the LORD.*

8. Abram now moves south some 20 miles (32 km) along the central highlands to *Bethel*, 'the house of God', and to *Ai* which means 'ruin'. The importance of Bethel as an early Canaanite religious centre is well attested archaeologically. Ai was probably already an abandoned site in Abram's day. Although nothing is said of any theophany to Abram at or near Bethel, Genesis records just such a theophany to Jacob at Bethel (see 28: 10-22). The opposite side of the coin to God's appearing at a sacred site is the worshipper's approach to God. So between Bethel and Ai Abram built an altar and *invoked the LORD by name*, that is, he worshipped the LORD. Again the narrative gives no indication of what the content of such an act of worship might have been.

The picture that we get of Abram in this section is that of a semi-nomad, whose natural wealth is in herds and flocks, moving, according to the seasonal availability of pasturage, along the well-watered central highlands and then down into the Negeb (verse 9), the southern-most part of the country.*

THE DESCENT TO EGYPT

There came a famine in the land, so severe that Abram 10
went down to Egypt to live there for a while. When he 11
was approaching Egypt, he said to his wife Sarai, 'I know
very well that you are a beautiful woman, and that when 12
the Egyptians see you, they will say, "She is his wife";
then they will kill me but let you live. Tell them that you 13

are my sister, so that all may go well with me because of
14 you and my life may be spared on your account.' When
Abram arrived in Egypt, the Egyptians saw that she was
15 indeed very beautiful. Pharaoh's courtiers saw her and
praised her to Pharaoh, and she was taken into Pharaoh's
16 household. He treated Abram well because of her, and
Abram came to possess sheep and cattle and asses, male and
17 female slaves, she-asses, and camels. But the LORD struck
Pharaoh and his household with grave diseases on account
18 of Abram's wife Sarai. Pharaoh summoned Abram and
said to him, 'Why have you treated me like this? Why
19 did you not tell me that she is your wife? Why did you
say that she was your sister, so that I took her as a wife?
20 Here she is: take her and be gone.' Then Pharaoh gave his
men orders, and they sent Abram away with his wife and
all that he had.

* The relationship between this story and the similar
stories in chapter 20 and 26: 1–11 has already been discussed
(see pp. 4–6). Its position here serves to underline a tension
which is ever present in the Genesis narratives. No sooner is
Abram in the land which the LORD promises to his descendants than he has to leave it through circumstances beyond his
control. The promise which seemed on its way to fulfilment,
now has a large question-mark placed beside it.

10. The move to Egypt is prompted by *famine in the land*.
Egypt had one great advantage over Canaan. Its prosperity
was based upon the dependable annual rise and fall of the
Nile, not upon seasonal rains which in Canaan might fail
and give rise to drought conditions. In going to Egypt
Abram was doing what many other semi-nomads did in
similar conditions. A report drawn up by an Egyptian frontier
official in the middle of the fourteenth century B.C. deals

with just such a situation. Writing to his superior, he says, 'We have finished letting the Bedouin tribes of Edom pass the fortress, to keep them alive and to keep their cattle alive' (cp. *A.N.E.T.* (see p. 317), p. 259).

11–20. This story of Abram and Sarai in Egypt is tantalizingly brief and leaves many unanswered questions. Sarai is said to be *a beautiful woman* (verse 11), yet if the chronological information given at 17: 17 is correct she must have been at the time of the journey to Egypt at least seventy years old. When we come to verse 17 no indication is given as to how Pharaoh knew that the *grave diseases* which struck his household were connected with Sarai's presence. Abram appears in the story in a very unfavourable light. In order to save his own skin, he tells Sarai to pass herself off as his sister. A marriage contract with a beautiful woman could always be arranged through her brother; a husband might have to be liquidated. The lie pays dividends. As a result of Sarai's presence in *Pharaoh's household* he receives *sheep and cattle and asses, male and female slaves, she-asses and camels* (verse 16). When faced with Pharaoh's indignant accusation, *Why did you not tell me that she is your wife?* he makes no reply – the silence of guilt. The parallel story in Gen. 20 tries to blunt the cutting edge of Abraham's deceit in several ways (see pp. 80–3), particularly by claiming that Sarah was in fact Abraham's half-sister: 'she is my father's daughter though not by the same mother; and she became my wife' (20: 12). Later Jewish sources continue the process of Abraham's rehabilitation. The Genesis Apocryphon, one of the Dead Sea Scrolls, justifies Abram's lie in advance by a God-sent dream, insists that Sarai was taken from Abram by force, and describes Abram's response to this as one of earnest prayer. Some modern scholars believe that behind the present form of the story lies the memory of a type of marriage involving a wife–sister relationship which is vouched for in the Nuzi texts (see pp. 13-14). Such a marriage in which the wife has the legal status of sister is said to be a particularly solemn and binding relationship. It has, however, been seriously questioned whether the Nuzi texts do in fact provide evidence for such a wife–sister status. In any case no one reading the story in Genesis would be likely to interpret it in such terms, since the plot hinges on the fact that Sarai, as Abram's sister, could not be his wife. The narrative has no interest in defending Abram. The threat to the promise comes not only from external circumstances but from the human frailty of the man to whom the promise has been made. Yet even here the providence of God is at work. Sarai is restored to Abram and they are deported from Egypt (verse 20). ✳

ABRAM AND LOT – THE QUARREL

13 Abram went up from Egypt into the Negeb, he and his
2 wife and all that he had, and Lot went with him. Abram
3 was now very rich in cattle and in silver and gold. From the Negeb he journeyed by stages to Bethel, to the place between Bethel and Ai where he had pitched his tent in
4 the beginning, where he had set up an altar on the first
5 occasion and had invoked the LORD by name. Now Lot was travelling with Abram, and he too possessed sheep
6 and cattle and tents. The land could not support them both together; for their livestock were so numerous that they
7 could not settle in the same district, and there were quarrels between Abram's herdsmen and Lot's. The Canaanites and the Perizzites were then living in the land.
8 So Abram said to Lot, 'Let there be no quarrelling between us, between my herdsmen and yours; for we are close
9 kinsmen. The whole country is there in front of you; let us part company. If you go left, I will go right; if you go
10 right, I will go left.' Lot looked up and saw how well-watered the whole Plain of the Jordan was; all the way to

Zoar it was like the Garden of the LORD, like the land of
Egypt. This was before the LORD had destroyed Sodom
and Gomorrah. So Lot chose all the Plain of the Jordan 11
and took the road on the east side. Thus they parted
company. Abram settled in the land of Canaan; but Lot 12
settled among the cities of the Plain and pitched his tents
near Sodom. Now the men of Sodom were wicked, great 13
sinners against the LORD.

✻   1–5. Abram now retraces his steps back up through the
Negeb to the sacred site between Bethel and Ai (see map
p. xiv). His wealth has increased because of his stay in Egypt.
He is now *very rich* not only *in cattle* but also *in silver and gold*.
This in contrast to Lot whose wealth is purely pastoral, *sheep
and cattle and tents*.

6–7. The quarrel which breaks out between Abram's herdsmen and Lot's is the kind of quarrel which must often have
arisen between semi-nomadic pastoral groups, a quarrel over
grazing rights. One area can only support a limited number of
sheep and cattle. In Gen. 36: 6–7, Jacob and Esau part company for a similar reason, although there is no mention of
any quarrel. The problem is intensified by the fact that Abram
and Lot are not the only people living off the land. As the
writer living long after the events described notes: *The
Canaanites and the Perizzites were then living in the land*. In
certain places the term *Canaanites* is used as a general term
for all the peoples living in the land of Canaan; in other
places it appears as the name of one among peoples who make
up the pre-Hebrew inhabitants of the land. The longest
such list, containing eleven names, including Canaanites and
Perizzites, occurs in 15: 19–21. *the Perizzites:* the name may
mean 'hamlet dwellers' as opposed to those who live in
fortified cities – a closely related word in Deut. 3: 5 being
translated by the N.E.B. as 'open settlements'. They always

appear linked with the Canaanites (see 34: 30) or as one item in a longer list.

8. Abram takes the initiative in suggesting that such a quarrel between kinsmen is unseemly. As the elder of the two he might have staked his claim first; instead he defers to Lot.

9. *If you go left, I will go right: left* and *right* may be used here simply to indicate opposite directions, or, as frequently elsewhere in the Old Testament, *left* may mean north and *right* south. *The whole country is there in front of you:* from near Bethel it is possible to look out over a wide sweep of the countryside, including the 'Plain (literally circle) of the Jordan' as far south as what is now the southern end of the Dead Sea.

10. *all the way to Zoar:* the site of Zoar is probably near the south-eastern end of the Dead Sea. It was the town to which Lot fled when Sodom and Gomorrah were destroyed (see chapter 19). *like the Garden of the LORD:* the fertility of the Jordan valley is compared to that of the Garden of Eden or Delight described in Gen. 2: 9 as full of beautiful and fruitful trees. The anonymous prophet who wrote Isa. 40–55 speaks of the LORD renewing his devastated homeland in the following terms:

'turning her wilderness into an Eden,
    her thirsty plains into a garden of the LORD'
                  (Isa. 51: 3).

like the land of Egypt: for Egypt as synonymous with fertility see the note on 12: 10. *This was before the LORD had destroyed Sodom and Gomorrah:* this editorial comment suggests that the incident was believed to have taken place before the Dead Sea existed and that what is now the Dead Sea was, prior to the geological upheaval which destroyed Sodom and Gomorrah, the southern end of the Plain of Jordan known, according to 14: 3, as the valley of Siddim. The site of biblical Sodom now lies under water near the southern end of the Dead Sea.

13. Lot settles near Sodom in what he believes to be the most fertile part of the country; it is also the most wicked. The *men of Sodom were wicked, great sinners against the LORD:* a comment which prepares the way for the story of the destruction of the cities of the plain in chapter 19.   ✻

PROMISE RENEWED

After Lot and Abram had parted, the LORD said to 14 Abram, 'Raise your eyes and look into the distance from the place where you are, north and south, east and west. All the land you can see I will give to you and to your 15 descendants for ever. I will make your descendants count- 16 less as the dust of the earth; if anyone could count the dust upon the ground, then he could count your descendants. Now go through the length and breadth of the land, for 17 I give it to you.' So Abram moved his tent and settled by 18 the terebinths of Mamre at Hebron; and there he built an altar to the LORD.

✻ To Abram, who seems to have been denied the best of the land by Lot's choice, certain elements of the initial promise given in 12: 2-3 are reiterated and expanded.

14-15. The theme of *the land* is made more explicit. As far as Abram can see in all directions is God's gift *to you and to your descendants for ever.*

16. The theme of a great nation is spelled out in terms of *descendants countless as the dust of the earth* (cp. 28: 14). Elsewhere in the Genesis narrative, the E tradition compares the number of Abram's descendants with the number of the stars in the sky (15: 5) or with 'the sand of the sea, which is beyond all counting' (32: 12; cp. 22: 17).

17. *Now go through the length and breadth of the land:* this may simply be an invitation to explore the land from one end to the other, or behind the expression there may lie an ancient

legal procedure in terms of which the physical traversing of a piece of land symbolized a legal claim to ownership.

18. *the terebinths of Mamre at Hebron:* for terebinths see the note at 12: 6. Mamre lies just north of Hebron in southern Palestine (see map p. xiv). It was a sacred site long before Abram came to Canaan. Some of the traditions concerning Abram centre on Mamre (see chapter 18 and 23: 17–20). In chapter 14 Mamre appears not as a place-name but as a personal name (verses 13, 24). ✳

ABRAM AS THE HEBREW CHIEFTAIN

14 It was in the time of Amraphel king of Shinar, Arioch king of Ellasar, Kedorlaomer king of Elam, and Tidal
2 king of Goyim. They went to war against Bera king of Sodom, Birsha king of Gomorrah, Shinab king of Admah, Shemeber king of Zeboyim, and the king of Bela, that is
3 Zoar. These kings joined forces in the valley of Siddim,
4 which is now the Dead Sea. They had been subject to Kedorlaomer for twelve years, but in the thirteenth year
5 they rebelled. Then in the fourteenth year Kedorlaomer and his confederate kings came and defeated the Rephaim in Ashteroth-karnaim, the Zuzim in Ham, the Emim in
6 Shaveh-kiriathaim, and the Horites in the hill-country from Seir[a] as far as El-paran on the edge of the wilderness.
7 On their way back they came to En-mishpat, which is now Kadesh, and laid waste all the country of the Amalekites and also that of the Amorites who lived in Hazazon-
8 tamar. Then the kings of Sodom, Gomorrah, Admah, Zeboyim, and Bela, which is now Zoar, marched out and drew up their forces against them in the valley of Siddim,

[a] *Prob. rdg.; Heb.* in their hill-country, Seir.

against Kedorlaomer king of Elam, Tidal king of Goyim, 9
Amraphel king of Shinar, and Arioch king of Ellasar,
four kings against five. Now the valley of Siddim was full 10
of bitumen pits; and when the kings of Sodom and
Gomorrah fled, they fell into them, but the rest escaped to
the hill-country. The four kings captured all the flocks 11
and herds of Sodom and Gomorrah and all their provisions, and went away. They also carried off Lot, Abram's 12
nephew, who was living in Sodom, and with him his
flocks and herds. But a fugitive came and told Abram the 13
Hebrew, who at that time was dwelling by the terebinths
of Mamre the Amorite. This Mamre was the brother of
Eshcol and Aner, who were allies of Abram. When 14
Abram heard that his kinsman had been taken prisoner,
he mustered[a] his retainers, men born in his household,
three hundred and eighteen of them, and pursued as far as
Dan. Abram and his followers surrounded the enemy by 15
night, attacked them and pursued them as far as Hobah,
north of Damascus; he then brought back all the flocks 16
and herds and also his kinsman Lot with his flocks and
herds, together with the women and the other captives.[b]
On his return from this defeat of Kedorlaomer and his 17
confederate kings, the king of Sodom came out to meet
him in the valley of Shaveh, which is now the King's
Valley.

Then Melchizedek king of Salem brought food and 18
wine. He was priest of God Most High,[c] and he pro- 19
nounced this blessing on Abram:

[a] *So Sam.; Heb.* emptied out.　　　　[b] *Lit.* the people.
[c] God Most High: *Heb.* El-Elyon.

'Blessed be Abram
by God Most High,
creator[a] of heaven and earth.
20   And blessed be God Most High,
who has delivered your enemies into your power.'

Abram gave him a tithe of all the booty.

21   The king of Sodom said to Abram, 'Give me the
22 people, and you can take the property'; but Abram said
to the king of Sodom, 'I lift my hand and swear by the
23 LORD, God Most High, creator of heaven and earth: not a
thread or a shoe-string will I accept of anything that is
24 yours. You shall never say, "I made Abram rich." I will
accept nothing but what the young men have eaten and
the share of the men who went with me. Aner, Eshcol,
and Mamre shall have their share.'

*   This chapter is something of an erratic boulder in the
Genesis landscape. It can be lifted very easily out of its present
context since it seems organically related neither to what
precedes it in chapter 13, nor to what follows it in chapter 15.
It is the only section in the narrative which seeks to relate
Abram to wider significant historical events in the ancient
Near East. Part of it reads like an extract from a rather formal
historical annal, yet when we try to uncover its historical
base we come up against insuperable difficulties.

The character of Abram in this chapter is curiously different
from that found elsewhere in Genesis. Only here does he
appear as a military chieftain capable of taking the field with
a considerable body of retainers. Only here is he called 'the
Hebrew' (see note on verse 13). The identity of the four
eastern rulers (verse 1) who march against their rebellious
subjects is something of a mystery. Many other names in the

[a] *Or* owner.

chapter, both personal and geographical, are equally elusive. Nor does the chapter itself read smoothly as a unity. The incident involving Melchizedek the priest–king of Salem (verses 18–20) seems unrelated to the rest of the chapter. The narrative flows much more naturally if verse 21 immediately follows verse 17. Stylistically the chapter belongs to none of the three major sources, J, E, and P, which make up the book of Genesis.

What lies behind this chapter? Has it any firm historical foundation? Why does it appear in its present context? What is its relationship to the other traditions about Abram? To none of these questions are there easy or obvious answers. There are those who would see this chapter as a completely fanciful, late story full of legendary material and utterly devoid of any historical roots, a story invented to show how the few, particularly if they are Jews, can successfully defeat the might of great world powers. It is hard, however, to believe that such a story would have required so much in the way of apparently trivial and irrelevant detail. It is far more likely that, in spite of some – at present – insoluble problems, the chapter does preserve the memory of a military foray in force which destroyed settlements in the Jordan valley. Whether this took place to crush a local rebellion, as verse 4 states, or with some other object in view, such as gaining control of the rich copper deposits south of the Dead Sea, must remain uncertain. Archaeological evidence of the destruction of Middle-Bronze-Age settlements in Transjordan and at the southern end of the Jordan valley around the late nineteenth and eighteenth centuries B.C., has been claimed in support of the historicity of the narrative. The interpretation of this evidence, however, is disputed and even if correctly dated, there is nothing which would necessarily connect it with the events described in this chapter.

On the assumption that there is a historical kernel, can we probe behind the present form of the chapter? It is noteworthy that verses 1–11 contain a story complete in itself –

the expedition of the four kings and their defeat of a local coalition – a story in which there is no reference to Abram. This is in marked contrast to the other traditions about Abram, in all of which he appears at the outset and is the focus of attention throughout. It is a reasonable assumption that originally the tradition had nothing to do with Abram. Lot's connection with the cities of the plain provides a neat connection between this tradition and the Abram stories. Abram's defeat of four eastern potentates, to the extent of pursuing them north of Damascus, would be a story eagerly relished by generations of Hebrews who had often good reason to fear the power of eastern imperialisms.

The Melchizedek incident has another purpose. The Genesis traditions link Abram with many important cities in Canaan, but there is no tradition linking him with what was to become the most important of all such cities, Jerusalem, the royal capital of the united monarchy under David and Solomon, and later capital of the southern kingdom of Judah. Ps. 110 claims that the king in Jerusalem was

'a priest for ever,
in the succession of Melchizedek' (verse 4).

Behind this claim there may lie objections to the king in Jerusalem exercising priestly functions on the grounds that he did not belong to the legitimate priestly family, the sons of Levi. If we assume that Salem is Jerusalem the objection is here countered by appealing to an old tradition, of which we are here but catching a glimpse, about a pre-Israelite priest–king in Jerusalem. It is particularly significant that Abram is depicted as receiving a blessing from, and offering a tithe to, Melchizedek, both actions which indicate Abram's inferior status. This would serve to bolster royal claims against any internal opposition from those who claimed to be the sons of Abram. There are other indications in Genesis of close links between the Abram and the Davidic royal traditions; note, for example, the claim made concerning Abram in 17: 6: 'and kings shall spring from you'.

We may, therefore, see in this chapter an ancient pre-Israelite historical kernel, which has been taken up into the Abram traditions and reshaped to serve later interests.

1. Much remains uncertain about the identity of the four kings. *Amraphel king of Shinar* used to be confidently identified with Hammurabi of Babylon, eighteenth century B.C., whose name is associated with the famous law code. Shinar is undoubtedly Babylon; but the identification of Amraphel with Hammurabi is linguistically extremely doubtful, and, in any case, several Hammurabis are now known to us. *Arioch king of Ellasar:* the name Arriuku appears as a Hurrian name in the Nuzi texts; and a place name Ila(n)zur in the Mari texts. Earlier attempts to identify Ellasar with the southern Babylonian town of Larsa have been given up. Further information about the texts from Mari and from Nuzi will be found in *The Making of the Old Testament*, pp. 8ff. *Kedorlaomer king of Elam:* Kedorlaomer is a good Elamite name, made up of the element Kudur meaning 'servant' and Lagomar, the name of a god. *Tidal king of Goyim:* Tidal may be identified with the Hittite name Tudhalias. Several kings of that name are known to us from Hittite records, Tudhalias I flourishing in the seventeenth century B.C. The descriptive title 'king of the *nations*', which is what *Goyim* means, is puzzling unless it should be taken as an honorific imperial title. We have no knowledge of four such kings ruling at the same time, nor of circumstances in which a *king of Elam*, the region north of the Persian Gulf in modern Iran, would lead such a punitive expedition westwards.

2. We are equally in the dark about the rulers of the cities of the plain who opposed them. The names of four of the cities occur together in Gen. 10: 19, while Zoar is mentioned in 13: 10. It is curious that the name of the *king of Bela* is not given. This may be an argument for the antiquity of the tradition; a later fictional writer would surely have had little difficulty in inventing a fifth name. Of the four names given, *Shinab* and *Shemeber* are unknown outside this passage while

Bera and *Birsha* look suspiciously like a play on the Hebrew words for 'evil' and 'wickedness'. *Bela, that is Zoar:* this is the first example of something which occurs frequently in this chapter. A place is given the name by which it was once known in tradition, and then it is identified for the readers by its contemporary equivalent. This may be done by an explanatory phrase: thus *Bela, that is Zoar;* 'the valley of Siddim, which is now the Dead Sea' (verse 3); 'El-paran on the edge of the wilderness' (verse 6); 'En-mishpat, which is now Kadesh' (verse 7); 'the valley of Shaveh, which is now the King's Valley' (verse 17). It may also be done by a double-barrelled name, the first element being the ancient name, the second element the name by which it is known elsewhere in the Old Testament: thus 'Ashteroth-Karnaim'; 'Shaveh-kiriathaim (verse 5); 'Hazazon-tamar (verse 7).

5. *the Rephaim* are included in the list of the pre-Israelite inhabitants of Canaan in 15: 20. In Deuteronomy they are described as giants (Deut. 3: 11) and are said to have been called Zamzummim by the Ammonites (Deut. 2: 20). *the Zuzim,* otherwise unknown to the Old Testament, may be identified with these Zamzummim. Deut. 2: 10 claims that *Emim* was the Moabite name for the Rephaim.

6. *the Horites:* this name was given to the peoples who once lived in the territory later occupied by the Edomites to the south of the Dead Sea (see 36: 20; Deut. 2: 12). They may be related to the Hurrians (see pp. 13-14). *in the hill-country from Seir:* this translation presupposes a slight alteration of the Hebrew text, a redivision of words. Some of the versions read 'in the hill-country of Seir', which would make equally good sense. As a place name *Seir* indicated the mountainous area of Edom.

7. *the Amalekites* are mentioned frequently in the Old Testament as the enemies of Israel. They attacked the Israelites under Moses during the period of the wilderness wandering prior to the settlement in Canaan (see Exod. 17: 8–16). The general route taken by the invading force is clear.

From north to south they move down the King's Highway, one of the main trade routes in Transjordan. Then from a point near the head of the Gulf of Akaba, they swing east to the desert oasis of Kadesh, whence they cut into the valley south of the Dead Sea where they successfully crush the local opposition (see *Old Testament Illustrations* map 31, p. 38).

10. *Now the valley of Siddim was full of bitumen pits:* bitumen deposits are still to be found on the bed of the Dead Sea. The presence of bitumen pits in the area is consistent with certain details in the story of the destruction of Sodom and Gomorrah in chapter 19: for example, the 'thick smoke rising high from the earth like the smoke of a lime-kiln' (19: 28; see note).

13. *Abram the Hebrew:* in documents spanning nearly a thousand years, and in areas as far apart as southern Mesopotamia and Egypt, we find references outside the Old Testament to *habiru*. The word does not describe a race, but a class of people, sometimes slaves, sometimes mercenaries, sometimes living on the fringes of settled communities and posing a threat to them. There has been much inconclusive discussion about the relationship, if any, between these *habiru* and the Hebrews. In the Old Testament the word Hebrew is used only on the lips of foreigners or in situations where the Hebrews are being contrasted with other peoples. That Abram would appear as just such a *habiru* in the eyes of the established communities in Canaan is not unlikely. The only other place in Genesis where the term *Hebrew* is used is in the Joseph story with its Egyptian background (see 39: 14; 40: 15; 43: 32). The names of Abram's allies are something of a puzzle. None of these names, *Mamre the Amorite, Eshcol and Aner*, appear elsewhere in the Old Testament as personal names, but they all occur as place-names. For *Mamre* see the note on 13: 18. *Eshcol*, which means 'grape cluster', occurs in the phrase 'the gorge of Eshcol' (Deut. 1: 24) and *Aner* in 1 Chron. 6: 70.

14. On hearing of Lot's capture, Abram *mustered his retainers*. This is a difficult phrase. The N.E.B. translation

follows the Samaritan text and makes a slight alteration in
the Hebrew verb assuming the common confusion of the
letters 'd' and 'r' in Hebrew. The verb in the traditional
Hebrew text can only mean 'emptied out' (see footnote).
The word rendered *retainers* occurs only here; a possible link
with an Egyptian word gives the meaning *retainers*. The more
traditional translation 'trained men' or 'trained servants'
assumes a link with the Hebrew verb 'to train'. *three hundred
and eighteen of them:* the Hebrew letters for 318 spell out the
name Eliezer who appears as the slave heir of Abram in 15: 2.
If an explanation of the precise number is needed, this is
rather more plausible than the line taken by the early Christian
apologist in the Epistle to Barnabas who, by converting the
number into Greek letters found a cryptic reference to Jesus
and the cross. *as far as Dan:* Judg. 18: 29 informs us that the
older name for *Dan* was Laish. It is perhaps surprising that
the older name has not been preserved in this case (see note
on verse 2).

15. Abram's pursuit of his defeated foes takes him *as far
as Hobah, north of Damascus*. Various places just north of
Damascus have been identified traditionally with Hobah, but
there is no certainty about the site, and no further reference
to it in the Old Testament.

17. *the valley of Shaveh which is now the King's Valley:*
according to 2 Sam. 18: 18, the King's Valley was not
far from Jerusalem. It contained a memorial pillar called
Absalom's Monument.

18. *Melchizedek:* possible reasons for the inclusion of this
Melchizedek incident have been already suggested. The
importance of Melchizedek is that he exercises the dual role
of priest and king. His name probably means 'Zedek' – the
name of a god – 'is my king'. *Salem* is probably an abbreviated form of Jerusalem; see the description of God in
Ps. 76: 2:

> 'his tent is pitched in Salem,
> in Zion his battle-quarters are set up'

Melchizedek was *priest of God Most High:* both elements in the Hebrew *El-Elyon,* '*God Most High*' are now known from sources outside the Old Testament to be divine names. It seems reasonable to assume that El-Elyon was one of the deities worshipped in Jerusalem in pre-Israelite times. What is surprising is that the narrative depicts Abram being blessed in the name of this pagan god. The difficulty seems to have been sensed since the Hebrew text of verse 22 adds 'the LORD', the peculiarly Hebrew personal name for God, before *God Most High:* the Greek (Septuagint) and Syriac (Peshitta) texts, however, do not read 'the LORD' in verse 22. The use of 'the LORD' side by side with *God Most High* points to the way in which Hebrew faith was prepared to take over the titles and attributes of other gods and apply them to Israel's own God, Yahweh.

19. *and he pronounced this blessing on Abram:* for benefits received the natural response was twofold, to bless the God who gave and to live in hope of future blessing (see Ps. 103). So the blessing pronounced by Melchizedek upon Abram looks in two directions, towards Abram and towards the God who has given Abram victory. *creator of heaven and earth:* the traditional rendering 'owner' or 'possessor' is given in the footnote. The verb, however, appears in Canaanite religious texts in a title of El which context suggests ought to be translated 'creator of earth', and this makes good sense here. The Melchizedek–Abram incident is to be further developed in the New Testament in the Letter to the Hebrews, where Melchizedek, as king and priest, becomes a type of the priesthood of Christ and Abram a type of the inferior Jewish priesthood descended from him (see Heb. 7: 1–10). In Heb. 7: 2 the name Melchizedek is incorrectly taken to mean 'king of righteousness', and Salem connected with the Hebrew word for 'peace'.

21–4. The chapter reaches its climax in Abram refusing to retain for himself any of the spoils of victory, in spite of the king of Sodom's offer. His allies may take their share, but he

will take nothing for himself. There is a curious contradiction
in the traditions here. Abram had no hesitation in becoming
rich at Pharaoh's expense (see 12: 16), but he will not allow
the king of Sodom the privilege of claiming '*I made Abram
rich.*' It is possible that the Abramic additions to this chapter
come from a later date than the story in 12: 10–20 and represent a further stage in the process of changing Abram into an
idealized figure. On the other hand Abram's rejection of
anything from the hand of the king of Sodom, may be
intended to preface God's total rejection of Sodom and the
other cities of the plain (see chapter 19). Abram will accept
nothing from a man God has doomed to destruction.   ✱

THE LORD'S COVENANT WITH ABRAM

15 After this the word of the LORD came to Abram in a
vision. He said, 'Do not be afraid, Abram, I am giving you
2 a very great reward.'[a] Abram replied, 'Lord GOD, what
canst thou give me? I have no standing among men, for
3 the heir to[b] my household is Eliezer of Damascus.' Abram
continued, 'Thou has given me no children, and so my
4 heir must be a slave born in my house.' Then came the
word of the LORD to him: 'This man shall not be your
5 heir; your heir shall be a child of your own body.' He
took Abram outside and said, 'Look up into the sky, and
count the stars if you can. So many', he said, 'shall your
descendants be.'

6   Abram put his faith in the LORD, and the LORD counted
7 that faith to him as righteousness; he said to him, 'I am
the LORD who brought you out from Ur of the Chaldees
8 to give you this land to occupy.' Abram said, 'O Lord

[a] I am giving...reward: *or* I am your shield, your very great reward.
[b] the heir to: *prob. rdg., cp. Pesh.; Heb. obscure.*

GOD, how can I be sure that I shall occupy it?' The LORD 9
answered, 'Bring me a heifer three years old, a she-goat
three years old, a ram three years old, a turtle-dove, and
a fledgling.' He brought him all these, halved the animals 10
down the middle and placed each piece opposite its corresponding piece, but he did not halve the birds. When the 11
birds of prey swooped down on the carcasses, Abram
scared them away. Then, as the sun was going down, a 12
trance came over Abram and great fear[a] came upon him.
The LORD said to Abram, 'Know this for certain, that 13
your descendants will be aliens living in a land that is not
theirs; they will be slaves, and will be held in oppression
there for four hundred years. But I will punish that 14
nation whose slaves they are, and after that they shall come
out with great possessions. You yourself shall join your 15
fathers in peace and be buried in a good old age; and the 16
fourth generation shall return here, for the Amorites will
not be ripe for punishment till then.' The sun went down 17
and it was dusk, and there appeared a smoking brazier and
a flaming torch passing between the divided pieces. That 18
very day the LORD made a covenant with Abram, and he
said, 'To your descendants I give this land from the River
of Egypt to the Great River, the river Euphrates, the 19
territory of the Kenites, Kenizzites, Kadmonites, Hittites, 20
Perizzites, Rephaim, Amorites, Canaanites, Girgashites, 21
Hivites,[b] and Jebusites.'

✡ In outline this chapter looks back to the concluding section of chapter 13 (verses 14–18) with its emphasis upon the reaffirmation of two of the strands in the promise to Abram.

Thus verses 1–5 return to the theme of 'countless descend-

[*a*] *Lit.* and fear with dense darkness. [*b*] *So Sam.; Heb. om.*

ants'; while verses 7–21 develop the theme of the promised
land. These sections are linked by a statement about Abram
and his attitude to God's promises (verse 6). But in another
respect there is a close thematic link with chapter 14. The
Abram who would accept no reward from the king of
Sodom, is now promised 'a very great reward' (verse 1)
from the LORD. The two sections of the chapter are basically
similar in pattern. Each begins with a pronouncement by the
LORD (verses 1 and 7). This is received with an expression of
doubt from Abram (verses 2 and 8). Each section ends with
a word of reassurance (verses 4–5 and 18–21). This is a pattern
which we find elsewhere in the Old Testament in the call
experience of the prophets. Thus Jer. 1: 4–8 – pronouncement
(verses 4–5), expression of doubt (verse 6), word of reassurance
(verses 7–8). The prophetic model is further underlined by
the way in which the first section is introduced, 'the word of
the LORD came to Abram in a vision' (verse 1), a statement
unparalleled elsewhere in Genesis, but closely paralleled in the
opening verses of prophetic books, for example Amos 1: 1;
Ezek. 1: 1–3. In this respect the section anticipates the description of Abram as 'a prophet' in 20: 7. All this is one sign
among many (see further the comment on verses 13–16) that
there are elements in this chapter from the E tradition,
although the main body of the material still reflects the J
tradition.

1. *After this:* a somewhat vague expression which indicates
a loose connection with what precedes (see 22: 20). The
N.E.B. translates the same expression differently in different
contexts; at 39: 7 'a time came when'; at 40: 1 'It happened
later.' *I am giving you a very great reward:* this translation
involves changing the vowels of the Hebrew text which
reads, as in the footnote, 'I am your shield, your very great
reward.' It is doubtful whether the change is necessary or an
improvement. Although not found elsewhere in Genesis,
the metaphor of God as a shield is known in the Old Testament, particularly in the Psalms:

'The LORD is my strength, my shield,
    in him my heart trusts' (Ps. 28: 7; cp. Ps. 3: 3)

2. Over against anything that God has promised to give, there stands the problem of Sarai's continuing barrenness. This is the ground of Abram's expression of doubt, although the precise meaning of certain words and phrases in this verse is far from certain. *I have no standing among men:* literally the Hebrew means 'I am going stripped (or barren).' The N.E.B. translation assumes that the stigma of being without a son has undermined Abram's status in the community. Other possible renderings are: 'I am still (or continue to be) childless' or 'I am destined to die childless', the verb 'to go' sometimes referring to death in the Old Testament. *the heir to my household is Eliezer of Damascus:* this translation involves following the Syriac in omitting from the Hebrew a word of very doubtful meaning. Even then it remains very questionable whether *Eliezer of Damascus* is a legitimate translation of the last words of the phrase. However uncertain the detail, the general meaning of the passage is clear from what follows. In default of a son, Eliezer, a slave born in the household, is Abram's heir.

It has been claimed that the legal background to this adoption of an heir is to be found in the Nuzi texts. From Nuzi we do possess texts which show someone being adopted as heir to an estate in return for undertaking certain filial responsibilities such as looking after the family property and providing proper burial for his adopting parents. There is, however, no evidence of a slave being adopted in these circumstances in the Nuzi texts. Moreover in the event of a son being subsequently born into the family, the rights of the adopted heir, although secondary to those of the son, are carefully safeguarded at Nuzi; in the Genesis story when Isaac is born, Eliezer disappears from the scene. The parallel, therefore, is not exact, though this incident may reflect adoption practices widespread in the ancient Near East.

4–5. Abram's doubts and hesitations are countered by a challenge, *count the stars if you can. So many...shall your descendants be.* See note on 13: 16.

6. This brief comment by the narrator is full of theological meaning and is intended to point us to the essence of Abram's character. *Abram put his faith in the LORD:* that is, he trusted the LORD, he said 'Amen' to the promises the LORD made – the word 'Amen' comes from the same root as the verb translated *put his faith in.* This attitude of faith involved not merely intellectual assent, but personal trusting, a commitment to someone upon whom you utterly rely. *the LORD counted that faith to him as righteousness:* on that trust is set the seal of the LORD's approval – the word translated *counted* being the word used by the priests in approving an offering presented to God (Num. 18: 27, 30). Abram has done 'the right thing' or is 'in the right relationship with' the LORD, *righteousness* signifying being 'in the right' in the light of accepted social custom or in terms of relationship with other people. Abram is thus viewed as the model for faith in the sense of the man who responds trustingly to what God offers, an idea very important to Paul (see Rom. 4; Gal. 3: 6).

Interestingly, this picture of Abram, the man of faith, links together two sections in both of which Abram expresses doubts: 'Lord GOD, what canst thou give me?' (verse 2); 'O Lord GOD, how can I be sure...?' (verse 8). Such doubts are not the opposite of faith. It is possible to trust God and yet live with very real uncertainties as to how God's purposes and promises are going to be fulfilled. The Old Testament gives us many such expressions of doubt set within the context of faith, not least in the Psalms (see, for example, Pss. 22 and 73).

7. The second section opens with a statement of self-identification by God, *I am the LORD who brought you out from Ur of the Chaldees,* a statement similar in form to other such statements such as the one which forms the prologue to the ten commandments: 'I am the LORD your God who

44

brought you out of Egypt' (Exod. 20: 2). The reference to
Ur of the Chaldees (Hebrew, *Kasdim*) is an anachronism from
the point of view of the age of Abram, since there is no evidence of a people called Kasdim in southern Mesopotamia
before the eleventh century B.C. The reference, of course,
would be meaningful to the Hebrew narrator and his later
readers.

9. Central to this section is the description of an ancient
rite which may lie behind one of the standard expressions in
the Old Testament for making a covenant, literally 'cutting'
a covenant. This is the expression used in verse 18: 'the
LORD made (literally 'cut') a covenant with Abram'. Although
the rite itself is hardly a sacrifice, it involves taking certain animals acceptable for sacrifice – *a heifer three years old, a she-
goat three years old, a ram three years old* – cutting them in
half and laying the halves opposite each other on the ground.
The contracting parties to the 'covenant' or agreement then
solemnly walk between the severed halves. From the one
other Old Testament reference (Jer. 34: 18–20) and extra-
biblical parallels, it seems that the rite was a form of drama-
tized curse. The parties as they walked between the severed
halves were in effect saying, 'May God do so to me if I
violate this solemn agreement.' There are, however, certain
peculiar features of the rite as described in this passage.

(i) Abram is very much the passive partner in the rite; 'a
trance came over Abram and great fear came upon him'
(verse 12). The word translated 'trance' is the word used in
Gen. 2: 21 of Adam lying passively asleep as a rib is taken
from him to be made into a woman. There is no indication
at any point in the narrative that Abram walks through between the severed halves of the animals.

(ii) The atmosphere surrounding the rite is very much one
of mystery. It takes place in the darkness, when 'The sun
went down' (verse 17), and between the severed pieces there
passes 'a smoking brazier and a flaming torch' (verse 17).
The word translated 'brazier' is found elsewhere in the Old

Testament meaning an earthenware stove or oven. What precisely is intended by this 'smoking brazier' and 'flaming torch' is not clear. They are, however, symbols of God's presence, since smoke and fire often convey this meaning in the Old Testament. In the book of Exodus, as the people journey in the wilderness, 'the LORD went before them, by day a pillar of cloud to guide them on their journey, by night a pillar of fire to give them light' (Exod. 13: 21). Smoke and fire are likewise associated with the LORD coming to his people at Mt Sinai (Exod. 19: 18; 20: 18). It is, therefore, the LORD alone who passes between the divided animals. He takes the initiative. He 'made a covenant with Abram' (verse 18). The word 'covenant' carries a wide range of meanings in the Old Testament. It can refer to an agreement between two parties to end a quarrel (Gen. 31: 43–4), or to a solemn pledge of friendship (1 Sam. 18: 3), or to a treaty between rulers or between a king and his subjects, or to a marriage contract. It is used, as here, to describe the relationship between God and his people, a relationship which is always believed to have been established by God and to rest on his initiative.

10–11. The place of the birds in the rite is not at all clear. The *birds of prey* who *swooped down on the carcasses* probably represent a threat to the rite, an evil omen which has to be averted.

13–16. These verses interrupt the narrative description of the rite and contain later theological comment, probably from the E tradition. They are designed to answer a question that must have troubled readers of the Abram stories. If God promised the land to Abram, why was there such a long delay in the land coming into the possession of Abram's descendants? Between the promise and its fulfilment there lay long years of exile and enslavement in Egypt. These years are here viewed as taking place within the providence of God. The occupation of the land is delayed, *for the Amorites will not be ripe for punishment till then* (verse 16). This statement assumes

that the destiny of all peoples lies in the hands of Israel's God
and that, in his own time, the wickedness of other peoples
calls forth inevitable judgement. Other Old Testament
passages claim that Abram's descendants occupied the land
because its earlier inhabitants forfeited it as the result of their
wickedness (see Deut. 9: 4–6; Lev. 18: 24–30). The name
Amorite, which means 'westerner', is used as a general name
for the pre-Israelite inhabitants of Canaan. In verse 21 it
appears as one item in a long list of such inhabitants.

18. The promised land is said to extend from *the River
of Egypt*, the Nile, to *the Great River, the river Euphrates*.
A slight alteration to the text would give the reading 'the
Brook of Egypt', a wadi south of Gaza which traditionally
marked the frontier. In this case the extent of the land would
correspond to that ascribed to the empire of David and
Solomon in its heyday (e.g. 1 Kings 4: 21).

19–21. This is an omnibus list of all the pre-Israelite
peoples thought to have once been settled in the land. About
some of the names in this list little is known. *Kenites* – the
name means 'smiths' – were supposed to be the descendants
of Moses' father-in-law. They settled alongside the tribe of
Judah in the Negeb (Judg. 1: 16). *Kenizzites:* like the Kenites,
a tribe settled in the Negeb. According to Gen. 36: 11 they
were related to the Edomites. *Kadmonites:* 'easterners'; there
are no other references to them in the Old Testament.
Hittites: the Hittite Empire, centred on Asia Minor, played
an important role in the politics of the ancient Near East
from the nineteenth to the thirteenth centuries B.C. There were
Hittite enclaves in Syria and Canaan for most of this period,
even when the Hittites were not the dominant power. Abram
purchased a burial cave from Ephron the Hittite (Gen. 23).
In a later age, lust drove David to eliminate Uriah the Hittite,
one of his own mercenary soldiers (2 Sam. 11). *Perizzites,
Canaanites:* see note on 13: 7. *Rephaim:* see note on 14: 5.
Amorites: see above on verses 15–16. *Girgashites:* a name
appearing only here and in similar lists (10: 15–16; Deut.

7: 1). *Hivites:* the N.E.B. here follows the Samaritan text, the Hebrew not containing this name. Old Testament tradition repeatedly confuses Hivites and Horites (Hurrians, see note 14: 6) – the words being very similar in Hebrew. In Gen. 36, Zibeon is called a Hivite in verse 2 (see the N.E.B. footnote) and a Horite in verse 20. *Jebusites:* the pre-Israelite inhabitants of Jerusalem (Josh. 15: 63). They may have been of Hurrian origin. ✳

HAGAR AND SARAI

16 Abram's wife Sarai had borne him no children. Now she
2 had an Egyptian slave-girl whose name was Hagar, and she said to Abram, 'You see that the LORD has not allowed me to bear a child. Take my slave-girl; perhaps I shall found a family through her.' Abram agreed to what
3 his wife said; so Sarai, Abram's wife, brought her slave-girl, Hagar the Egyptian, and gave her to her husband Abram as a wife.*a* When this happened Abram had been
4 in Canaan for ten years. He lay with Hagar and she conceived; and when she knew that she was with child, she
5 despised her mistress. Sarai said to Abram, 'I have been wronged and you must answer for it. It was I who gave my slave-girl into your arms, but since she has known that she is with child, she has despised me. May the LORD
6 see justice done between you and me.' Abram replied to Sarai, 'Your slave-girl is in your hands; deal with her as you will.' So Sarai ill-treated her and she ran away.

7 The angel of the LORD found her by a spring of water
8 in the wilderness on the way to Shur, and he said, 'Hagar, Sarai's slave-girl, where have you come from

[a] Or concubine.

48

and where are you going?' She answered, 'I am running away from Sarai my mistress.' The angel of the LORD 9 said to her, 'Go back to your mistress and submit to her illtreatment.' The angel also said, 'I will make your 10 descendants too many to be counted.' And the angel 11 of the LORD said to her:

> 'You are with child and will bear a son.
> You shall name him Ishmael,*a*
> because the LORD has heard of your ill-treatment.
> He shall be a man like the wild ass, 12
> his hand against every man
> and every man's hand against him;
> and he shall live at odds with*b* all his kinsmen.'

She called the LORD who was speaking to her by the name 13 El-Roi,*c* for she said, 'Have I indeed seen God and still live*d* after that vision?' That is why men call the well 14 Beer-lahai-roi;*e* it lies between Kadesh and Bered. Hagar 15 bore Abram a son, and he named the child she bore him Ishmael. Abram was eighty-six years old when Hagar 16 bore Ishmael.

* Verses 3, 15 and 16 come from the P source with its formal style and its fondness for precise chronological detail; note the 'ten years' of verse 3 and the reference to Abram being 'eighty-six years old' in verse 16. The rest of the chapter continues the J tradition and is an excellent example of the writer's purpose and greatness. A rich variety of material has been gathered together. An aetiological interest (see p. 15)

[a] *That is* God heard.   [b] *Or* live to the east of...
[c] *That is* God of a vision.
[d] God and still live: *prob. rdg.; Heb.* hither.
[e] *That is* the Well of the Living One of Vision.

is evident at three points in the chapter. An explanation is given of the name Ishmael (verse 11); the proud, fierce character of the Ishmaelite desert tribesmen is accounted for by the character of their ancestor (verse 12); and verse 14 gives a reason for a certain well being called Beer-lahai-roi. But this aetiological interest lies only on the fringe of the narrative; its central concern is focussed elsewhere. The opening words of the chapter provide the clue: 'Abram's wife Sarai had borne him no children.' This echoes the brief note in Gen. 11: 30: 'Sarai was barren; she had no child'; and Abram's complaint in 15: 3: 'Thou hast given me no children.' Already we have been led to assume that if there is to be a great nation coming from Abram it will come through the birth of a child to Abram and Sarai. Surely now the time is ripe. Abram's doubts have been countered; God's promises have been strongly reaffirmed (chapter 15). But no; the obstacle still remains, 'Sarai had borne him no children.' Human ingenuity seeks a way round this impasse. Sarai will 'found a family' by giving Abram her Egyptian slave-girl Hagar as a concubine. It works. Hagar bears a son, Ishmael; but the narrative makes it plain that Ishmael is not the son in whom God's promises to Abram are to find their fulfilment. The tension is increased. Repeated promises, but how and when will they become reality? If human ingenuity fails, what is left? The chapter leaves us waiting all the more anxiously for the answers yet to come.

On a more human level the three central characters are deftly sketched. Abram caught between two women; Sarai frustrated, then tormented with jealousy; Hagar, her slave, proud and spitefully tactless.

1. *an Egyptian slave-girl whose name was Hagar:* there is surely studied irony here. In Egypt, Abram had received female slaves as part of the reward for his deceit in passing Sarai off as his sister and allowing her to enter Pharaoh's household; now, at Sarai's suggestion, it is an Egyptian slave-girl who is to 'found a family' for Abram.

2. The custom of a childless wife giving her husband a slave concubine appears again in the patriarchal narratives in 30: 3 where Rachel says to Jacob, 'Here is my slave-girl Bilhah. Lie with her, so that she may bear sons to be laid upon my knees, and through her I too may build up a family.'

A similar custom is found in extra-biblical legal texts. The Code of Hammurabi legislates for the situation where a citizen is married to a priestess and she remains childless. He is then permitted to take a concubine, but it is specifically laid down that the concubine may not claim equality with the priestess wife. If she attempts to do so, she is to be degraded to the status of a slave. In the Nuzi texts there are marriage contracts which state that if the wife fails to produce children, she is under obligation to provide a concubine for her husband and she has legal authority over any children born of that relationship.

3. *gave her to her husband Abram as a wife:* since the Hebrew word translated 'wife' may equally refer to a second wife in the household, the translation 'concubine', given in the footnote, perhaps more truly indicates the relationship here.

4. Childlessness was a tragedy in the ancient Near East, and the childless wife was only too liable to be despised (see the story of Hannah in 1 Sam. 1: 1–6). Hagar, however, oversteps the mark. Though she is Abram's concubine, she is still Sarai's slave. Abram recognizes Sarai's continuing right to treat her as a slave-girl. The one remedy available to a slave faced with severe ill-treatment is flight; so Hagar 'ran away' (verse 6).

7. It is hardly surprising that the narrative thinks of an Egyptian slave-girl fleeing south towards the frontier with Egypt. There *by a spring of water in the wilderness on the way to Shur* she was confronted by *The angel of the LORD*. The site of Shur (see 20: 1; 25: 18) is uncertain; it may have been a frontier post. The word translated 'angel' means 'someone sent', a messenger. We must not think of the angel of the LORD in this narrative as some heavenly, winged creature

distinct from God. The narrative itself does not clearly distinguish between the angel of the LORD and the LORD. The angel of the LORD finds Hagar (verse 7); the angel of the LORD speaks to her (verses 10–11); but according to verse 13 it was 'the LORD who was speaking to her'. A similar switch back and forth between 'God' and 'the angel of God' occurs in a parallel story about Hagar in 21: 14–21. The angel of the LORD is simply one of the forms in which the LORD appears. He is the LORD himself, graciously reaching out to touch the life of Hagar in her hour of need. The broad compassion of the narrative is noteworthy. An Egyptian slave-girl and her unborn son, destined to be the ancestor of a group of desert tribes who never belonged to Israel, are within the LORD's care and protection.

9. *Go back:* the slave-girl has no legal right to freedom. Legally she still belongs to Sarai; she must return, even if it means returning to *ill-treatment*.

10. The harshness of this directive is softened by a promise which echoes the promise previously made to Abram; '*I will make your descendants too many to be counted.*' This verse may be a later addition to the narrative to take account of the importance of the Ishmaelite tribes. Verses 9–11 certainly read rather awkwardly, verses 9 and 11 beginning, 'the angel of the LORD said to her', and the intervening verse beginning, *The angel also said.*

11. This is a traditional formula for the announcement of the birth and future destiny of an important child. It is heard again heralding the birth of Isaac in 17: 19 and in the famous passage in Isaiah: 'A young woman is with child, and she will bear a son, and will call him Immanuel' (Isa. 7: 14). The name *Ishmael*, literally 'God heard', is explained by linking it with Hagar's experience, *the LORD has heard of your ill-treatment.*

12. Since it was believed that the ancestor of a group lived on in his descendants and that their character was a reflection of his, a thumb-nail sketch of the Ishmaelites is given in this

verse. Ishmael is to be *a man like the wild ass*, freely and wildly roaming across the desert steppe, a man often in conflict with others; *he shall live at odds with all his kinsmen*. The Hebrew phrase translated *at odds with* may be more literally rendered 'upon (or 'against') the face of'. It is a phrase capable of many meanings. As indicating direction it can mean 'to the east of', hence the footnote here, and the N.E.B. text at 25: 18 where Ishmael's sons are said to have 'settled to the east of his brothers'. It can also mean 'alongside of'. Context here, however, suggests an element of conflict and defiance in the expression, hence *at odds with*. The same phrase in Deut. 21: 16 is translated by the N.E.B. 'in contempt of'.

13–14. Linked to Hagar's encounter with the LORD is a story explaining the name of a well, *Beer-lahai-roi*, literally, 'the Well of the Living One of Vision' or as most of the versions and English translations take it 'the Well of the Living One who sees me'. That this well, which lay *between Kadesh and Bered*, was in southern Palestine is clear. The oasis of Kadesh is some 50 miles (80 km) south of Beersheba; Bered, however, is otherwise unknown. Tradition has, perhaps correctly, identified Beer-lahai-roi with a well some 12 miles (19 km) north-west of Kadesh. The name is said to derive from the way in which Hagar addressed the LORD as *El-Roi*, 'God of Vision' or 'God who sees me'. *El-Roi* may indeed have been the traditional title by which a god was worshipped at some southern sanctuary. The explanation given in verse 13, however, for Hagar thus addressing the LORD, is far from clear. The Hebrew text may be literally rendered, 'Have I indeed seen here, after he has seen me (or 'after a vision').' The emended text, followed by the N.E.B. makes good sense, '*Have I indeed seen God and still live after that vision?*' It was widely believed in ancient times that to see God was a fatal experience. Even Moses, according to Exod. 33: 20, was not permitted to see God's face, 'for no mortal man may see me and live'. As a special privilege Moses was allowed to catch a glimpse of God's back. Even this explanation of the text, however, underlines how loosely this final aetiological incident is linked to the main narrative. There is nothing in the previous verses to suggest that Hagar saw the LORD. All we are told is that the angel of the LORD spoke to her. ✶

THE COVENANT AND ITS SIGN

✶ Chapter 17 comes from the P tradition and parallels the J traditions on either side of it. The one reference to the LORD in 17: 1 probably acts as a link with the preceding J material. As a whole, the chapter looks back to chapter 15 in so far as verses 1–14 contain the P account of God's covenant with Abram, and forward to 18: 1–15 since verses 15–22 describe an incident involving incredulous laughter at the announcement of the coming birth of Isaac. ✶

17 When Abram was ninety-nine years old, the LORD appeared to him and said, 'I am God Almighty.[a] Live
2 always in my presence and be perfect, so that I may set my covenant between myself and you and multiply your
3 descendants.' Abram threw himself down on his face, and
4 God spoke with him and said, 'I make this covenant, and I make it with you: you shall be the father of a host of
5 nations. Your name shall no longer be Abram,[b] your name shall be Abraham,[c] for I make you father of a host
6 of nations. I will make you exceedingly fruitful; I will make nations out of you, and kings shall spring from you.
7 I will fulfil my covenant between myself and you and your descendants after you, generation after generation, an everlasting covenant, to be your God, yours and your

[a] God Almighty: *Heb.* El-Shaddai.   [b] *That is* High Father.
[c] *That is* Father of a Multitude.

descendants' after you. As an everlasting possession I will 8
give you and your descendants after you the land in which
you now are aliens, all the land of Canaan, and I will be
God to your descendants.'

God said to Abraham, 'For your part, you must keep 9
my covenant, you and your descendants after you,
generation by generation. This is how you shall keep my 10
covenant between myself and you and your descendants
after you: circumcise yourselves, every male among you.
You shall circumcise the flesh of your foreskin, and it 11
shall be the sign of the covenant between us. Every male 12
among you in every generation shall be circumcised on
the eighth day, both those born in your house and any
foreigner, not of your blood but bought with your money.
Circumcise both those born in your house and those 13
bought with your money; thus shall my covenant be
marked in your flesh as an everlasting covenant. Every 14
uncircumcised male, everyone who has not had the flesh
of his foreskin circumcised, shall be cut off from the kin of
his father. He has broken my covenant.'

* This P account of God's covenant with Abram has its
own distinctive emphasis. Here there is no description of any
ancient covenant-making rite; nor is the expression 'to cut
a covenant' used. There is no attempt to describe, even
symbolically, the presence of God; merely the laconic statement at the beginning, 'the LORD appeared to him' (verse 1),
and at the end, 'When he had finished talking with Abraham,
God ascended and left him' (verse 22). Yet this covenant is
equally rooted in God's gracious initiative. It is something
God gives; it is always described as 'my (that is, God's)
covenant between myself and you' (verses 2, 10) or simply
'my covenant' (verses 7, 13). Nowhere is this more strongly

emphasized than in verse 4, 'I make this covenant, and I make it with you', literally 'I, behold my covenant with you...' Further, in its own language, this covenant is a reaffirmation of the two promise themes of chapter 15, innumerable descendants and a homeland: God will 'multiply your descendants' (verse 2), 'you shall be the father of a host of nations' (verse 4), and 'the land in which you now are aliens, all the land of Canaan' is to be given to Abram and his descendants as 'an everlasting possession' (verse 8). In other respects, however, this covenant strikes notes which have not yet been heard.

(i) The covenant is called 'an everlasting covenant' (verses 7, 13, 19). It is made not only with Abram but with generations yet to come. It is to span the entire history of the people who spring from Abram. It is not merely something given once; it is a relationship which God will 'fulfil' (verses 7, 21) or perhaps better maintain or establish. It involves a relationship in terms of which generation after generation will know the God of Abram as their God, 'I will be God to your descendants' (verse 8). In this respect, and in its emphasis upon 'kings shall spring from you' (verse 6, see also verse 16 where it is said of Sarah, 'the kings of many people shall spring from her') the P covenant tradition has close links with the tradition concerning the covenant made with David and the royal family. In 2 Sam. 23: 5 David says 'he (that is God) has made a pact with me for all time', literally, 'an everlasting covenant'.

(ii) Although the covenant is God's gift, Abram is not entirely a passive partner. He is called to a responsive obedience:' you must keep my covenant' (verse 9); an obedience obligatory on all succeeding generations and spelled out in terms of circumcision.

1. With typical precision the P narrator notes Abram's age, *ninety-nine years old*. This means that when Isaac is born a year later, Abram is a good round one hundred years old. *I am God Almighty*: Hebrew *El-Shaddai*, another compound name

for the deity in which the first element is *El*, compare *El-Elyon* (14: 18) and *El-Roi* (16: 13). Traditionally the second element, *Shaddai*, has been rendered *Almighty* on very doubtful grounds. More recently attempts have been made to link it with the Akkadian word for mountain, that is 'the mountain one', but the significance of the full title remains uncertain. *Live always in my presence:* literally, 'walk before me'. The same expression is found in Ps. 116: 9, where in response to God's gracious protection, the psalmist says:

> 'I will walk in the presence of the LORD
> in the land of the living.'

It denotes a life characterized by trust and obedience. *and be perfect:* the same word *perfect* is used of Noah in 6: 9 and there translated 'blameless' by the N.E.B. The word is commonly found in the language of worship to denote a sacrifice without blemish, and therefore acceptable to God (see Exod. 12: 5). What is to make Abram acceptable is the life of trust and obedience.

2. *so that I may set my covenant between myself and you:* this translation seems to imply that God gives the covenant to Abram as the reward for his obedience and trust. It would be better to omit *so that* and translate 'I will set my covenant.' The command to Abram indicates the life to which he is called in terms of the covenant God is about to give. Abram's obedience is not the reason for the covenant, but the response to it.

4–5. *you shall be the father of a host of nations. Your name shall no longer be Abram, your name shall be Abraham:* a name is not merely a convenient identity-disk in the ancient world. A person's name contains something of himself, his character, his personality, his destiny. In particular, the solemn bestowing of a new name is intended to indicate, perhaps in some sense to ensure, that person's future. Associated with the giving of the covenant in the P tradition is the bestowing of a new name upon Abram. The name Abram means 'High Father'

(see the N.E.B. footnote) or 'the Father is exalted', possibly
in origin a divine title. The new name Abraham is linguistically
no more than a dialectic variant of Abram, with the same
meaning. But this passage links the name Abraham with the
phrase *father of a host*, Hebrew *ab hamon*. There is no scientific,
linguistic basis for this, but the fact that the name Abraham
was popularly interpreted to mean *father of a host* shows how
strongly tradition emphasized the element of the great nation,
the many descendants who were to come from this one man.

9–14. From what God has given, the narrative now turns
to what Abraham and his descendants must give: *For your
part, you must keep my covenant* (verse 9). What keeping the
covenant means is immediately specified in terms of circumcision, which is to be obligatory upon *Every male among you
in every generation* (verse 12), and is to take place *on the eighth
day*. Circumcision was practised in the ancient Near East by
many peoples, including the Egyptians and most of Israel's
immediate neighbours. The Philistines were regarded as the
odd people out in not practising it (see 1 Sam. 14:6). Normally
circumcision was a rite practised about the age of puberty or
immediately preceding marriage. What the Old Testament
does is to take this widely practised rite of initiation and trans-
form its meaning until it becomes the sign of one of the
fundamentals of Israel's faith. Circumcision is here *the sign of the
covenant between us* (verse 11): the visible and ineradicable
mark that a man belongs to God's chosen community.
Further, the act of circumcision is transferred from puberty
to the eighth day after birth, to stress the fact that the covenant relationship is something received, not something that
depends upon personal choice and decision. To remain un-
circumcized henceforth is regarded as a breach of the covenant. Such a man *shall be cut off from the kin of his father* (verse 14)
that is, he will be excluded or excommunicated from the
community of faith. Since circumcision as an act is not tied
to any land or to any building, it became increasingly important for Jews, particularly when they were exiled from their

homeland and scattered across the world. It was the constant
reminder of the relationship into which God in his grace had
called them.   *

THE PROMISE OF A SON TO SARAI

God said to Abraham, 'As for Sarai your wife; you shall   15
call her not Sarai,*a* but Sarah.*b* I will bless her and give   16
you a son by her. I will bless her and she shall be the
mother of nations; the kings of many people shall spring
from her.' Abraham threw himself down on his face; he   17
laughed and said to himself, 'Can a son be born to a man
who is a hundred years old? Can Sarah bear a son when
she is ninety?' He said to God, 'If only Ishmael might live   18
under thy special care!' But God replied, 'No. Your wife   19
Sarah shall bear you a son, and you shall call him Isaac.*c*
With him I will fulfil my covenant, an everlasting covenant with his descendants after him. I have heard your   20
prayer for Ishmael. I have blessed him and will make him
fruitful. I will multiply his descendants; he shall be father
of twelve princes, and I will raise a great nation from him.
But my covenant I will fulfil with Isaac, whom Sarah will   21
bear to you at this season next year.' When he had finished   22
talking with Abraham, God ascended and left him.

* 15. Just as Abram received a new name symbolic of the
hope that was in him, so now, *As for Sarai your wife; you shall
call her not Sarai, but Sarah*. Linguistically Sarai and Sarah
are merely different forms of the feminine word meaning
Princess. But it is likely that at a popular level the form Sarai
was thought to reflect a Hebrew verb meaning 'to mock'.
The change is thus from one whose name was Mockery

[a] *That is* Mockery.   [b] *That is* Princess.   [c] *That is* He laughed.

(see the N.E.B. footnote), and object of scorn because of her childlessness (cp. the note on 16: 4 and Peninnah's attitude to Hannah in 1 Sam. 1: 6), to one whose name is Princess, an appropriate name for one from whom 'the kings of many people shall spring' (verse 16).

16. *I will bless her and give you a son by her:* in the P tradition the concept of blessing is often closely associated with fertility (see verse 20 and Gen. 1: 28).

17-18. *Abraham...laughed:* the verb translated 'laughed' (Hebrew *yitsḥaq*), prepares the way for the naming of the coming child Isaac, Hebrew *yitsḥaq*, 'he laughed' (verse 19; cp. the N.E.B. footnote). All the traditions in Genesis explain the name Isaac in this way. (In the J tradition in 18: 13 the name Isaac is linked with Sarah's laugh, not merely an incredulous but a bitter laugh, born of repeated frustration. In the E tradition in 21: 6 the name comes from Sarah's happy laughter after she has given birth to Isaac: 'God has given me good reason to laugh, and everybody who hears will laugh with me.') The promise of a son through Sarah has been so long delayed that Abraham can only respond to the announcement with sheer incredulity which expresses itself through laughter: *'Can a son be born to a man who is a hundred years old? Can Sarah bear a son when she is ninety?'* He is certain only of the son he already has, Ishmael; so he makes a plea for the future based solely on Ishmael: *'If only Ishmael might live under thy special care!'* or 'be acceptable to you', Hebrew literally 'be before you'.

20. The door is firmly closed on Ishmael as the bearer of the promise. Nevertheless, as at 16: 10, a great future is predicted for Ishmael. *I have heard your prayer for Ishmael*, again a play on the word *Ishmael*, 'God heard' (see the note on 16: 11). He is to be *father of twelve princes* or chieftains. The family tree of Ishmael in Gen. 25: 12-16 gives the names of the sons of Ishmael, 'twelve princes according to their tribal groups' (25: 16).

21. However great Ishmael's future may be, the future of

the covenant and God's promises lies with Isaac, *whom Sarah will bear to you at this season next year*. In spite of the misplaced attempt by human ingenuity to sidestep Sarah's barrenness (see 16: 1–6), in spite of Abraham's incredulity, the fulfilment of the promise draws near, and, in the circumstances, it can only be an act of sheer divine grace. *

THE FIRST CIRCUMCISION

Then Abraham took Ishmael his son, everyone who had 23 been born in his household and everyone bought with money, every male in his household, and he circumcised them that very same day in the flesh of their foreskins as God had told him to do. Abraham was ninety-nine years 24 old when he circumcised the flesh of his foreskin. Ishmael 25 was thirteen years old when he was circumcised in the flesh of his foreskin. Both Abraham and Ishmael were 26 circumcised on the same day, and all the men of his house- 27 hold, born in the house or bought with money from foreigners, were circumcised with him.

* The demands of the covenant are now met. In language consciously echoing verses 10–13 there takes place the circumcision of all those in Abraham's household, Abraham himself, his son Ishmael, and all his male servants both those *born in his household*, sons of those already slaves, and those *bought with money*. Thus the covenant relationship is sealed. God's initiative has been answered by an appropriate human response. *

THE PROMISE OF A SON TO SARAH

18 The LORD appeared to Abraham by the terebinths of Mamre. As Abraham was sitting at the opening of his

2 tent in the heat of the day, he looked up and saw three men standing in front of him. When he saw them, he ran from the opening of his tent to meet them and bowed low

3 to the ground. 'Sirs,' he said, 'if I have deserved your favour, do not pass by my humble self without a visit.

4 Let me send for some water so that you may wash your

5 feet and rest under a tree; and let me fetch a little food so that you may refresh yourselves. Afterwards you may continue the journey which has brought you my way.'

6 They said, 'Do by all means as you say.' So Abraham hurried into the tent to Sarah and said 'Take three measures of flour quickly, knead it and make some cakes.'

7 Then Abraham ran to the cattle, chose a fine tender calf

8 and gave it to a servant, who hurriedly prepared it. He took curds and milk and the calf he had prepared, set it before them, and waited on them himself under the tree

9 while they ate. They asked him where Sarah his wife was,

10 and he said, 'There, in the tent.' The stranger said, 'About this time next year I will be sure to come back to you, and Sarah your wife shall have a son.' Now Sarah was listening at the opening of the tent, and he was close beside it.

11 Both Abraham and Sarah had grown very old, and Sarah

12 was past the age of child-bearing. So Sarah laughed to herself and said, 'I am past bearing children now that

13 I am out of my time, and my husband is old.' The LORD said to Abraham, 'Why did Sarah laugh and say, "Shall

14 I indeed bear a child when I am old?" Is anything impossible for the LORD? In due season I will come back to you,

about this time next year, and Sarah shall have a son.'
Sarah lied because she was frightened, and denied that she 15
had laughed; but he said, 'Yes, you did laugh.'

☆ This section contains the parallel in the J tradition to the 'Promise of a son to Sarah' theme. It tells a story with graphic vividness, and disarming simplicity. As Abraham sits, perhaps somewhat drowsily, 'in the heat of the day' (verse 1), suddenly out of the heat haze appear three men. Hospitality is offered and accepted. Hurriedly a meal is prepared. The conversation turns to Sarah. Eavesdropping, she hears the promise of a son. Bitterly she laughs, then promptly denies her laughter. Disarmingly simple, it is yet a profoundly mysterious story. Who are the three men? 'The LORD appeared to Abraham' claims verse 1; then he sees 'three men' (verse 2). They speak...they eat...they ask (verses 5, 8, 9); then 'The stranger said' (verse 10), but in verse 13 it is again the LORD who addresses Abraham. We sense here the same kind of problem which we saw in 16: 7–13 with its movement back and forth between the LORD and the angel of the LORD. The reader is not left long in the dark. He is quickly expected to know that the 'three men' and 'the stranger' are to be identified. Part of the charm of the story, however, is that at the outset Abraham did not, and could not, know.

The story inevitably recalls similar stories in other cultures of how a god or gods, often in disguise, visit a humble home, receive hospitality and reward it sometimes by announcing the coming birth of a child. The classic parallel is in Ovid's *Fasti*, book 5, lines 447–83, where three gods Jupiter, Neptune and Mercury visit a childless peasant and in return for hospitality grant him a son. If the J narrator is using an ancient folk-tale motif, he is adapting it to his own purposes, to underline that God's purposes can be, and often are, fulfilled in strange and, from the human point of view, seemingly impossible ways.

1. *the terebinths of Mamre:* see note on 13: 18. *in the heat*

of the day: the time when any sensible man would be resting in the shade *at the opening of his tent*.

2–3. As the code of hospitality demands, Abraham immediately invites the *three men* to enter his tent, to refresh themselves after their journey, and to share a meal. His attitude to them is deferential: *Sirs:* the Hebrew text here is ambiguous, probably deliberately so. The consonants could be read as 'my lord', 'sir' (singular) or 'my lords', 'sirs' (plural) or as traditionally vocalized, LORD, YHWH. *my humble self:* literally 'your servant' a common form of depreciatory self-description in the ancient Near East in both biblical and extra-biblical texts. In 19: 2 'my humble home' is literally 'the house of your servant'. It is hard to understand why the N.E.B. at 19: 19 translates literally 'your servant' when 'my humble self' would have been again appropriate.

6–8. In the cool of the shade *under the tree* the visitors share a meal which is rather more than the little food modestly offered in verse 5. Newly baked *cakes* of bread, meat, the choice meat of a *fine tender calf, curds and milk* constitute a typical substantial meal for the semi-nomadic herdsman.

9–10. The conversation turns to Sarah, who, as was the custom, had remained in the seclusion of the tent while the men ate. She overhears the promise of a son *About this time next year* or with a slight change of vowels 'nine months hence', literally 'about the time of a pregnant woman'. Apart from two occurrences in this chapter (see verse 14), this phrase is otherwise found only in 2 Kings 4: 16, and its precise meaning is not wholly clear.

11–12. The narrator's comment on the age of Abraham and Sarah – they *had grown very old* – and on the fact that Sarah was *past the age of child-bearing*, prepares the way for Sarah's response. *Sarah laughed to herself and said:* the fact that Sarah *laughed to herself* probably points to the pent-up bitterness in her thoughts (see note on 17: 17). It would thus be better to translate 'and thought' instead of *and said. now that I am out of my time:* the word translated *time* occurs only here in the Old Testament; it probably means sexual pleasure.

13–14. Sarah may have 'laughed to herself', but the LORD knows, so immediately Abraham is confronted with the question *Why did Sarah laugh...?* It is a strange question. Laughter would be the normal glad response to the announcement of the birth of a child. But Sarah's laughter has a bitter undertone. What the LORD attributes to Sarah in this verse is not quite the same as she said in verse 12, but the meaning is similar. The narrative climaxes in the words, *Is anything impossible for the LORD?* Human ingenuity had failed; in the nature of things, given Abraham and Sarah's age, the future seemed hopeless. But into the humanly impossible, there breaks a divine possibility. It can happen through God's grace (see Mark 10: 27).

15. *Sarah lied because she was frightened:* although the LORD addresses Abraham, Abraham remains silent. The bitter, disbelieving response was Sarah's. Guilty and afraid in face of the LORD's accusing 'Why?', she denies that she ever made such a response. She had the excellent example of her husband to follow. Abraham had done precisely the same, lied because he was frightened, when he passed Sarah off as his sister in Egypt (12: 10–20). *Yes, you did laugh:* good idiomatic English for the Hebrew which the older versions render more literally, 'No, (but) you did laugh.' Deceit may run in the family, but it cannot be sustained in the presence of the LORD. The J narrator has few illusions about the leading characters in his story. Both Abraham and Sarah are all too human in their weakness, yet it is to them that the promises were made, and through them that they are to be fulfilled.

The story of Abraham is moving to its climax, but many strands in the narrative remain unresolved. What, for example, about Lot? This question is answered in 18: 16–33 and chapter 19, a narrative masterly in its construction, in which the J narrator makes use of certain very old traditions, notably one about the violent destruction of some of the cities of the plain. As in the case of chapter 14, the story of the destruction of Sodom and Gomorrah is probably much older than the Abraham traditions. It is here being used to develop certain themes which were of lasting significance for Israel's faith. It becomes in Old Testament tradition (cp. Deut. 29: 23; Isa. 1: 9–10) a symbol of God's judgement and its awesome consequences. ✡

ABRAHAM PLEADS FOR SODOM AND GOMORRAH

16 The men set out and looked down towards Sodom, and
17 Abraham went with them to start them on their way. The
LORD thought to himself, 'Shall I conceal from Abraham
18 what I intend to do? He will become a great and powerful
nation, and all nations on earth will pray to be blessed as
19 he is blessed. I have taken care of him on purpose that he
may charge his sons and family after him to conform to
the way of the LORD and to do what is right and just; thus
20 I shall fulfil all that I have promised for him.' So the LORD
said, 'There is a great outcry over Sodom and Gomorrah;
21 their sin is very grave. I must go down and see whether
their deeds warrant the outcry which has reached me.
22 I am resolved to know the truth.' When the men turned
and went towards Sodom, Abraham remained standing
23 before the LORD. Abraham drew near him and said,
'Wilt thou really sweep away good and bad together?
24 Suppose there are fifty good men in the city; wilt thou
really sweep it away, and not pardon the place because of
25 the fifty good men? Far be it from thee to do this—to kill
good and bad together; for then the good would suffer
with the bad. Far be it from thee. Shall not the judge of all
26 the earth do what is just?' The LORD said, 'If I find in the
city of Sodom fifty good men, I will pardon the whole
27 place for their sake.' Abraham replied, 'May I presume to
28 speak to the Lord, dust and ashes that I am: suppose there

are five short of the fifty good men? Wilt thou destroy
the whole city for a mere five men?' He said, 'If I find
forty-five there I will not destroy it.' Abraham spoke 29
again, 'Suppose forty can be found there?'; and he said,
'For the sake of the forty I will not do it.' Then Abraham 30
said, 'Please do not be angry, O Lord, if I speak again:
suppose thirty can be found there?' He answered, 'If
I find thirty there I will not do it.' Abraham continued, 31
'May I presume to speak to the Lord: suppose twenty can
be found there?' He replied, 'For the sake of the twenty
I will not destroy it.' Abraham said, 'I pray thee not to be 32
angry, O Lord, if I speak just once more: suppose ten can
be found there?' He said, 'For the sake of the ten I will not
destroy it.' When the LORD had finished talking with 33
Abraham, he left him, and Abraham returned home.

✶ The same ambiguity and mystery which we noted in the
previous section continues. At the outset we are told that
'The men', presumably the three men Abraham had entertained, 'set out and looked down towards Sodom'. There
follows a dialogue between Abraham and the LORD, in the
course of which the LORD says, 'I must go down' (that is, to
Sodom), which is immediately followed by the statement that
'the men turned and went towards Sodom' (verse 22). Then
we are told, 'the two angels (messengers) came to Sodom'
(19: 1). Later they are described as 'the two men' (19: 10, 12)
and 'the angels' (19: 15). In every case whether men or
angels, three or two, they are closely identified with the LORD.
   16. Like a gracious host Abraham sees his visitors on their
way. The narrative then immediately switches to the LORD
and what is going on in the LORD's mind.
   17–19. *Shall I conceal from Abraham what I intend to do?*: it is
characteristic of Israel's God, the God of Abraham, that he

acts not only in ways that men can understand, but that he makes his intentions known beforehand to certain men who are privy to his counsel. It is the conviction of the prophet Amos, and indeed of the entire prophetic tradition, that:

> 'the Lord GOD does nothing
> without giving to his servants the prophets knowledge of his plans' (Amos 3: 7).

Not only is Abraham the recipient of God's promise, but he has a responsibility placed upon him. *I have taken care of him* or 'I have chosen him' – the Hebrew verb 'know', used here, could carry either meaning – to instruct coming generations so that they may keep *the way of the LORD*, that is, live the kind of life the LORD expects. This life can only be described in terms of doing *what is right and just*, literally, righteousness and justice. Righteousness and justice are the great, insistent prophetic demands (see for example Amos 5: 24) for a society so ordered under God that the rights and needs of all are met.

20. What the LORD reveals to Abraham is his intention to destroy Sodom and Gomorrah (see map p. xiv). *There is a great outcry over Sodom and Gomorrah; their sin is very grave:* the word translated *outcry* indicates an agonized cry or plea for help from the oppressed, or it describes the grievous circumstances which prompt the cry. Although the N.E.B. uses the same translation *outcry* in verse 21, the Hebrew words in verses 20 and 21 are slightly different. The distinction is probably intentional. Instead of *There is a great outcry over Sodom and Gomorrah*, we should read 'The outrage (the outrageous conduct) of Sodom and Gomorrah is very great' and then retain *outcry* in verse 21. What this outrage was is uncertain. In 13: 13 the people of Sodom are described in general terms as 'wicked, great sinners against the LORD'. In the narrative which follows in chapter 19 the example given of such wickedness is sexual deviation (19: 5). Elsewhere in the Old Testament their evil is that of a callously affluent

68

society unconcerned for the poor and the needy (see Ezek.
16: 49). There is never, however, any suggestion that their
wickedness is other than social and moral.

21-2 The LORD proposes to begin legal proceedings by
carrying out an investigation to see whether the *outcry* over
Sodom and Gomorrah is justified. The men, therefore *went
towards Sodom* but *Abraham remained standing before the LORD*.
This translation presupposes one of the early scribal correc-
tions to the traditional Hebrew text which read, 'The LORD
remained standing before Abraham'. This reading, however,
was thought to detract from the majesty and dignity of the
LORD, so it was altered. The traditional text, however, makes
perfectly good sense, particularly in a narrative which is
highly anthropomorphic in its references to the LORD:
witness the way in which verse 17 makes the LORD debate
with himself. The men depart, but the LORD himself remains
to converse with Abraham. The fact that the LORD remained
with Abraham is probably the reason why the three men of
the narrative until now, become the two angels and the two
men who appear in Sodom according to chapter 19.

23-32. These verses, which obviously do not belong to the
old Sodom story, but represent the narrator's reflections on it,
touch upon ideas which are very important in the thought
of the Old Testament.

(i) *Shall not the judge of all the earth do what is just?* (verse 25:)
this not only assumes that the LORD, Israel's God, is a universal
god, but also that he acts responsibly in ways which can be
understood by, and which commend themselves to, the
moral sense of men. God is concerned with *what is just*, or he
is nothing. From this conviction Israel never wavered. It was
not an easy conviction to sustain. Some of the deepest crises
of faith in Israel centred round situations in which the facts
of experience seemed to call in question the belief that God is
just (see Ps. 73; Jer. 12: 1-3; and notably Job).

(ii) It follows that there must be something inherently
wrong in a situation where the LORD is prepared to *sweep*

69

away good and bad together (verse 23). *Good* and *bad* are inadequate renderings here. It is better to stress the legal background to the Hebrew words, and translate 'innocent' and 'guilty'. The moral dilemma being faced is, 'Why should the innocent be destroyed with the guilty?'

(iii) Men do not live as mere individuals; they belong to communities. There is a strong sense of corporate responsibility stressed in many parts of the Old Testament. In particular responsibility for evil and the inevitable punishment which it brings fall not merely on the individual but on the group or the community to which he belongs. Should not the principle also work in the opposite direction? Should it not be possible for the innocent to act as a saving remnant within the community? Can the goodness of the innocent preserve the community from destruction; and how small can the innocent remnant be and still remain effective? *Suppose there are fifty good* (innocent) *men in the city* (verse 24). With ever increasing daring and with mounting hesitation since he knows that at some point he may be pushing against a limit, Abraham reduces the number; *forty five* (verses 27–8) ...*forty* (verse 29)...*thirty* (verse 30)...*twenty* (verse 31)... *ten* (verse 32). Why the argument stops at ten is not clear. The narrative which follows makes it clear that Sodom was destroyed because there was not a single innocent man in the city. The attack on Lot's guests is carried out by 'everyone without exception' (19: 4).

Behind the urgent issues raised in this section there lies a truth which was often evident to men of faith in Israel. The people as a whole, the nation descended from Abraham, never truly fulfilled its destiny by following the way of the LORD: but always within the nation there was a faithful remnant, often not easily identifiable, yet of vital importance for the future of the people. ✶

THE WICKEDNESS OF SODOM

The two angels came to Sodom in the evening, and Lot **19** was sitting in the gateway of the city. When he saw them he rose to meet them and bowed low with his face to the ground. He said, 'I pray you, sirs, turn aside to my 2 humble home, spend the night there and wash your feet; you can rise early and continue your journey.' 'No,' they answered, 'we will spend the night in the street.' But Lot 3 was so insistent that they did turn aside and enter his house. He prepared a meal for them, baking unleavened cakes, and they ate them. Before they lay down to sleep, 4 the men of Sodom, both young and old, surrounded the house—everyone without exception. They called to Lot 5 and asked him where the men were who had entered his house that night. 'Bring them out', they shouted, 'so that we can have intercourse with them.'

Lot went out into the doorway to them, closed the door 6 behind him and said, 'No, my friends, do not be so 7 wicked. Look, I have two daughters, both virgins; let me 8 bring them out to you, and you can do what you like with them; but do not touch these men, because they have come under the shelter of my roof.' They said, 'Out of 9 our way! This man has come and settled here as an alien, and does he now take it upon himself to judge us? We will treat you worse than them.' They crowded in on the man Lot and pressed close to smash in the door. But the two 10 men inside reached out, pulled Lot in, and closed the door. Then they struck the men in the doorway with blindness, 11 both small and great, so that they could not find the door.

✻ 1. *The two angels came to Sodom in the evening:* that the messengers were not merely men is clearly indicated by this phrase. It must have been well into the afternoon before they shared the meal with Abraham (chapter 18), yet in the evening they are entering Sodom, 40 miles (64 km) distant from Mamre and over very difficult terrain. *Lot was sitting in the gateway of the city:* the open space just inside the gate corresponds to our city-centre. There the community met for common action, business was transacted, local justice administered (cp. Amos 5: 10–15 where N.E.B. renders the word for 'gate' as 'court').

2–3. Lot's attitude to the visitors is very similar to that of Abraham. He is deferential, he insists, in spite of their protestations to the contrary, that they should accept his hospitality. They are to spend the night with him; a meal is prepared. *unleavened cakes:* probably have no religious significance, although in later Israel unleavened bread did. It probably indicates flat rolls of bread, hurriedly prepared, in contrast to the fine flour used in Abraham's household.

4–5. It must be assumed that the two messengers appear young and physically attractive. The men of the city, both *young and old...everyone without exception* gather round Lot's house demanding that his guests be made available for homosexual relationships.

6–8. Lot takes his duties under the code of hospitality seriously. He must protect his guests at all costs. He goes out to reason with the mob, and *closed the door behind him.* He is prepared to offer his own *two daughters, both virgins* to gratify the lust of the mob, provided they leave his guests unmolested. Although daughters in Israel belonged absolutely to their fathers and were his to dispose of, it is hard to believe that the reader's eyebrows were not expected to be raised at this offer. It has been argued that Lot knew there was no real danger in the offer since the men of Sodom were only interested in homosexual relationships, but this is doubtful. There may be an element of poetic justice intended in that in the

last glimpse we have of Lot, we see him lying besotted in
a cave with these same two daughters having an incestuous
relationship with him (see 19: 30–8). A similar story to this
is related in Judg. 19.

9. Although dwelling in Sodom, Lot is still *an alien*,
temporarily resident in the city. The citizens, therefore, are
not prepared to allow the scruples of this alien to dictate what
they may or may not do.

10–11. Lot who tried to protect his guests, is now saved
by these same guests, who reveal their more than human
power. Lot is pulled inside and the door closed, *Then they
struck the men in the doorway with blindness*. The word translated *blindness* is not the common Hebrew word indicating
total loss of sight. The only other place in the Old Testament
where this word is used is 2 Kings 6: 18 where again the
condition is caused by the use of supernatural power. The
word may be a loan word from an Akkadian root signifying
dazzling brightness. A blinding light emanates from Lot's
divine visitors temporarily incapacitating them *so that they
could not find the door*. *both small and great:* every Tom, Dick
and Harry. *

THE DESTRUCTION OF SODOM AND GOMORRAH

The two men said to Lot, 'Have you anyone else here, 12
sons-in-law, sons, or daughters, or any who belong to you
in the city? Get them out of this place, because we are 13
going to destroy it. The outcry against it has been so great
that the LORD has sent us to destroy it.' So Lot went out 14
and spoke to his intended sons-in-law.[a] He said, 'Be
quick and leave this place; the LORD is going to destroy the
city.' But they did not take him seriously.

As soon as it was dawn, the angels urged Lot to go, say- 15

[a] *Or* his sons-in-law, who had married his daughters.

ing, 'Be quick, take your wife and your two daughters who are here, or you will be swept away when the city is
16 punished.' When he lingered, they took him by the hand, with his wife and his daughters, and, because the LORD had spared him, led him on until he was outside the city.
17 When they had brought them out, they said, 'Flee for your lives; do not look back and do not stop anywhere in the Plain. Flee to the hills or you will be swept away.'
18, 19 Lot replied, 'No, sirs. You have shown your servant favour and you have added to your unfailing care for me by saving my life, but I cannot escape to the hills; I shall
20 be overtaken by the disaster, and die. Look, here is a town, only a small place, near enough for me to reach quickly. Let me escape to it—it is very small—and save
21 my life.' He said to him, 'I grant your request: I will not
22 overthrow this town you speak of. But flee there quickly, because I can do nothing until you are there.' That is
23 why the place was called Zoar.[a] The sun had risen over
24 the land as Lot entered Zoar; and then the LORD rained down fire and brimstone from the skies on Sodom and
25 Gomorrah. He overthrew those cities and destroyed all the Plain, with everyone living there and everything
26 growing in the ground. But Lot's wife, behind him, looked back, and she turned into a pillar of salt.

27 Next morning Abraham rose early and went to the
28 place where he had stood in the presence of the LORD. He looked down towards Sodom and Gomorrah and all the wide extent of the Plain, and there he saw thick smoke rising high from the earth like the smoke of a lime-kiln.

[a] *That is* Small.

Thus, when God destroyed the cities of the Plain, he 29
thought of Abraham and rescued Lot from the disaster,
the overthrow of the cities where he had been living.

* 12–14. Lot is now warned by the messengers of the
impending doom of the city. He is advised to flee, taking with
him the other members of his family group, *sons-in-law,
sons, or daughters*. This assumes that Lot had married daughters
as well as the two whom he had been prepared to sacrifice.
The language of verse 14, however, is not clear: *intended
sons-in-law*, literally 'sons-in-law, takers of his daughters',
could mean either sons-in-law who intended to take his
daughters, or, as in the footnote, sons-in-law who had married
(taken) his daughters. It is perhaps clearest if we follow the
footnote. His married daughters remain in the city, since their
husbands *did not take him* (Lot) *seriously*. The unmarried
daughters flee with their father.

16. Lot hesitated to leave the doomed city. He and his
family have to be forcibly led out of the city. If we ask why
Lot escaped disaster, then the only reason given is that it
was *because the LORD had spared him*. It is never claimed, as
it was in the case of Noah (see 6: 9), that it was because of his
character or his attitude to God. It remains a mystery rooted
in the pity that God had for him. The priestly note at 19: 29
claims that Lot was rescued because God 'thought of
Abraham'; his relationship to Abraham, the recipient of
God's promise, saved him.

17. *Flee for your lives:* the word translated *flee* occurs five
times in this brief section. Thrice the N.E.B. translates *flee*
(twice in verse 17, once in verse 22), twice it translates
'escape' (verses, 19, 20). Since the last two letters in the verb
are *l–t*, its use here is probably a deliberate play on the name
Lot.

18. *No, sirs:* or 'No, LORD' (see note on 18: 2–3).

75

20. Lot is unwilling to take to the hills; he prefers the security of a nearby *town, only a small place... it is very small.* Twice the word *small* is used. In sound it resembles the name Zoar in Hebrew. Thus a popular explanation is given as to why a certain place near Sodom was called Zoar, 'small town' (see the N.E.B. footnote on verse 22).

23–8. Briefly, in six verses, the destruction of Sodom and Gomorrah is described. The Jordan valley or plain is part of a great geological rift extending down into Africa, and the language of these verses would be consistent with a severe earthquake, accompanied with lightning which ignited bitumen and probably petroleum deposits in the area and triggered off a widespread conflagration with *thick smoke rising high from the earth like the smoke of a lime-kiln* (verse 28). The *fire and brimstone* of verse 24 is best taken as one idea, sulphurous fire. The exact location of Sodom and Gomorrah is still disputed, but it is not unreasonable to assume that they lie under what is now the shallow southern end of the Dead Sea, the area which was once the valley of Siddim (see the note on 14: 10). The last major earthquake in the area probably decisively changed the topography and led to an extension of the Dead Sea southwards.

26. At the south-west end of the Dead Sea there is a long plateau of rock-salt, called traditionally Mount Sodom. The reference to Lot's wife being *turned into a pillar of salt* has an aetiological flavour about it. It explained the existence of a curiously shaped rock formation which once was part of the landscape. But there is also a deeper meaning. Warned to flee and not to look back (verse 17), Lot's wife chose to disobey as the awesome reality of God's judgement was falling upon the wickedness of Sodom and Gomorrah. The judgement thus engulfs her; she *looked back*, the consequences were fatal.

27–8. As if to remind us that this is not merely the story of the destruction of Sodom and Gomorrah, but part of the traditions about Abraham and his relationship with the LORD, the final glimpse is one of Abraham on the hills near Hebron looking south towards the rising pall of smoke. It is a measure of the greatness of the narrator that he has no comment to make on what may have been passing in Abraham's mind. He leaves him there silently contemplating the consequences of human wickedness. ✳

THE ORIGIN OF THE MOABITES
AND THE AMMONITES

Lot went up from Zoar and settled in the hill-country 30 with his two daughters, because he was afraid to stay in Zoar; he lived with his two daughters in a cave. The 31 elder daughter said to the younger, 'Our father is old and there is not a man in the country to come to us in the usual way. Come now, let us make our father drink wine and 32 then lie with him and in this way keep the family alive through our father.' So that night they gave him wine to 33 drink, and the elder daughter came and lay with him, and he did not know when she lay down and when she got up. Next day the elder said to the younger, 'Last night I lay 34 with my father. Let us give him wine to drink again tonight; then you go in and lie with him. So we shall keep the family alive through our father.' So they gave their 35 father wine to drink again that night, and the younger daughter went and lay with him, and he did not know when she lay down and when she got up. In this way both 36 Lot's daughters came to be with child by their father. The 37 elder daughter bore a son and called him Moab; he was the ancestor of the present Moabites. The younger also 38 bore a son, whom she called Ben-ammi; he was the ancestor of the present Ammonites.

* There is much that is uncertain about this curious episode.

30. *Lot went up from Zoar:* after refusing to flee to the hills (verse 19), he now *settled in the hill-country with his two daughters* and lived *in a cave* (verse 30). He left Zoar *because he was afraid to stay in Zoar*, yet no explanation of this fear is given. Probably this underlines Lot's continuing distrust of God. The small town, graciously provided for him by God (verse 21), does not measure up to Lot's standards of security. Where was this cave? It is vaguely described as being in the hill-country, but which hill-country on which side of the Dead Sea? In view of the Moabite links in the story, the hills of Moab to the east of the Dead Sea are probably intended. Was there once a cave there known as Lot's cave?

31–8. *there is not a man in the country to come to us in the usual way:* there is no necessary hint of moral censure implied on Lot's daughters for plying their father with wine till each in turn has an incestuous relationship with him. They are being commended for taking the only possible course open to them to ensure the future in a situation where, as far as they knew, they were the sole survivors of catastrophe. Two things seem clear in this story.

(i) Although, typically, the J narrator makes no comment, the final picture that we get of Lot lying in a drunken stupor in a cave and being used by his daughters, is in the sharpest contrast to the first mention of Lot setting out with Abraham as Abraham responds to God's call (12: 5). There are those for whom the pilgrimage of faith ends tragically. In Lot's case the tragedy is traceable to the wrong and selfish decision he took to grasp for himself the best of the land (13: 10–11).

(ii) The incident has an aetiological interest. It provides an explanation of the names Moabite and Ammonite, given to two tribes on Israel's eastern desert border. *Moab* (verse 37) is regarded as derived from the Hebrew words translated *through our father* (verse 34), and *by their father* (verse 36) in both of which the basic Hebrew is *me'ab*.

Ammonites (verse 38) is regarded as deriving from the name

which the younger daughter gave to her son *Ben-ammi*,
intended to be interpreted as 'son of my kin'. The Hebrew
word '*am* which normally in the Old Testament means
'people' is used here in the sense which it still has in Arabic,
to mean the nearest male relative, usually an uncle, but here
a father. Behind the present form of the story, there may
lie an earlier Moabite–Ammonite tradition which proudly
remembered that they were descended from the sole survivors
of a catastrophe. The Hebrews may have reshaped the tradition to stress the somewhat dubious origins of the Moabites
and the Ammonites.   ✶

ABRAHAM AND ABIMELECH

Abraham journeyed by stages from there into the Negeb, **20**
and settled between Kadesh and Shur, living as an alien in
Gerar. He said that Sarah his wife was his sister, and 2
Abimelech king of Gerar sent and took her. But God 3
came to Abimelech in a dream by night and said, 'You
shall die because of this woman whom you have taken.
She is a married woman.' Now Abimelech had not gone 4
near her; and he said, 'Lord, wilt thou destroy an innocent
people? Did he not tell me himself that she was his sister, 5
and she herself said that he was her brother. It was with a
clear conscience[a] and in all innocence that I did this.' God 6
said to him in the dream, 'Yes: I know that you acted
with a clear conscience. Moreover, it was I who held you
back from committing a sin against me: that is why I did
not let you touch her. Send back the man's wife now; he 7
is a prophet, and he will intercede on your behalf, and you
shall live. But if you do not send her back, I tell you that
you are doomed to die, you and all that is yours.' So 8

[a] *Lit.* in complete sincerity.

Abimelech rose early in the morning, summoned all his servants and told them the whole story; the men were
9 terrified. Abimelech then summoned Abraham and said to him, 'Why have you treated us like this? What harm have I done to you that you should bring this great sin on me and my kingdom? You have done a thing that ought
10 not to be done.' And he asked Abraham, 'What was your
11 purpose in doing this?' Abraham answered, 'I said to myself, There can be no fear of God in this place, and they
12 will kill me for the sake of my wife. She is in fact my sister, she is my father's daughter though not by the same
13 mother; and she became my wife. When God set me wandering from my father's house, I said to her, "There is a duty towards me which you must loyally fulfil: wherever we go, you must say that I am your brother."'
14 Then Abimelech took sheep and cattle, and male and female slaves, gave them to Abraham, and returned his
15 wife Sarah to him. Abimelech said, 'My country lies
16 before you; settle wherever you please.' To Sarah he said, 'I have given your brother a thousand pieces of silver, so that your own people may turn a blind eye on it all, and
17 you will be completely vindicated.' Then Abraham interceded with God, and God healed Abimelech, his wife, and
18 his slave-girls, and they bore children; for the LORD had made every woman in Abimelech's household barren on account of Abraham's wife Sarah.

* The relationship between this story from the E tradition and the J narratives in chapters 12 and 26, which it closely parallels, has been discussed on pp. 4–6. The present chapter has most of the characteristics of the E tradition. It consistently uses 'God', *'elohim*, not 'the LORD'. It is in certain

respects more self-consciously reflective than the J tradition; notice the attempts made to justify Abraham's conduct and the stress on Abimelech's innocence. It describes Abraham as 'a prophet' (20: 7), probably a sign of the influence of prophetic thinking on the E tradition (see comment on chapter 15).

1. *Abraham journeyed...from there:* presumably from Mamre (see 18: 1); though we cannot be sure what preceded this story in the E tradition. *settled between Kadesh and Shur, living as an alien in Gerar:* Abraham is depicted as pasturing his flocks in the south, in the steppe area between Kadesh and Shur (see the note at 16: 7). During this period he resides for a spell in the town of Gerar, a southern Palestinian town not far from Gaza (see map p. xiv).

2. *Abimelech:* the name means 'Melech is my father': *melek* is the Hebrew word for 'king': here it is the name or title of a deity. In the parallel narrative in chapter 26, involving Isaac and Rebecca, he is called 'the Philistine king at Gerar' (26: 1), which can only be an anachronistic description since the Philistines did not settle on the coastal plain till early in the twelfth century B.C. That the same king is intended in both chapters seems likely, since a commander-in-chief called Phicol appears in both incidents (see 21: 22 and 26: 26). The patriarchal traditions preserved the memory of an incident involving a patriarch, his wife and Abimelech; in one version of the tradition it involved Abraham and Sarah, in another Isaac and Rebecca.

3. *You shall die:* according to Deut. 22: 22 the penalty for adultery with a married woman is death for both the man and the woman.

4. *Lord, wilt thou destroy an innocent people?:* this echoes Abraham's question in 18: 23. It occurs here on the lips of a foreign ruler as if to underline the universal validity of the belief that God must do what is just.

5. Not only does the narrative seek to justify Abraham's conduct (verses 11–13), but it exonerates Abimelech from all blame. He acts *with a clear conscience and in all innocence.* The

phrase translated *with a clear conscience* uses the same Hebrew word as was translated 'perfect' at 17: 1. The N.E.B. footnote 'in complete sincerity' is not so much a literal translation as an alternative interpretation. In view of the emphasis upon innocence – literally 'the cleanness of my hands' – the text gives the better rendering.

6. Not the act itself, but the reason which led to the act is regarded as of supreme importance. Because Abimelech acted *with a clear conscience* God prevented him from *committing a sin against me*. How God prevented him is not stated, unless the dream itself is supposed to have intervened before Abimelech touched Sarah.

7. *he is a prophet, and he will intercede on your behalf:* the function of the prophet in the Old Testament is twofold. He is God's messenger with God's word to declare to the community of his day. He also identifies himself with his people, and on their behalf he prays to God. See, for example, Amos 7: 1–6 where the prophet faced with visions which spell the doom of Israel, says 'O Lord GOD, forgive...'

7–9. The sense of corporate responsibility which we noted in the comment on 18: 23–32 is well illustrated here. Not only Abimelech, but all that he has, his servants, his kingdom, are under God's judgement.

11–12. For Abraham's self-justification as expressed here see pp. 5–6.

13. *There is a duty towards me which you must loyally fulfil:* the words *duty* and *loyally* are attempts to catch the flavour of the Hebrew word *ḥesed*, a word of wide-ranging meaning, but often pointing to the responsibilities which spring out of a relationship. Sarah has to show her wifely duty to Abraham by agreeing to say that she is his sister. When *ḥesed* is used of God, it indicates that which keeps God true to the covenant relationship he established with Abraham and his descendants. The N.E.B. frequently translates 'love' (see Ps. 136), the Revised Standard Version 'steadfast love' and the Authorized Version 'mercy'.

16. In Old Testament law the penalty for a sexual offence against a woman is usually a monetary payment to her nearest male relative, often her father. The same principle seems to operate here. A potential wrong has been done to Abraham; monetary compensation is given *so that your own people may turn a blind eye on it*. The exact translation of the Hebrew phrase, literally 'a covering of the eyes', is uncertain, though it may have a legal background.

18. This verse, which alone uses *the LORD*, fits uneasily into the rest of the story. Nothing so far has prepared us for the situation in which the women in Abimelech's household are smitten with barrenness. It may have been thought appropriate that since Sarah was still barren, a similar affliction should befall Abimelech's women. The story could end fittingly with verse 17, which notes Abraham fulfilling the prophetic function ascribed to him in verse 7. ✻

THE BIRTH OF ISAAC

The LORD showed favour to Sarah as he had promised, **21** and made good what he had said about her. She con- 2 ceived and bore a son to Abraham for his old age, at the time which God had appointed. The son whom Sarah 3 bore to him, Abraham named Isaac.[a] When Isaac was 4 eight days old Abraham circumcised him, as God had commanded. Abraham was a hundred years old when his 5 son Isaac was born. Sarah said, 'God has given me good 6 reason to laugh, and everybody who hears will laugh with me.' She said, 'Whoever would have told Abraham that 7 Sarah would suckle children? Yet I have borne him a son for his old age.' The boy grew and was weaned, and on 8 the day of his weaning Abraham gave a feast.

[a] *That is* He laughed.

✶ The three main narrative sources combine to describe the long-awaited event, the birth of a son to Abraham and Sarah. It comes here with peculiar appropriateness. God withholds and then gives fertility to Abimelech's household, now he fulfils his promise to Abraham in the birth of a son. This child is the pledge of the future fulfilment of all God's promises. Verses 1–2 are usually assigned to the J strand, verses 3–5 to P, and the rest of the chapter to E.

1. *The LORD showed favour to Sarah:* literally 'visited Sarah'; the particular colour given the word 'visited', whether friendly and gracious or hostile, depends on context. *made good what he had said about her:* better 'did for her what he said he would do'.

4. The child is born, named Isaac, and circumcised in the terms laid down by the covenant of chapter 17.

6. Here the name of Isaac is explained by the joyful laughter with which Sarah greets the birth of her son (see comment at 17: 17; 18: 12–15). *everybody who hears will laugh with me:* this translation assumes that all Sarah's acquaintances will share in her rejoicing. This seems better than to interpret it, as some translations do, as indicating derisive laughter: others laughing over Sarah, saying mockingly, 'fancy old Sarah having a child, at her age'.

8. From 2 Macc. 7: 27 it is evident that it was not unusual for a child to be suckled for three years. Weaning marked an important stage in the child's development, and would be recognized by a family celebration. ✶

THE EXPULSION OF HAGAR AND ISHMAEL

9 Sarah saw the son whom Hagar the Egyptian had borne
10 to Abraham laughing at him, and she said to Abraham, 'Drive out this slave-girl and her son; I will not have this slave-girl's son sharing the inheritance with my son
11 Isaac.' Abraham was vexed at this on his son Ishmael's

account, but God said to him, 'Do not be vexed on 12
account of the boy and the slave-girl. Do what Sarah says,
because you shall have descendants through Isaac. I will 13
make a great[a] nation of the slave-girl's son too, because he
is your own child.'

Abraham rose early in the morning, took some food and 14
a waterskin full of water and gave it to Hagar; he set the
child on her shoulder and sent her away, and she went
and wandered in the wilderness of Beersheba. When the 15
water in the skin was finished, she thrust the child under a
bush, and went and sat down some way off, about two 16
bowshots away, for she said, 'How can I watch the child
die?' So she sat some way off, weeping bitterly. God 17
heard the child crying, and the[b] angel of God called from
heaven to Hagar, 'What is the matter, Hagar? Do not be
afraid: God has heard the child crying where you laid
him. Get to your feet, lift the child up and hold him in 18
your arms, because I will make of him a great nation.'
Then God opened her eyes and she saw a well full of 19
water; she went to it, filled her waterskin and gave the
child a drink. God was with the child, and he grew up and 20–21
lived in the wilderness of Paran. He became an archer, and
his mother found him a wife from Egypt.

* In many respects this section covers the same ground as
the J tradition in chapter 16. It tells of Sarah's jealousy over
Hagar and her son, of their consequent expulsion, and of
God's care for them in their hour of need. In other respects,
however, the traditions are very different, and not only as
to whether the incident took place before or after Isaac's birth.
Hagar appears rather differently in this section. Gone is the

[a] *So Sam.; Heb. om.* [b] *Or an.*

provocative and tactless pride; there remains only a mother desperately seeking to protect her child. So with Abraham: instead of telling Sarah to do as she likes with Hagar, Abraham is disturbed at Sarah's attitude, and only a word from God makes him accede to her request. He seeks to protect Hagar and Ishmael. He provides them with food and water as they leave his household (verse 14).

9. *laughing at him:* Hebrew simply has *laughing*; the Septuagint adds 'with Isaac her son'. The word *laughing* is ambiguous. It may mean, as the N.E.B. renders, *laughing at him*, which may be taken as partial justification for Sarah's attitude; or it may be rendered 'playing with him', in which case the mere sight of the two children playing together was enough to spark off Sarah's jealousy.

10. There are indications in certain law codes in the ancient Near East of attempts to safeguard the rights of the children of a slave wife to a share in the family inheritance. In certain cases this right could be waived in return for freedom. The Code of Lipit-Ishtar, a Mesopotamian compilation of laws from the nineteenth century B.C. stipulates that in a family with a wife and a slave as wife, each with children, when 'the father granted freedom to the slave and her children, the children of the slave shall not divide the estate with the children of their master' (*A.N.E.T.* (see p. 317), p. 160). This has been taken to justify Sarah's attitude. But to *Drive out* Hagar and Ishmael is not the same as giving them their freedom; nor can we ignore the fact that Sarah's attitude is rooted in jealousy and in her unwillingness to see *this slave-girl's son sharing the inheritance with my son Isaac.*

12-13. Abraham's distress is countered by a twofold reassurance from God:

(i) the future lies with Isaac;

(ii) although Hagar and Ishmael are driven out, Ishmael will still become the ancestor of a *great nation* (verse 13) – *great* seems to have been accidentally omitted from the Hebrew text at this point; it occurs in the parallel statement in verse 18 (for a similar promise concerning Ishmael see 17: 20).

14. *he set the child on her shoulder and sent her away:* if we follow the chronological information given at 16: 16, Ishmael must be at least fifteen, and indeed seventeen if Isaac was not weaned until he was three. This would make the N.E.B. rendering of an awkward Hebrew sentence highly unlikely. The following verses, however, where Hagar 'thrust the child under a bush', then left, unwilling to watch him die (verse 15); where God hears 'the child crying' (verse 17); where Hagar is told to 'lift the child up and hold him in your arms' (verse 18), all presuppose that Ishmael is still a young child. This makes it likely that this story is totally independent of the J tradition in chapter 16. If so, then the N.E.B. translation may stand. It would also be possible to render 'he set it (i.e. the food) on her shoulder and sent her away with the child'.

15–18. The scene is movingly described – the last of the water gone, the distraught mother who cannot bear to look at her dying child, the angel of God bringing a word of hope. Note the twice occurring *God heard...God has heard* (verse 17), again a play on the name Ishmael (see 16: 11).

20. *God was with the child:* compare 39: 23 where the success which came to Joseph in his Egyptian prison is attributed to the fact that 'the LORD was with Joseph'.

21. *the wilderness of Paran:* according to Num. 13: 26, the oasis of Kadesh (see 20: 1) was in the wilderness of Paran, a desert plateau to the south of Canaan. *He became an archer:* this assumes that in the desert steppe region of Paran, Ishmael supported himself by hunting and perhaps plundering. The picture is that of the somewhat lawless Bedouin of the desert. *his mother found him a wife from Egypt:* normally it was the duty of the father to arrange a marriage for his son, but Hagar has to assume this responsibility. The fact that Ishmael marries an Egyptian is intended to indicate decisively that Ishmael cannot be the bearer of the promise made by God to Abraham. Abraham is to take great pains to ensure that Isaac marries from among his own kin (see chapter 24).   *

BEERSHEBA

22 Now about that time Abimelech, with Phicol the commander of his army, addressed Abraham in these terms;
23 'God is with you in all that you do. Now swear an oath to me in the name of God, that you will not break faith with me, my offspring, or my descendants. As I have kept faith with you, so shall you keep faith with me and with the country where you have come to live as an alien.'
24, 25 Abraham said, 'I swear.' It happened that Abraham had a complaint against Abimelech about a well which
26 Abimelech's men had seized. Abimelech said, 'I do not know who did this. You never told me, and I have heard
27 nothing about it till now.' So Abraham took sheep and cattle and gave them to Abimelech; and the two of them
28, 29 made a pact. Abraham set seven ewe-lambs apart, and when Abimelech asked him why he had set these lambs
30 apart, he said, 'Accept these from me in token that I dug
31 this well.' Therefore that place was called Beersheba,[a]
32 because there the two of them swore an oath. When they had made the pact at Beersheba, Abimelech and Phicol the commander of his army returned at once to the
33 country of the Philistines, and Abraham planted a strip of ground[b] at Beersheba. There he invoked the LORD, the
34 everlasting God, by name, and he lived as an alien in the country of the Philistines for many a year.

✶ This section contains another story linking Abraham with Abimelech. It is connected with the surrounding material by a vague time reference 'Now about that time'. It is used to

[a] *That is* Well of Seven *and* Well of an Oath.
[b] *Or* planted a tamarisk.

provide an explanation or rather two explanations of the place-name Beersheba (see map p. xiv). The narrative begins by assuming that, during his stay in the Negeb, Abraham had prospered to such an extent that Abimelech thought it prudent to conclude with him a mutual non-aggression pact 'As I have kept faith with you, so shall you keep faith with me' (verse 23). The initiative in the incident lies with Abimelech. The narrative seems to be claiming that even this pagan ruler recognized the greatness of Abraham, a greatness rooted in his relationship with God: 'God is with you in all that you do' (verse 22). Verses 22-4 read like a complete story in themselves. Verse 25 begins another incident of which the link with the previous verses is far from clear. Here it is Abraham who makes the first move. He has a complaint to lodge. Abimelech's men have seized a well. Perhaps this incident is intended to provide a specific illustration of the violation of the pact between the two. This dispute is resolved by 'a pact' (verse 27), by Abimelech accepting from Abraham a gift of 'seven ewe-lambs' (verse 28), and by the two of them swearing an oath (verse 31).

There are certain very rough edges in this story. Beersheba can mean either 'The Well of Seven' or 'The Well of an Oath', and both explanations seem to be offered. At one moment Abraham is giving Abimelech 'sheep and cattle' (verse 27), at the next 'seven ewe-lambs' (verse 28). It is likely that at a popular level more than one story would be current as to why the name Beersheba was given to a certain place. Two seem to have been combined here. The J tradition at Gen. 26: 23-33 provides a third, linking it with an oath taken by Isaac and Abimelech.

22. *Phicol the commander of his army:* apart from the reference in verse 32 and his appearance in the parallel story in 26: 26, nothing is known about Phicol.

26. *I do not know who did this:* whether justifiably or not, Abimelech professes total ignorance of the incident over the well.

27. The *sheep and cattle* may have been intended as the animals to be used in solemnizing the agreement by a rite similar to that described in chapter 15. *the two of them made a pact:* the word *pact* is the same Hebrew word translated 'covenant' in chapters 15 and 17. The N.E.B. prefers to retain 'covenant' for the specifically religious usages of the word, where God is involved as one party to the agreement: elsewhere it uses words like *pact* or 'agreement'.

28-30. By accepting the *seven ewe-lambs*, Abimelech was recognizing Abraham's generosity and at the same time conceding Abraham's claim to the well.

32. *the country of the Philistines:* see note on 20: 2.

33. *Abraham planted a strip of ground at Beersheba:* it is difficult to see what the words *planted a strip of ground* are intended to convey. It is better to follow the footnote and read 'planted a tamarisk' tree. The tamarisk is a small, hardwood tree with evergreen leaves. As such it was probably thought an appropriate tree to be associated with the worship of a god called *the everlasting God*, Hebrew *El-ʿOlam*. A god *El-ʿOlam* may have been worshipped near Beersheba long before the Hebrew patriarchs ever came to Canaan. The cult is now identified with the worship of the LORD (see comment on 14: 18). The title *the everlasting God* would convey for the Hebrews not the idea of a god of eternity, if by that we mean something qualitatively different from our world of time, but rather a god who is related to all time: past, present and future.

34. Abraham in this narrative is, in many ways, at the height of his power: father of a son, Isaac, respected by a foreign ruler, establishing the worship of the LORD wherever he goes. In one respect, however, he remains insecure. Instead of having – as God promised – a land as his possession, he continues to live *as an alien in the country of the Philistines*. Events now threaten to increase his insecurity. The one tangible token he possesses of the fulfilment of God's promises is Isaac. God now commands him to sacrifice Isaac.   ✻

THE TESTING OF ABRAHAM

The time came when God put Abraham to the test. **22**
'Abraham', he called, and Abraham replied, 'Here I am.'
God said, 'Take your son Isaac, your only son, whom you 2
love, and go to the land of Moriah. There you shall offer
him as a sacrifice on one of the hills which I will show
you.' So Abraham rose early in the morning and saddled 3
his ass, and he took with him two of his men and his son
Isaac; and he split the firewood for the sacrifice, and set
out for the place of which God had spoken. On the third 4
day Abraham looked up and saw the place in the distance.
He said to his men, 'Stay here with the ass while I and the 5
boy go over there; and when we have worshipped we will
come back to you.' So Abraham took the wood for the 6
sacrifice and laid it on his son Isaac's shoulder; he himself
carried the fire and the knife, and the two of them went
on together. Isaac said to Abraham, 'Father', and he an- 7
swered, 'What is it, my son?' Isaac said, 'Here are the fire
and the wood, but where is the young beast for the sacrifice?' Abraham answered, 'God will provide himself with 8
a young beast for a sacrifice, my son.' And the two of them
went on together and came to the place of which God 9
had spoken. There Abraham built an altar and arranged
the wood. He bound his son Isaac and laid him on the
altar on top of the wood. Then he stretched out his hand 10
and took the knife to kill his son; but the angel of the 11
LORD called to him from heaven, 'Abraham, Abraham.'
He answered, 'Here I am.' The angel of the LORD said, 12
'Do not raise your hand against the boy; do not touch
him. Now I know that you are a God-fearing man. You

have not withheld from me your son, your only son.'

13 Abraham looked up, and there he saw a[a] ram caught by its horns in a thicket. So he went and took the ram and
14 offered it as a sacrifice instead of his son. Abraham named that place Jehovah-jireh;[b] and to this day the saying is:
15 'In the mountain of the LORD it was provided.' Then the angel of the LORD called from heaven a second time to
16 Abraham, 'This is the word of the LORD: By my own self I swear: inasmuch as you have done this and have not
17 withheld your son, your only son, I will bless you abundantly and greatly multiply your descendants until they are as numerous as the stars in the sky and the grains of sand on the sea-shore. Your descendants shall possess
18 the cities[c] of their enemies. All nations on earth shall pray to be blessed as your descendants are blessed, and this because you have obeyed me.'

19   Abraham went back to his men, and together they returned to Beersheba; and there Abraham remained.

✶ Traditionally this section has been called 'The Binding of Isaac', from the statement in verse 9: 'He bound his son Isaac and laid him on the altar on top of the wood.' This story has captured the imagination and haunted the conscience of both Jews and Christians across the centuries. As a piece of literature from the E tradition, it is remarkable for its restrained economy of words, its ability to depict with a few deft touches a scene almost unbearable in its emotional intensity. What was passing through Abraham's mind as, carrying fire and knife and with the wood piled on Isaac's back, father and son walked towards the place of sacrifice? We are not told. What did father and son have to say to each

[a] a: *so many MSS.; others* behind.
[b] *That is* the LORD will provide.   [c] *Lit.* gates.

other on that last journey? Nothing, apparently, except one puzzled question asked by Isaac and an evasive reply (verses 7–8). We may admire the literary skill of the narrative, but do we not, at the same time, recoil from its content? Was the God of Abraham really a god who demanded human sacrifice? If so, must we not then dismiss the story as an unfortunate hangover from a primitive barbarism offensive to our moral sensitivity? What criteria are we to use in interpreting this narrative?

It has been read as a polemic against human sacrifice and as justification for replacing human sacrifice by the offering of an animal such as a ram (see verses 13, 14). There is sporadic evidence for human sacrifice, particularly from Canaanite sources, during the second millennium B.C. and later. 2 Kings 3: 27 describes how the king of Moab was prepared, in a crisis, to sacrifice his eldest son. The powerful efficacy of such a sacrifice is seen in the consternation it causes in the ranks of the Israelite army. Even in Israel, in situations of reviving paganism, human sacrifice was practised (see 2 Kings 21: 6; Jer. 19: 5). It is, however, rigorously forbidden in the law (see Deut. 18: 10; Lev. 18: 21), as pagan and inconsistent with true obedience to the LORD. As a protest against human sacrifice, however, the narrative is far from satisfactory. In one way it is unnecessary, since the practice of substituting the life of an animal for the life of man, was already well known in the ancient Near East by patriarchal times. Further the narrative presupposes that God can and on occasion does, demand human sacrifice, a strange way of condemning the practice.

It has been read as a cultic legend explaining both the worship of God at a place called Jehovah-jireh (verse 14) and the popular saying associated with that worship. It is odd, however, that the actual site is so elusive, particularly when it claims to originate in a key incident in Abraham's life. It is described as taking place on 'one of the hills' in 'the land of Moriah' (verse 2). Later tradition was to identify this hill with Mt Zion and the temple site in Jerusalem. This was done on the basis of 2 Chron. 3: 1 where Solomon is said to have built the house of the LORD in Jerusalem on Mt Moriah. This is no more than the fruit of later piety. If the site had been known to be Jerusalem at the time when this narrative was written there would have been some indication of this fact in the text. The textual tradition in verse 2 is very varied. The Septuagint translates 'Moriah' in the same way as it translated 'Moreh' in 12: 6, while the Syriac renders 'the land of the Amorites'.

No approach to the narrative can be adequate which does not set it firmly within its context in the Abraham traditions. This should be evident from the present form of the narrative. It begins by declaring 'God put Abraham to the test' (verse 1) and ends with a solemn reaffirmation of God's promise to Abraham (verses 15–18). The testing of Abraham lies in this, that he is commanded by God to sacrifice that which alone guarantees the future, his only son, God's own gift to him. When he set out from Harran, Abraham had to leave his own country and kinsmen (12: 1) and thus break his ties with the past; now he is asked to renounce his son and thus break his ties with the future. This is the moment when that faith which Abraham put in the LORD (15: 6) faces its supreme challenge. To hold on to God's dearest gift or to obey God's command, this is the dilemma he faces. Only in the moment of obedience, does Abraham discover that what he was prepared to renounce is given back to him. If this was the dark hour of Abraham's life, there were to be many such dark hours in the life of his descendants. Men had to learn to live in faith, stripped of many of the God-given things they most cherished – their promised land, the temple in which they worshipped God in Jerusalem. Sometimes in faith they had to be prepared to renounce life itself, rather than disobey God – see the famous story of the seven brothers in 2 Macc. 7. Abraham is their model, the man of disinterested faith who is prepared to obey God at whatever cost. To see Abraham as the model for faith does not, however, deal with all the difficulties in the story. This faith speaks to us from an alien world. What to us is unthinkable, that God would demand human sacrifice, is not unthinkable to Abraham. He makes no protest. Later Old Testament passages do question this basic assumption in the narrative.

'What shall I bring when I approach the LORD?

Shall I offer my eldest son for my own wrongdoing,
  my children for my own sin?

God has told you what is good;
  and what is it that the LORD asks of you?
  Only to act justly, to love loyalty
  to walk wisely before your God'

(Mic. 6: 6–8, cp. Jer. 7: 31).

A deeper insight and a fuller knowledge of God, however, only come to those prepared to live to the limit of the vision they possess, however imperfect that vision may be.

1. *God put Abraham to the test:* this provides the reader with the clue to the meaning of what follows. Lest there be any doubt that it is God's doing, the word God occurs in the emphatic position at the beginning of the sentence, as if to say 'It was God who...' The reader knows, but Abraham of course does not and cannot know, that this is the reason for God's strange demand. *Here I am:* the Hebrew phrase occurs three times in the course of the narrative, twice as Abraham responds to God (verses 1 and 11), once as he responds to Isaac (verse 7), where the N.E.B. renders 'What is it...?' Our natural English equivalent is often simply 'Yes?' or 'What do you want?'

2. *your son Isaac, your only son, whom you love:* this three-fold description underlines the enormity of the sacrifice Abraham is asked to make. This is no ordinary child, but Isaac; *your only son* does not quite catch the full flavour of the original which conveys a sense of uniqueness perhaps better rendered by 'your one and only son'. Strictly speaking,

95

Isaac is not Abraham's *only son*, but he is that special son in whom all his God-promised hopes for the future are centred. *you shall offer him as a sacrifice:* more precisely as a whole-offering (see Lev. 1), the essence of which is that the offering is given entirely to God on the altar.

3–6. The simple matter-of-factness of the narrative here is in sharp contrast to its emotional intensity. After a two days' journey, father and son stride off alone, leaving the servants with the ass. The *firewood* is strapped on Isaac's back; Abraham carries *the fire and the knife*. *fire* probably means firestone or flint, the tools needed to light a fire.

7–8. The silence of the walk is broken by one poignant question: *where is the young beast for the sacrifice?* Abraham's reply, *God will provide himself with a young beast for a sacrifice*, must not be taken as a confident expression of faith that there is a way out of the appalling dilemma. He is being evasive. He does not know. How can he? He can only try to conceal his breaking heart behind conventionally pious words. The words *God will provide himself*, literally 'will see for himself' – compare our idiom 'to see to it' – prepare the way for the name given to the place in verse 14.

9–11. In cold and almost clinical detail, and without a word spoken between father and son, the final scene is depicted – the altar built, the wood ready for lighting, Isaac bound and laid upon the altar, the knife raised to strike. The fatal blow is checked as *the angel of the LORD called to him from heaven*. For *the angel of the LORD* see the comment on 16: 7.

12. *Now I know that you are a God-fearing man:* the purpose of the test is now revealed to Abraham. He has proved to be a God-fearing man. This is not a general description of Abraham's piety or the depth of his religious feelings; it indicates his willingness to obey God at whatever cost.

13. There is no necessary implication that the ram suddenly and miraculously appeared. It may have been there all the time. Only now, with the tension broken, does Abraham look up and see it. The traditional Hebrew text reads here

'ram behind (or after)'. Some Hebrew manuscripts, however, correctly read 'a', the reading 'after' coming from the common confusion of the letters 'r' and 'd'.

14. *Jehovah-jireh:* that is, 'the LORD will provide' (see the N.E.B. footnote). Usually the N.E.B. renders the four-letter Hebrew personal name for God, YHWH, by 'the LORD'. It retains the incorrect 'Jehovah' (see p. 7) in certain place-names; cp. Exod. 17: 15; Judg. 6: 24; Ezek. 48: 35. The place-name here is supposed to be explained by the fact, noted at verse 8, that God would provide the animal for the sacrifice. This is also claimed to be the explanation of the popular saying associated with this place of worship, '*In the mountain of the LORD it was provided.*' Both the place-name and the popular saying, however, are ambiguous. The name Jehovah-jireh could equally well mean 'the LORD sees'; and the popular saying could be rendered, 'In the mountain of the LORD he is seen (or he appears).' This would stress the special sanctity of the site as a place where the LORD had revealed himself to Abraham.

15–18. These verses are an appendix to the main narrative, somewhat artificially joined to it by claiming that the angel of the LORD spoke to Abraham *a second time* (verse 15). They reiterate the main themes in God's promises to Abraham (cp. 12: 3 and 13: 16), but in language significantly different from that found elsewhere. There is no parallel elsewhere in patriarchal narratives to the introductory words, *This is the word of the LORD*, literally, 'oracle of the LORD', though the phrase occurs frequently in prophetic books in the Old Testament, notably Jeremiah: nor to the solemn assertion, *By my own self I swear* (verse 16), nor to the statement, *Your descendants shall possess the cities* (literally 'gates') *of their enemies* (verse 17) that is, will conquer their enemies. That God's promises to Abraham should be confirmed as the climax to this narrative is natural enough. Why they should be expressed in this particular form is unclear. *and this because you have obeyed me* (verse 18): Abraham has been tested and has not failed. On this basis of obedient faith the future is to be built. This narrative marks the end of Abraham's spiritual experience. God has spoken to him for the last time.   *

THE FAMILY OF NAHOR

20 After this Abraham was told, 'Milcah has borne sons to
21 your brother Nahor: Uz his first-born, then his brother
22 Buz, and Kemuel father of Aram, and Kesed, Hazo,
23 Pildash, Jidlaph and Bethuel; and a daughter, Rebecca, has been born to Bethuel.' These eight Milcah bore to
24 Abraham's brother Nahor. His concubine, whose name was Reumah, also bore him sons: Tebah, Gaham, Tahash and Maacah.

* This brief list contains the names of the twelve sons of Abraham's brother Nahor, eight born to his wife Milcah, four born to his concubine Reumah. Thus we are introduced to a league of twelve Aramaean tribes, just as 25: 12–18 lists twelve Ishmaelite tribes and Jacob–Israel becomes the father of twelve Israelite tribes (see 35: 23–6; 49). Many of the names in the list are shadowy. Eight of them are not otherwise mentioned in the Old Testament. Uz (verse 21) is connected with the Horites in 36: 28–30, while the land of Uz appears in Job 1: 1 and Lam. 4: 21. Buz is listed with other peoples 'who roam the fringes of the desert' in Jer. 25: 23. Maacah (verse 24) appears as an Aramaean place-name in 2 Sam. 10: 6, 8. The one break in the formal listing of the sons of Nahor is the reference to *a daughter, Rebecca...born to Bethuel* (verse 23). This prepares the way for the narrative in chapter 24.   *

THE CAVE OF MACHPELAH

Sarah lived for a hundred and twenty-seven years,[a] and **23** 1,2
died in Kiriath-arba, which is Hebron, in Canaan.
Abraham went in to mourn over Sarah and to weep for
her. At last he rose and left the presence of the dead. He 3
said to the Hittites,[b] 'I am an alien and a settler among 4
you. Give me land enough for a burial-place, so that I
can give my dead proper burial.' The Hittites answered 5
Abraham, 'Do, pray, listen to what we have to say, sir. 6
You are a mighty prince among us. Bury your dead in the
best grave we have. There is not one of us who will deny
you his grave or hinder you from burying your dead.'
Abraham stood up and then bowed low to the Hittites, 7
the people of that country. He said to them, 'If you are 8
willing to let me give my dead proper burial, then listen
to me and speak for me to Ephron son of Zohar, asking 9
him to give me the cave that belongs to him at Machpelah, at the far end of his land. Let him give it to me for
the full price, so that I may take possession of it as a burial-
place within your territory.' Ephron the Hittite was sitting 10
with the others, and he gave Abraham this answer in the
hearing of everyone as they came into the city gate: 'No, 11
sir; hear what I have to say. I will make you a gift of the
land and I will also give you the cave which is on it. In the
presence of all my kinsmen I give it to you; so bury your
dead.' Abraham bowed low before the people of the 12
country and said to Ephron in their hearing, 'If you really 13
mean it—but do listen to me! I give you the price of the

[a] *So Sept.; Heb. adds* the years of the life of Sarah.
[b] *Lit.* the sons of Heth.

14 land: take it and I will bury my dead there.' And Ephron
15 answered, 'Do listen to me, sir: the land is worth four
hundred shekels of silver. But what is that between you
16 and me? There you may bury your dead.' Abraham came
to an agreement with him and weighed out the amount
that Ephron had named in the hearing of the Hittites, four
hundred shekels of the standard recognized by merchants.
17 Thus the plot of land belonging to Ephron at Machpelah
to the east of Mamre, the plot, the cave that is on it, every
18 tree on the plot, within the whole area, became the legal
possession of Abraham, in the presence of all the Hittites
19 as they came into the city gate. After this Abraham buried
his wife Sarah in the cave on the plot of land at Machpelah to the east of Mamre, which is Hebron, in Canaan.
20 Thus the plot and the cave on it became Abraham's possession as a burial-place, by purchase from the Hittites.

✳ It seems a trivial incident; merely the purchase by
Abraham of a plot of land containing a cave in which to bury
his wife. Within the framework of the Genesis stories, however, it has its own particular significance. Stress is laid on the
fact that Abraham is 'an alien and a settler' (verse 4). He
possesses no land, and as an alien he probably has no legal
right to any. He thus has to approach the local Hittite community to cede him land in which to bury Sarah. Community
permission granted, he then approaches Ephron the Hittite to
negotiate the sale of a particular plot of land at Machpelah.
There follows a typical piece of oriental bargaining, humor-
ously described. As an opening gambit Ephron offers the land
as a gift. But he knows that Abraham will understand that
this is a polite way of suggesting a sale. Once Abraham responds as expected, Ephron says 'Well, let's say four hundred
shekels' – probably an exorbitant price – 'what's that between

friends?' Abraham is in no position to haggle; the very offer of the sale is a privilege to an alien. In language that seems to echo that of a formal legal document (verses 17–18), the land 'became the legal possession of Abraham'. The land is then immediately used as a burial place for Sarah, thus finally sealing the transference of ownership. The alien has now a legal foothold in the land which God has promised to him. To live as an alien, waiting for the realization of God's promise, may be an act of faith, but to die with the promise wholly unfulfilled and to be buried in foreign soil, would be tragedy. So the plot of land at Machpelah and the cave, in which not only Sarah, but later Abraham, Isaac, Rebecca, Leah and Jacob are to be buried, become the visible sign that one day the whole land will become the possession of Abraham's descendants. Thus what on one level seems to be purely a piece of secular, commercial haggling, becomes for the P narrator a story of deep religious significance.

1. The Hebrew of this opening verse is somewhat repetitive, though its meaning is not in doubt. The N.E.B. follows the simplified Greek text. With typical precision, the P tradition notes Sarah's age at her death, *a hundred and twenty-seven years*.

2. *Kiriath-arba, which is Hebron*: for this twofold designation of a place by its earlier and its contemporary name, see comment on chapter 14. One Old Testament tradition links the earlier name of the city with a man called Arba: 'city of Arba' (see Josh. 15: 13 and the gazetteer in the volume on Joshua in this series, p. 197). *arba*, however, is also the Hebrew word for 'four' and the old name may have indicated a city with four districts. Hebron (see map p. xiv), which lies some 19 miles (30½ km) south-west of Jerusalem, played an important role in Hebrew history. It is particularly associated with David's rise to power (see 2 Sam. 2–4).

Abraham's mourning, whatever its personal emotional content, was a necessary part of the conventional, public ritual surrounding death.

3. *the Hittites:* literally, 'the sons of Heth'; see the comment on 15: 20.

6. *You are a mighty prince:* literally, 'a prince of God'. The N.E.B. translation assumes that 'of God' is to be rendered adjectivally, as in 30: 8 where an expression similarly containing 'of God' is translated 'a fine trick' (see further the comment on 1: 2 in *Genesis 1–11* in this series). The Hittites are thus depicted as acknowledging Abraham's personal prowess and reputation. A Hebrew reader, however, would be more likely to take the phrase more literally, since he would think of Abraham's greatness in terms of his relationship with God.

8. *Ephron son of Zohar:* he appears only in this narrative and in references to it (see 25: 9).

10. *Ephron the Hittite was sitting with the others:* that is in the open space just inside the city gates where business and legal matters were formally transacted. *as they came into the city gate:* the precise meaning of this phrase here and in verse 18, is disputed. It may, as the N.E.B. translation assumes, mean all his fellow citizens who were passing by at this particular moment, or it may have a more restricted meaning and indicate all those who shared legal responsibility with him, the gate being the place where justice was dispensed by the leading citizens.

15. *four hundred shekels of silver:* this may well be an exorbitant price, though we lack knowledge as to the precise weight, and hence the value, of the silver shekel in Abraham's day. In a later age Omri paid two talents, i.e. 6000 shekels for the hill of Samaria on which he built his new capital (1 Kings 16: 24). Jeremiah, admittedly in a situation where the market value of land must have been minimal, bought a field for 17 shekels of silver (Jer. 32: 9).

16. *of the standard recognized by merchants:* literally, 'passing over to the merchant'; the going rate of exchange acceptable among traders of the day.

17. *Machpelah:* the site has been traditionally, and probably

correctly, identified with the cave underneath the mosque
which now stands in Hebron, though the tombs there, locally
called those of Abraham, Isaac and Jacob, are mediaeval at
the earliest.

17–18. There has been considerable discussion about the
precise legal background to some of the phrases in these
verses. Parallels have been sought and claimed in Hittite,
Babylonian, Hurrian and Canaanite legal texts. That the
language may reflect in a general way legal terminology
surrounding land transference is hardly surprising, but
attempts to prove more than this are not convincing.   ✵

A WIFE FOR ISAAC

By this time Abraham had become a very old man, and **24**
the LORD had blessed him in all that he did. Abraham said 2
to his servant, who had been long in his service and was in
charge of all his possessions, 'Put your hand under my
thigh: I want you to swear by the LORD, the God of 3
heaven and earth, that you will not take a wife for my son
from the women of the Canaanites in whose land I dwell;
you must go to my own country and to my own kindred 4
to find a wife for my son Isaac.' The servant said to him, 5
'What if the woman is unwilling to come with me to this
country? Must I in that event take your son back to the
land from which you came?' Abraham said to him, 'On 6
no account are you to take my son back there. The LORD 7
the God of heaven who took me from my father's house
and the land of my birth, the LORD who swore to me that
he would give this land to my descendants—he will send
his angel before you, and from there you shall take a wife
for my son. If the woman is unwilling to come with you, 8
then you will be released from your oath to me; but you

9 must not take my son back there.' So the servant put his
hand under his master Abraham's thigh and swore an
oath in those terms.

10 The servant took ten camels from his master's herds,
and also all kinds of gifts from his master; he set out for
Aram-naharaim*a* and arrived at the city where Nahor
11 lived. Towards evening, the time when the women come
out to draw water, he made the camels kneel down by the
12 well outside the city. He said, 'O LORD God of my master
Abraham, give me good fortune this day; keep faith with
13 my master Abraham. Here I stand by the spring, and the
14 women of the city are coming out to draw water. Let it be
like this: I shall say to a girl, "Please lower your jar so that
I may drink"; and if she answers, "Drink, and I will
water your camels also", that will be the girl whom thou
dost intend for thy servant Isaac. In this way I shall know
that thou hast kept faith with my master.'

15 Before he had finished praying silently,*b* he saw
Rebecca coming out with her water-jug on her shoulder.
She was the daughter of Bethuel son of Milcah, the wife of
16 Abraham's brother Nahor. The girl was very beautiful, a
virgin, who had had no intercourse with a man. She went
down to the spring, filled her jar and came up again.
17 Abraham's servant hurried to meet her and said, 'Give me
18 a sip of water from your jar.' 'Drink, sir', she answered,
and at once lowered her jar on to her hand to let him
19 drink. When she had finished giving him a drink, she
said, 'Now I will draw water for your camels until they
20 have had enough.' So she quickly emptied her jar into the

[a] *That is* Aram of Two Rivers.
[b] *So Sam., cp. verse 45; Heb. om.; lit.* in his heart.

water-trough, hurried again to the well to draw water and
watered all the camels. The man was watching quietly to 21
see whether or not the LORD had made his journey successful. When the camels had finished drinking, the man 22
took a gold nose-ring weighing half a shekel, and two
bracelets for her wrists weighing ten shekels, also of gold,
and said, 'Tell me, please, whose daughter you are. Is 23
there room in your father's house for us to spend the
night?' She answered, 'I am the daughter of Bethuel, the 24
son of Nahor and Milcah; and we have plenty of straw 25
and fodder and also room for you to spend the night.' So 26
the man bowed down and prostrated himself to the
LORD. He said, 'Blessed be the LORD the God of my master 27
Abraham, who has not failed to keep faith and truth with
my master; for I have been guided by the LORD to the
house of my master's kinsman.'

The girl ran to her mother's house and told them what 28
had happened. Now Rebecca had a brother named 29–30
Laban; and, when he saw the nose-ring, and also the
bracelets on his sister's wrists, and heard his sister Rebecca
tell what the man had said to her, he ran out to the man at
the spring. When he came to him and found him still
standing there by the camels, he said, 'Come in, sir, whom 31
the LORD has blessed. Why stay outside? I have prepared
the house, and there is room for the camels.' So he 32
brought the man into the house, unloaded the camels and
provided straw and fodder for them, and water for him
and all his men to wash their feet. Food was set before 33
him, but he said, 'I will not eat until I have delivered my
message.' Laban said, 'Let us hear it.' He answered, 'I am 34
the servant of Abraham. The LORD has greatly blessed my 35

master, and he has become a man of power. The LORD has given him flocks and herds, silver and gold, male and
36 female slaves, camels and asses. My master's wife Sarah in her old age bore him a son, to whom he has given all that
37 he has. So my master made me swear an oath, saying, "You shall not take a wife for my son from the women of
38 the Canaanites in whose land I dwell; but you shall go to my father's house and to my family to find a wife for
39 him." So I said to my master, "What if the woman will
40 not come with me?" He answered, "The LORD, in whose presence I have lived, will send his angel with you and will make your journey successful. You shall take a wife for
41 my son from my family and from my father's house; then you shall be released from the charge I have laid upon you. But if, when you come to my family, they will not give her to you, you shall still be released from the
42 charge." So I came to the spring today, and I said, "O LORD God of my master Abraham, if thou wilt make my
43 journey successful, let it be like this. Here I stand by the spring. When a young woman comes out to draw water, I shall say to her, 'Give me a little water to drink from
44 your jar.' If she answers, 'Yes, do drink, and I will draw water for your camels as well', she is the woman whom
45 the LORD intends for my master's son." Before I had finished praying silently, I saw Rebecca coming out with her water-jar on her shoulder. She went down to the spring and drew some water, and I said to her, "Please
46 give me a drink." She quickly lowered her jar from her shoulder and said, "Drink; and I will water your camels as well." So I drank, and she also gave my camels water.
47 I asked her whose daughter she was, and she said, "I am

the daughter of Bethuel, the son of Nahor and Milcah."
Then I put the ring in her nose and the bracelets on her
wrists, and I bowed low and prostrated myself before the 48
LORD. I blessed the LORD the God of my master Abraham,
who had led me by the right road to take my master's
niece for his son. Now tell me if you will keep faith and 49
truth with my master. If not, say so, and I will turn
elsewhere.'*a*

Laban and Bethuel answered, 'This is from the LORD; 50
we can say nothing for or against. Here is Rebecca her- 51
self; take her and go. She shall be the wife of your
master's son, as the LORD has decreed.' When Abraham's 52
servant heard what they said, he prostrated himself on the
ground before the LORD. Then he brought out gold and 53
silver ornaments, and robes, and gave them to Rebecca,
and he gave costly gifts to her brother and her mother. He 54
and his men then ate and drank and spent the night there.
When they rose in the morning, he said, 'Give me leave
to go back to my master.' Her brother and her mother 55
said, 'Let the girl stay with us for a few days, say ten days,
and then she shall go.' But he said to them, 'Do not detain 56
me, for the LORD has granted me success. Give me leave to
return to my master.' They said, 'Let us call the girl and 57
see what she says.' They called Rebecca and asked her if 58
she would go with the man, and she said, 'Yes, I will go.'
So they let their sister Rebecca and her nurse go with 59
Abraham's servant and his men. They blessed Rebecca 60
and said to her:

'You are our sister, may you be the mother of myriads;
   may your sons possess the cities*b* of their enemies.'

[a] *Lit.* to right or to left.   [b] *Lit.* gate.

61 Then Rebecca and her companions mounted their camels at once and followed the man. So the servant took Rebecca and went his way.

62 Isaac meanwhile had moved on as far as Beer-lahai-roi
63 and was living in the Negeb. One evening when he had gone out into the open country hoping to meet them,[a] he
64 looked up and saw camels approaching. When Rebecca raised her eyes and saw Isaac, she slipped hastily from her
65 camel, saying to the servant, 'Who is that man walking across the open towards us?' The servant answered, 'It is
66 my master.' So she took her veil and covered herself. The
67 servant related to Isaac all that had happened. Isaac conducted her into the tent[b] and took her as his wife. So she became his wife, and he loved her and was consoled for the death of his mother.

* On this, the longest single narrative in the patriarchal traditions, it is tempting to say all comment is superfluous. A superb story, moving in its charm and simplicity, is told with all the skill we associate with the J narrator. Abraham, in advanced old age, commissions a trusted servant to find a wife for Isaac. Two conditions are laid down:

(i) she must not be 'a woman of the Canaanites'; she must come from among Abraham's own kindred back home in north-west Mesopotamia. This reflects the belief that Abraham knows himself to be an alien in the land of the Canaanites. The future, under God, lies not with the indigenous population but with that alien family whom God has chosen. Later generations would certainly read into this attitude the insidious threat that Canaanite religion and culture posed to the Hebrews;

[a] hoping...them: *or* to relieve himself.
[b] *Prob. rdg.; Heb. adds* Sarah his mother.

(ii) on no account is Isaac to return to Abraham's home country. That would mean undoing the pilgrimage which Abraham had begun when he left Harran for Canaan.

The character of the trusted servant is deftly drawn. He is not told how to find a wife for Isaac, only where to go. Arriving at his destination he makes for the public well and prays, not for a miracle, but for guidance in using his own sound commonsense to lead him to the right woman. He looks for someone both generous and thoughtful. Rebecca appears. She amply fulfils his criteria, with the added bonus that she is both beautiful and chaste (verse 16). Once the servant discovers that she is a relative, a grand-daughter of Abraham's brother, he is certain that his mission has succeeded. Welcomed by the family, he refuses to accept hospitality until he tells of his commission. Events move quickly. The marriage is arranged. Rebecca herself agrees to leave the very next day. The final scene (verses 62–7), although obscure in certain points of detail, describes the first meeting and the marriage of Isaac and Rebecca.

The narrative, however, is not without its difficulties. It is strange that nothing is said at the end about Abraham welcoming Rebecca or commending his faithful servant. The returning servant refers to Isaac as 'my master' (verse 65). The opening scene reads very much like the instructions of a man who knows himself to be very near death, and is therefore unable personally to arrange an appropriate marriage for his son. Perhaps we are being invited to infer that between the servant's departure and his return – a period which must have been at least two to three months – Abraham died. True, the notice of Abraham's death 'at a good old age, after a very long life' is found in the next chapter (25: 8), but that comes from the P tradition with its fondness for summarizing and chronicling events.

Rebecca is introduced as 'the daughter of Bethuel, son of Milcah' (verse 15), but is her father still alive at the time of the story? After her meeting with Abraham's servant,

Rebecca runs 'to her mother's house' (verse 28), the welcome is prepared by Laban, her brother (verses 29–32) and costly gifts are presented 'to Rebecca...to her brother and her mother' (verse 53). There is only one reference to Bethuel being involved in the family discussions. Verse 50 states 'Laban and Bethuel answered'. The order of names here is unusual, the son being mentioned before the father. It is possible that the words 'and Bethuel' have been added to the text by someone who did not realize that the narrative works on the assumption that Bethuel is dead.

The Nuzi texts may throw some light on the role played by Laban. Among them are marriage contracts in which the brother acts in arranging a sister's marriage. These texts may assume the death of the father or they may reflect an original fratriarchal type of society where legal authority and responsibility rested with the brother. In such contracts, the girl involved gives her formal consent to the marriage It is interesting that Rebecca is consulted to see whether she is willing to 'go with the man' (verse 58). Such difficulties do not, however, obtrude and they certainly do not spoil the reader's enjoyment of one of the world's great match-making stories.

2. *Abraham said to his servant:* if this had been the Eliezer of chapter 15 we would have expected this fact to be noted. It is noteworthy that an anonymous servant plays the leading role in the story. On his lips we hear the first prayer in the book of Genesis (see verses 12–14). *Put your hand under my thigh:* the only other occurrence of this phrase in the Old Testament is Gen. 47: 29, where Jacob, on his death-bed, asks his son Joseph similarly to take a solemn oath. The meaning of the action is not certain. The hands placed upon the reproductive organs may indicate that the whole family who issue from that man are implicated in the oath. In this case, it would indicate that the whole family of Abraham, through the line of Isaac, would be prohibited from marrying a woman of the Canaanites.

3. *the LORD, the God of heaven and earth:* that is, the God

of the entire world; compare 14: 22 where the LORD is identified with 'God Most High, creator of heaven and earth'. Such descriptions of God in universalistic terms are not common in the patriarchal narratives. This description may have seemed appropriate to the narrator at the point where the servant is about to set out on a long journey, taking him beyond the bounds of Canaan to traverse other countries. The Septuagint, probably correctly, reads similarly at verse 7 where the Hebrew reads only 'the LORD the God of heaven'.

7. *he will send his angel* (messenger) *before you:* although Abraham does not tell the servant how he will identify the woman who is to be Isaac's wife, he assures him that he will be providentially guided in his choice.

10. *The servant took ten camels from his master's herds:* it has been suggested that this must be an anachronism since the domestication of the camel only took place late in the second millennium B.C. There are, however, sporadic references to camels in earlier documents. It would, in any case, be thought appropriate for a man of Abraham's standing to possess camels. *Aram-naharaim:* 'Aram of Two Rivers', (see the N.E.B. footnote and map p. xiii), the two rivers being the Euphrates and the Tigris. The region indicated by this phrase is the area of north-west Mesopotamia, lying to the east of the Euphrates. Both Mari and Harran are in this area. The lengthy journey is passed over in silence. Nor is the name of the city, to which the servant comes, given: it is simply referred to as *the city where Nahor lived.* To have reached Abraham's kinsmen is all that is important for the narrative. According to 11: 31 the city would be Harran.

11. The daily scene at the well where, towards evening, the women come to draw water is skilfully recreated.

12–14. *O LORD God of my master Abraham:* one of a series of descriptive titles, characteristic of the patriarchal, which link God with the head of the patriarchal family (see p. 12). The servant's prayer asks for no miracle. He prays for guidance, but assumes that commonsense must be actively involved in the situation. The servant has already decided upon the criteria for a suitable wife for Isaac. To give water to a stranger at the well would be an act of common courtesy: to offer to water his camels would show costly generosity and uncommon thoughtfulness. Such is the woman for whom he looks. *keep faith with my master Abraham:* see comment on 21: 23.

15. *praying silently:* the Hebrew text reads simply 'speaking'. Both the Samaritan text and Septuagint add 'in his heart (mind)', as does the Hebrew in the servant's recapitulation of the narrative in verse 45. The servant displays a marvellous calmness and patience. In verse 21 he is described as 'watching quietly', while Rebecca fulfils his expectations, a phrase which probably conveys something of the feeling of a man watching with bated breath to see what will happen.

16. Add to generosity and thoughtfulness the fact that Rebecca *was very beautiful, a virgin,* and the ideal wife is at hand.

22. The personal presents for Rebecca, *a gold nose-ring weighing half a shekel, and two bracelets for her wrists weighing ten shekels, also of gold,* would indicate more than a reward for services rendered. They are intended to show the servant's further interest in Rebecca.

27. His prayer for guidance answered, the servant now offers a prayer of thanksgiving for the successful accomplishment of his mission thus far.

28–32. After the disclosure that Rebecca is one of Abraham's kin, events move swiftly. Rebecca *ran to her mother's house,* and her brother Laban *ran out to the man at the spring.* The servant is welcomed, provision made for his camels, and water provided *for him and all his men to wash their feet.* The narrative has concentrated so exclusively upon the servant and his role that this is the first time there has been any mention of the men who accompanied him on the journey.

In verses 29–30 the N.E.B. follows many modern commentators in changing the order of the phrases in the traditional text. Traditionally the words *he ran out to the man at the spring* occur immediately after *Laban.* We may retain the traditional order and read at the beginning of verse 30 'he had seen' instead of the N.E.B. *and, when he saw*.

Although many commentators have seen in Laban's action a hint of greed, anticipating the character of Laban in chapters 29–31, this does not seem a necessary inference. Laban is naturally anxious to meet the man who has so honoured Rebecca. The demands of hospitality account for the rest of his actions.

34–49. The servant's long recapitulation of his mission is characteristic of narrative style in the ancient world. Similar examples can be found in the Babylonian Epic of Gilgamesh and in the Homeric poems.

49. *I will turn elsewhere:* or perhaps, 'I will decide what to do', literally, I will turn 'to right or to left' (see the N.E.B. footnote).

50. *This is from the LORD; we can say nothing for or against:* the servant has convinced them that what has happened is the LORD's will. Thereafter it is not for Laban – assuming *and Bethuel* to be an addition to the text – either to disapprove or to approve. He must simply accept.

53. *he gave costly gifts to her brother and her mother:* although the word translated *gifts* is not the technical word for the bride-price, in a society where marriage was a form of purchase, there can be little doubt that this is what is intended here.

55. *for a few days, say ten days:* literally, 'days or ten', probably an idiomatic expression for 'ten days or so'.

59. *her nurse:* an older woman who acts as travelling companion and confidante. There is a brief reference in 35: 8 to her death; she is there named Deborah.

60. The blessing pronounced upon Rebecca by her family is the blessing one might expect in a tribal situation; that Rebecca should be the mother of a large and strong tribe, *the mother of myriads*, a tribe noted for its military prowess, *may your sons possess the cities* (literally, 'gates') *of their enemies* (cp. 22: 17).

62. The Hebrew text here is far from clear in its geograph-

ical intention. The phrase *had moved on as far as* is little more
than a guess. Some of the versions read 'came into the desert
of Beer-lahai-roi'. Perhaps we should read 'had come from
Beer-lahai-roi'. For Beer-lahai-roi, see the comment at
16:13-14.

63. *hoping to meet them*: the Hebrew word behind this
translation is a puzzle. Most of the ancient versions take it to
mean something like 'meditating' or 'talking'. It might
indicate that Isaac had gone out for a stroll; or as the N.E.B.
footnote 'to relieve himself' indicates, it may be a deliberate
euphemism.

65. The putting on of the *veil* may be part of the prepara-
tion of the coming wedding ceremony, but the word, used
only here and in 38:14, 19, may denote a special shawl, here
used to conceal the face. There is no evidence for veils in
Old Testament times like those of Moslem women in recent
centuries.

67. After the word *tent* the Hebrew text adds 'Sarah his
mother'. Possibly the words have been accidentally misplaced
from the end of the verse. Thus the chapter would conclude
with the words 'and was consoled for the death of Sarah his
mother'.

Sarah may be dead; but God's promises must continue. The
future now lies with Isaac and his relationship with Rebecca.
But first, the history of the other descendants of Abraham
who are not the inheritors of the promise must be summar-
ized. ✱

THE FAMILY OF ABRAHAM

25 [a] Abraham married another wife, whose name was Ke-
2   turah. She bore him Zimran, Jokshan, Medan, Midian,
3   Ishbak and Shuah. Jokshan became the father of Sheba and
    Dedan. The sons of Dedan were Asshurim, Letushim and
4   Leummim, and the sons of Midian were Ephah, Epher,

[a] *Verses 1–4: cp. 1 Chron. 1: 32, 33.*

Enoch, Abida, and Eldaah. All these were descendants of
Keturah.

Abraham had given all that he had to Isaac; and he had 5, 6
already in his lifetime given presents to the sons of his
concubines, and had sent them away eastwards, to a land
of the east, out of his son Isaac's way. Abraham had lived 7
for a hundred and seventy-five years when he breathed 8
his last. He died at a good old age, after a very long life, and
was gathered to his father's kin. His sons, Isaac and 9
Ishmael, buried him in the cave at Machpelah, on the land
of Ephron son of Zohar the Hittite, east of Mamre, the 10
plot which Abraham had bought from the Hittites. There
Abraham was buried with his wife Sarah. After the death 11
of Abraham, God blessed his son Isaac, who settled close
by Beer-lahai-roi.

This is the table of the descendants of Abraham's son 12
Ishmael, whom Hagar the Egyptian, Sarah's slave-girl,
bore to him. These are the names of the sons of Ishmael 13[a]
named in order of their birth: Nebaioth, Ishmael's eldest
son, then Kedar, Adbeel, Mibsam, Mishma, Dumah, 14
Massa, Hadad,[b] Teman,[c] Jetur, Naphish and Kedemah. 15
These are the sons of Ishmael, after whom their hamlets 16
and encampments were named, twelve princes according
to their tribal groups. Ishmael had lived for a hundred and 17
thirty-seven years when he breathed his last. So he died
and was gathered to his father's kin. Ishmael's sons 18
inhabited the land from Havilah to Shur, which is east of
Egypt on the way to Asshur, having settled to the east of
his brothers.

✶ This section rounds off the traditions about Abraham.

[a] *Verses 13–16: cp. 1 Chron. 1: 29–31.*
[b] *Or, with one MS.,* Harar.   [c] *So Sept.; Heb.* Tema.

Central to it, at verses 7–10, is a note from the P sourc
describing the death and burial of Abraham. He dies 'a
a good old age, after a very long life' and is buried by hi
sons in the family vault at Machpelah. It is assumed tha
Ishmael, in spite of the expulsion narrative in 21: 1–21
returns to share in the funeral rites. The section as a whole
however, is as much concerned with the future as with th
past. On either side of the account of Abraham's death ther
are statements which clearly point to the future which lie
with Isaac. Abraham 'had given all that he had to Isaac
(verse 5) and 'God blessed his son Isaac' (verse 11). Supremel
what God had given to Isaac through Abraham was his plac
in the outworking of God's promises and the blessing
associated with them.

Before the narrative continues with the family history o
Isaac, what is known of Abraham's other sons is briefl
sketched. From the point of view of the main theme of th
patriarchal narratives these other sons represent cul-de-sacs
yet they are witness to the fact that from this one man man
descendants were to spring. So verses 1–4 list the descendant
of Abraham by his wife Keturah, and verses 12–18 give th
family history of Ishmael.

1–4. These verses from the J source are somewhat loosel
structured. They list the sons of Abraham born to *anothe
wife...Keturah*, whom, we must assume, he married afte
the death of Sarah. Six sons are named and further informa
tion given about the families of two of them, Jokshan an
Midian, and about *the sons of Dedan* of the next generation
The same list, with the omission of the reference to the son
of Dedan appears in 1 Chron. 1: 32–3. Many of the names ar
shadowy but all seem to represent tribal groups who live
in the desert steppe to the east of Canaan and southwards a
far as the Arabian peninsula.

3. *Sheba and Dedan* appear in Ezekiel's list of the merchant
of the world of his day, Dedan as a dealer in 'coarse woollen
for saddle-cloths', Sheba as 'offering the choicest spices

very kind of precious stone and gold' (Ezek. 27: 20, 22). *Asshurim:* a desert tribe not to be confused with the Assyrians. The place-name Asshur in verse 18 should be similarly interpreted.

4. *the sons of Midian:* the Midianites touch Hebrew history at many points. Moses, for example, fled from the Egyptian court to the land of Midian and married a Midianite girl, daughter of the priest of Midian named Reuel (Exod. 2: 11–22). The priest appears in Exod. 18 (here named Jethro), acknowledging Yahweh as supreme God (verses 10–11) and counselling Moses. Such a closeness of relationship contrasts strangely with the picture of marauding, camel-riding Midianites who were a thorn in the flesh of the Hebrews during the early period of the settlement in Canaan (Judg. 6–8).

5–6. *Abraham had given all that he had to Isaac: given* is used here in a strictly legal sense, meaning 'bequeathed'. Isaac had thus been designated as Abraham's legal heir. Like a generous father, however, Abraham had *already in his lifetime* made provision for *the sons of his concubines.* Since only Hagar had previously been noted as Abraham's concubine we must either assume that he had other concubines not mentioned in the narrative or that the plural *concubines* is used, following Hebrew idiom, in an abstract sense to mean concubinage. The emphasis upon the other sons being *sent...away eastwards* serves to underline the unique position and status of Isaac.

7. *Abraham had lived for a hundred and seventy-five years:* what traditional information or speculation, if any, lay behind this precise figure we do not know. It can hardly be accidental however, that Abraham dies exactly one hundred years after he sets out from Harran (see 12: 5).

8–9. *He died at a good old age, after a very long life:* the phrase *after a very long life* may be more literally rendered 'old and satisfied (or fulfilled)'. A premature, childless death was tragedy, but to die at a ripe old age, surrounded by a goodly family, was the natural end of a fulfilled life. *gathered to his*

117

father's kin: a characteristic way of describing what happer at death (cp. 35: 29; 49: 29). It stresses the oneness of th family group across the generations and probably impli being buried in a family tomb. Abraham was buried along side Sarah *in the cave at Machpelah* in what was to become th family tomb.

12. *This is the table of the descendants of:* the typical phra; used by the P tradition to introduce a piece of family histor The Authorized Version and the Revised Version rende 'These are the generations of. . .' The N.E.B. varies betwee *This is the table of the descendants of.* . . and 'These are th descendants of. . .' (see 10: 1).

13–15. Twelve *sons of Ishmael* are listed, just as there wer twelve sons of Nahor (22: 20–4) and twelve sons of Jaco (35: 23–6). Leagues of twelve tribes seem to have been con mon in the ancient Near East. It has been suggested, followin a later Greek analogy, that there was a religious reason fc this; each tribe being responsible on a monthly rota fc providing for worship at a central sanctuary. The evidenc for this, however, is far from conclusive. About most of th names in this list – which occurs again in 1 Chron. 1: 29–30 we have little information. Such evidence as we have link them with the Arabian peninsula. Kedar appears in Ezekiel list of merchants as 'the source of your commerce in lamb rams, and he-goats' (Ezek. 27: 21). Nebaioth is mentione alongside Kedar as providing rams acceptable as sacrifici; offerings in Isa. 60: 7. The variant readings *Hadad* or 'Harar (see the N.E.B. footnote) or, in the Syriac version, 'Hadar show the very common confusion of the Hebrew letters 'r and 'd' in manuscripts. It is difficult to see why the N.E.F follows the Septuagint reading *Teman* against the Hebrev 'Tema'. Elsewhere in the Old Testament Teman is liste with the Edomites (see 36: 11; Amos 1: 12). Tema, probabl to be identified with the well-known Arabian oasis of Teima is mentioned together with Kedar and Dedan in an oracl dealing with the Arabs in Isa. 21: 13–17.

16. *twelve princes:* the word translated *princes* here and in 7: 20 indicates anyone of high status. Although in certain contexts it may have a religious meaning it is doubtful whether here it means anything more than tribal chieftains.

18. *from Havilah to Shur:* cp. 1 Sam. 15: 7. The precise identity of Havilah is uncertain. Various oases in Arabia and elsewhere have been suggested. For Shur see comment on 16: 7. The general area indicated probably centres on the northern fringe of the Arabian peninsula.

having settled to the east of his brothers: a similar phrase in 16: 12 is translated by the N.E.B. 'shall live at odds with all his kinsmen' (see note there). It could here mean 'having lived at odds with his kinsmen', but this seems less probable in the context. The same wording is used for *east of Egypt*. ✶

THE FAMILY OF ISAAC

This is the table of the descendants of Abraham's son 19 Isaac. Isaac's father was Abraham. When Isaac was forty 20 years old he married Rebecca the daughter of Bethuel the Aramaean from Paddan-aram and the sister of Laban the Aramaean. Isaac appealed to the LORD on behalf of his wife 21 because she was barren; the LORD yielded to his entreaty, and Rebecca conceived. The children pressed hard on 22 each other in her womb, and she said, 'If this is how it is with me, what does it mean?' So she went to seek guidance of the LORD. The LORD said to her: 23

> 'Two nations in your womb,
>   two peoples, going their own ways from birth!
>   One shall be stronger than the other;
>   the older shall be servant to the younger.'

When her time had come, there were indeed twins in her 24

25 womb. The first came out red, hairy all over like a ha
26 cloak, and they named him Esau.[a] Immediately afte
   wards his brother was born with his hand grasping Esa
   heel, and they called him Jacob.[b] Isaac was sixty years o
   when they were born.

※ 19. *This is the table of the descendants of Abraham's s
Isaac: see note on verse 12. The occurrence of this phrase he
is unusual since instead of introducing a fairly factual list
the sons of Isaac, it leads into a piece of family lore concerni
the birth of rival twins. The reason may lie in the mergi
of different sources, with an introduction from the P sour
leading into narrative from the J source in verses 21–6.

   20. This verse looks back to the narrative in chapter :
Paddan-aram as a place-name occurs only in the P traditic
concerning Isaac and Jacob (cp. 28: 1–9 and 48: 7). The nam
which may mean 'Road (or Field) of Aram' is probab
intended to indicate a specific place in the general area
Aram-naharaim.

   21. The theme of a wife's barrenness plays a promine
part in the patriarchal stories. The acute tensions – domes
and theological – of this situation, noted in the Abrahar
Sarah stories are not stressed here, though they might ha
been. The chronological information given in verses 20 a
26 that Isaac was forty years old when he married Rebecc
and sixty when the twins were born, would indicate th
Rebecca had known the frustration and strain of sterility f
twenty years. The interest in this section, however, focuss
not on the Isaac–Rebecca relationship but on the contrastii
and conflicting characters of the sons she conceived. *Isa
appealed to the LORD...the LORD yielded to his entreaty:* th
translation hardly catches the flavour of the original in whi
the same verb occurs in both phrases: we might rend

[a] *That is* Covering.   [b] *That is* He caught by the he

'Isaac entreated the LORD...the LORD let himself be entreated.'

22–6. Three themes, which appear elsewhere in the Genesis traditions and more widely in the Old Testament, are to be found in these verses.

(i) Esau and Jacob are depicted not merely as individuals. They are the ancestors who give their names to two tribal groups.

> 'Two nations in your womb,
> two peoples, going their own ways from birth!'
>
> (verse 23)

The traditions about Esau and Jacob have a strong tribal interest. They are pointers to the history of, and the relationship between, the sons of Esau, the Edomites (cp. 36: 9–43) who occupied territory south of the Dead Sea, and the Israelites, the sons of Jacob/Israel (cp. 35: 10).

(ii) The important status, the birthright, which belongs to the eldest son in the family is described, and how in certain circumstances that status may pass to another member of the family is explained. The eldest son has both responsibilities and privileges, the responsibility of being the embodiment of the family name and fortune, the link with the future, the privilege of being next to his father in status and of receiving a double portion in the share out of the family inheritance (see Deut. 21: 17. The texts discovered at Nuzi, 150 miles (241 km) north of Baghdad (see *The Making of the Old Testament*, p. 10, in this series) also provide evidence for the eldest son receiving a double portion).

(iii) Popular explanations are given of certain names. Thus at the birth of the twins we are told 'The first came out red' (verse 25). The Hebrew word for red is *'adom* (here *'admoni*), a play on the theme of Esau as ancestor of the Edomites. Another explanation of the word Edom, again linking it with Hebrew *'adom*, but this time referring to the 'red broth' which Jacob gives to Esau, is to be found in verse 30. The key word in the description of Esau as 'hairy all over like a hair cloak' (verse 25) is the Hebrew *se'ar*, a play on the name fo the hill-country of Seir, the home of the Edomites. Th N.E.B. footnote renders the name Esau as 'covering assuming a connection with a Hebrew verb *'asah* 'to cover But this is very doubtful; in fact the meaning of the name uncertain. The combining of elements here, and evidenc elsewhere in the Old Testament, strongly suggest that Esa and Edom were originally distinct, equated only at som stage in Old Testament times. Similarly the name of Jaco is explained by reference to the Hebrew word *'aqab*, 'heel the one 'born with his hand grasping Esau's heel' (verse 26 see the N.E.B. footnote).

Another popular, but different, explanation of the nam Jacob is given in 27: 36. From similar types of names in th ancient Near East it is likely that Jacob is in fact an abbrevia tion of Jacob-el, meaning 'May God protect', but popula story-telling is not bound by the rules of linguistics.

22. Relations between the Israelites and the Edomites wer often troubled and bitter (see Obadiah). This is reflected i many of the incidents in the traditions concerning Jacob an Esau. Here it is traced back to their pre-natal condition, the *pressed hard on each other in her womb. So she went to seek guid ance of the LORD:* we are not told how Rebecca sough guidance of the LORD. Elsewhere in the Old Testament th same phrase is often used to describe someone going to sacred site or temple to consult God. The narrative, howeve is concerned not with how it is done, but with the reply sh receives, a reply which controls the destiny of two nations.

23. *the older shall be servant to the younger:* thus reversing the normal roles, Jacob usurping the position which wa Esau's by right. This reversal of roles is attributed to a decre of the LORD prior to the birth of the twins. The tradition which follow have no illusions about Jacob. Favourite son o a doting mother, he is a cold, calculating schemer, prepare to drive a hard bargain with Esau (verses 27–34) and to deceiv

his aged, blind father (chapter 27). He has little to learn in the art of oneupmanship (see 30: 25–43). He is no idealized figure; he reaps a bitter harvest from his actions. Yet this is the man who becomes Israel (see 32: 28), the inheritor of the promises made to Abraham, the man through whom God's purposes and promises are to be handed on to future generations. *

ESAU SELLS HIS BIRTHRIGHT

The boys grew up; and Esau became skilful in hunting, 27 a man of the open plains, but Jacob led a settled life and stayed among the tents. Isaac favoured Esau because he 28 kept him supplied with venison, but Rebecca favoured Jacob. One day Jacob prepared a broth and when Esau 29 came in from the country, exhausted, he said to Jacob, 30 'I am exhausted; let me swallow some of that red broth': this is why he was called Edom.[a] Jacob said, 'Not till you 31 sell me your rights as the first-born.' Esau replied, 'I am at 32 death's door; what use is my birthright to me?' Jacob 33 said, 'Not till you swear!'; so he swore an oath and sold his birthright to Jacob. Then Jacob gave Esau bread and 34 the lentil broth, and he ate and drank and went away without more ado. Thus Esau showed how little he valued his birthright.

* This section ought to be read together with chapter 27. The theme of both is basically the same: how Jacob deprived Esau of what was his by right. In both Jacob appears in a most unfavourable light, taking advantage of Esau's exhausted condition in this section, and shamelessly tricking blind Isaac into giving him a dying father's benediction which should

[a] *That is* Red.

have gone to the eldest son, in chapter 27. Esau, however, is depicted very differently in the two sections. Here he appears as a somewhat boorish, insensitive man, willing to trade anything to satisfy his immediate pangs of hunger. In chapter 27 he is a somewhat piteous figure, desperately trying to salvage something from a brother's treachery and not unnaturally bearing that brother a bitter grudge.

What is at stake here is Esau's 'rights as the first-born', probably the right to receive a double portion of the family inheritance and confirmation of status as head of the family on his father's death. Certainly the deal Esau makes with Jacob does not seem to alter his status during his father's lifetime. Up to the last Isaac believes that he is bestowing the rightful eldest son's blessing upon Esau. But there is a deeper undercurrent. This is no mere family saga; it is the story of a pilgrimage of faith. Just as Abraham bequeathed to Isaac his place in the outworking of God's promises, so now the question is who inherits these promises from Isaac. Although he acts with cold, calculating self-interest, Jacob, unknown to himself, is serving a higher purpose. Esau, on the other hand renounces, under the pressure of immediate needs, something of which he does not know the value.

27. Esau and Jacob symbolize two different ways of life; Esau the hunter, a man of the open plains and Jacob the shepherd, who leads a more settled life.

29–31. The harshness of the hunter's life is underlined. If he does not kill he returns home hungry and *exhausted*. Jacob drives a hard bargain; *some of that red broth* or stew for *your rights as the first-born*.

33. '*Not till you swear!*' a solemn oath had as much binding force as a carefully drawn up and legally attested document.

34. *and went away without more ado*: although the words *without more ado* are not in the Hebrew text, they serve to bring out what is implicit in the text. Esau's sole concern was to satisfy his immediate bodily needs. Having done so, *he ate and drank and went away*, totally unconcerned about what he has given away. *

124

ISAAC AT GERAR AND BEERSHEBA

✶ Chapter 26 gathers together all the traditions which centre primarily on Isaac. The traditions are brief, varied and at almost every point overlap with traditions already linked with Abraham:

verses 2–6 repeat and expand the theme of the promises made to Abraham in 12: 1–3 and 15: 7;

verses 7–11 contain a version of the wife–sister theme which has already occurred twice in the Abraham stories (see 12: 10–20 and chapter 20);

verses 12–22 bring Isaac into conflict with the Philistines in a dispute over access to wells, as is the case with Abraham in 21: 25–30;

verses 23–33 link Isaac with Beersheba and provide an explanation of the origin of the name Beersheba; cp. the Abraham tradition in 21: 22–34.

Common to both traditions are the Philistine king, Abimelech, and his army commander, Phicol.

If, as some scholars believe, these overlapping stories are variant versions of one tradition, then the comparatively minor role which Isaac now has in the tradition may be the result of Abraham becoming the dominant figure and attaching to himself stories which were once told about Isaac. The entire chapter, with the possible exception of verses 34–5, comes from the J source. ✶

THE PROMISE CONFIRMED TO ISAAC

There came a famine in the land—not the earlier famine in **26** Abraham's time—and Isaac went to Abimelech the Philistine king at Gerar. The LORD appeared to Isaac and 2 said, 'Do not go down to Egypt, but stay in this country as I bid you. Stay in this country and I will be with you 3 and bless you, for to you and to your descendants I will give all these lands. Thus shall I fulfil the oath which

4 I swore to your father Abraham. I will make your descendants as many as the stars in the sky; I will give them all these lands, and all the nations of the earth will
5 pray to be blessed as they are blessed—all because Abraham obeyed me and kept my charge, my commandments, my
6 statutes, and my laws.' So Isaac lived in Gerar.

7   When the men of the place asked him about his wife, he told them that she was his sister; he was afraid to say that Rebecca was his wife, in case they killed him because
8 of her; for she was very beautiful. When they had been there for some considerable time, Abimelech the Philistine king looked down from his window and saw Isaac
9 and his wife Rebecca laughing together. He summoned Isaac and said, 'So she is your wife, is she? What made you say she was your sister?' Isaac answered, 'I thought
10 I should be killed because of her.' Abimelech said, 'Why have you treated us like this? One of the people might easily have gone to bed with your wife, and then you
11 would have made us liable to retribution.' So Abimelech warned all the people, threatening that whoever touched this man or his wife would be put to death.

✻ It is interesting to compare the structure of this passage with 12: 10–20. Both passages begin on the same note – famine. But whereas in chapter 12 there immediately follows the brief account of the journey to Egypt and the threat to Sarai, here, between the famine and the threat to Isaac's wife Rebecca, there comes a theophany – the LORD appeared to Isaac. The purpose of this theophany is twofold:

(i) to ensure that Isaac does not attempt to escape the coming of famine by going down to Egypt. Canaan has by now been clearly designated as the land promised by God to

Abraham. Isaac must not jeopardize the promise by leaving Canaan. It is characteristic of the restraint of the narrator that he does not tell us how Isaac did survive the famine. He simply comments 'So Isaac lived in Gerar' (verse 6).

(ii) to confirm and to develop the promises made to Abraham. The key elements in these promises are repeated – blessing, the giving of the land, descendants as numerous 'as the stars in the sky' – but two new elements appear:

(a) the dependability of the promise is rooted in an oath which the LORD swore to 'your father Abraham'. Just as Esau unwittingly renounced his share in the promise by a solemn oath (25: 33), so the continuance of the promise depends upon a deliberate and unchangeable oath sworn by the LORD;

(b) Abraham is cited as an example of the kind of response which is expected from the human side, the response of obedience (see verse 5).

1. *not the earlier famine in Abraham's time:* since famine was not an unusual occurrence in Canaan, dependent as it was upon the somewhat fickle annual rainfall, there is nothing strange in the repetition of the famine motif. By referring to the famine in Abraham's time the narrator is deliberately drawing our attention to the parallel with 12: 10–20. *Abimelech the Philistine king at Gerar:* see note on 20: 2.

4. *pray to be blessed as they are blessed:* although the form of the verb 'to bless' in Hebrew is different from that found in 12: 3, the meaning is similar.

5. *kept my charge, my commandments, my statutes, and my laws:* the words *commandments, statutes* and *laws* define what is involved in the charge or mandate that Abraham was called to keep, in terms which would be familiar to later generations in Israel whose life was governed by such statutes and laws, given, according to tradition, to Israel through Moses (see Deut. 4: 1–2).

7–11. For the relationship between this account of the hazarding of a patriarch's wife and the similar stories in chapters 12 and 20 see pp. 4–6. Here the threat to Rebecca is potential rather than actual. Abimelech does not touch her. When he accidentally discovers her true relationship to Isaac, he takes immediate steps to safeguard his own community. Isaac's excuse for his double dealing is as lame as Abraham's in 12: 10–13.

8. *saw Isaac and his wife Rebecca laughing together:* another play on the name Isaac (see 17: 17) and one much more strongly emphasized in the Hebrew text where the word *laughing* comes immediately after *Isaac. laughing* could be rendered 'playing', i.e. 'making love', which seems more probable.

10. *then you would have made us liable to retribution:* the word translated *retribution* also means 'guilt', particularly in a situation where tangible restitution can be assessed for a wrong done. Under the Mosaic law (see Lev. 20: 10) the penalty for both adulterer and adulteress is death. ✷

TROUBLE WITH THE PHILISTINES

12 Isaac sowed seed in that land, and that year he reaped a
13 hundred-fold, and the LORD blessed him. He became more and more powerful, until he was very powerful
14 indeed. He had flocks and herds and many slaves, so that
15 the Philistines were envious of him. They had stopped up all the wells dug by the slaves in the days of Isaac's father
18 Abraham, and filled them with earth. Isaac dug them again, all those wells dug in his father Abraham's time, and stopped up by the Philistines after his death, and he called them by the names which his father had given them.

16   Then Abimelech said to him, 'Go away from here; you
17 are too strong for us.' So Isaac left that place and encamped
19*a* in the valley of Gerar, and stayed there. Then Isaac's

[a] *Verse 18 transposed to follow 15.*

slaves dug in the valley and found a spring of running
water, but the shepherds of Gerar quarrelled with Isaac's 20
shepherds, claiming the water as theirs. He called the well
Esek,[a] because they made difficulties for him. His men 21
then dug another well, but the others quarrelled with him
over that also, so he called it Sitnah.[b] He moved on from 22
there and dug another well, but there was no quarrel over
that one, so he called it Rehoboth,[c] saying, 'Now the
LORD has given us plenty of room and we shall be fruitful
in the land.'

12. *Isaac sowed seed in that land:* this is the first reference to
a patriarch sharing in the activities of the settled farming
community. It was not uncommon for semi-nomadic groups
to settle seasonally in an area and reap a crop before moving on.
he reaped a hundredfold: a reasonable return in a year of plenty
(see Mark 4: 8).

14. Isaac's real wealth, however, is calculated in nomadic
terms, *flocks and herds and many slaves.* This gives him status
as a powerful clan leader, an evident sign of the LORD's
blessing. *so that the Philistines were envious of him:* this suggests
a motive for the attempt to deny Isaac access to wells in the
area. It is a comment which must often have evoked a wry
smile from Hebrew readers of the story on the many occasions when they found themselves subject to foreign régimes,
enviable because of their military power and cultural achieve-
ments.

15–19. The N.E.B. reordering of these verses to make
verse 18 follow immediately after verse 15 seems to give
a more natural sequence of events but is not strictly necessary
once we recognize that verse 15 is an aside alluding to events

[a] *That is* Difficulty.   [b] *That is* Enmity.
[c] *That is* Plenty of room.

which are no longer part of the Abraham stories. This aside is then picked up in the present narrative in verse 18.

18-22. he called them by the names which his father had given them: this reference to the names of the wells prepares the way for a series of brief notes (verses 19-22) which provide an aetiology or explanation of the names of certain other springs or wells in the area. The first two names *Esek* (verse 20) and *Sitnah* (verse 21) are traced back to the quarrel between the shepherds of Isaac and the local shepherds of Gerar. *Esek* means 'difficulty' (see the N.E.B. footnote) or 'challenge' and plays upon the meaning of the verb from the same root translated *they made difficulties for him* (or 'they challenged him'). *Sitnah* has no corresponding verb in the text but its meaning 'enmity' (see the N.E.B. footnote) or 'opposition' picks up the general atmosphere of quarrelling present in the narrative. The third name *Rehoboth* (verse 22) means 'room' (see the N.E.B. footnote), perhaps 'ample room'; it plays upon the similar-sounding verb translated *has given us plenty of room.* The exact location of these wells is uncertain, though there is a valley some 19 miles (30½ km) south-west of Beersheba called the Wadi Ruheibeh which may retain an echo of the name Rehoboth. The material here, however, has not been preserved solely to give an explanation of the names of three wells. Isaac is moving around in the land promised by God to Abraham and his descendants. Obstacles bar the way to the fulfilment of this promise. The Philistines are hostile. They stop up wells; they dispute watering rights with Isaac. Isaac moves on, trusting in the LORD to remove the obstacles, and the LORD provides him with undisputed room in which to settle and prosper. *

ISAAC AT BEERSHEBA

23, 24 Isaac went up country from there to Beersheba. That same night the LORD appeared to him there and said, 'I am the God of your father Abraham. Fear nothing, for

I am with you. I will bless you and give you many descendants for the sake of Abraham my servant.' So Isaac 25 built an altar there and invoked the LORD by name. Then he pitched his tent there, and there also his slaves dug a well. Abimelech came to him from Gerar with Ahuzzath 26 his friend and Phicol the commander of his army. Isaac 27 said to them, 'Why have you come here? You hate me and you sent me away.' They answered, 'We have seen 28 plainly that the LORD is with you, so we thought, "Let the two of us put each other to the oath and make a treaty that will bind us." We have not attacked you, we have 29 done you nothing but good, and we let you go away peaceably. Swear that you will do us no harm, now that the LORD has blessed you.' So Isaac gave a feast and they 30 ate and drank. They rose early in the morning and 31 exchanged oaths. Then Isaac bade them farewell, and they parted from him in peace. The same day Isaac's 32 slaves came and told him about a well that they had dug: 'We have found water', they said. He named the well 33 Shibah.[a] This is why the city is called Beersheba[b] to this day.

* Two incidents, both closely paralleled in the Abraham traditions, are associated with Isaac's stay at Beersheba. The first (verses 23–5), centres upon a theophany 'the LORD appeared to him there'. Just as Abraham, seemingly denied part of the promised land by Lot's selfish choice, is reassured by a word from the LORD (13: 14–18), so now to Isaac, facing Philistine opposition, there comes reassurance through the repetition of the promise of blessing and many descendants. In each case the patriarch's response to the LORD takes

[a] *That is* Oath.   [b] *That is* Well of an Oath.

the form of the building of an altar which marks the place as one of continuing and lasting importance as a centre for the worship of the LORD. The prophet Amos refers to Beersheba as an important religous centre in his day (Amos 5: 5; 8: 14).

24. *the God of your father Abraham:* see p. 12. *Fear nothing, for I am with you:* see the introductory comments on chapter 15, on such words of reassurance, p. 42. *for the sake of Abraham my servant:* that is, in order that the promises made to Abraham may find their fulfilment.

25. The commonsense realism of the narrative is well illustrated in this verse: *an altar* and *a well*, a place to worship the LORD and the provision of the necessity for sustaining life. Round these Isaac's life revolves.

26-33. The second incident at Beersheba records a treaty with Abimelech. The notes on the parallel Abraham narrative in 21: 22-34 should be consulted. This Isaac tradition focusses on 'the oath' (verse 28) as the explanation of the name Beersheba, 'Well of an Oath' (see the N.E.B. footnote). Likewise the name given to the well dug by Isaac's slaves, Shibah (verse 33), is best explained in context as 'Oath' (see the N.E.B. footnote), though it could also mean 'seven' or 'plenty', and some of the early versions (e.g. the Vulgate; see p. xii) follow these explanations. This section forms a fitting climax to the Isaac traditions. It reiterates what is of central significance in Isaac's life, 'the LORD is with you' (verse 28), and it stresses that this fact is now recognized by the Philistines and their ruler Abimelech who in previous incidents had been anything but friendly.

26. *Ahuzzath his friend:* Ahuzzath appears only here in the Old Testament, though some of the versions introduce him into the parallel narrative in chapter 21. *friend* is probably better translated in its more technical sense of counsellor or adviser; the 'King's Friend' appears as one of the officials at Solomon's court listed in 1 Kings 4: 5. ✲

ESAU'S WIVES

When Esau was forty years old he married Judith daughter 34
of Beeri the Hittite, and Basemath daughter of Elon the
Hittite; this was a bitter grief to Isaac and Rebecca. 35

✷ This brief note from the priestly source prepares the
way for the concluding verse of chapter 27 and the opening
section of chapter 28. Tradition seems to have preserved more
than one explanation as to why it was Jacob and not Esau
who became Isaac's heir and thus the inheritor of the promises
first made to Abraham. Here it is suggested that Esau excluded
himself by marrying foreign wives, unlike Jacob who,
according to chapter 29, followed in his father's footsteps by
marrying from among his own kinsfolk in Harran.

34. *Judith daughter of Beeri the Hittite, and Basemath daughter
of Elon the Hittite:* the information given here and in 28: 9 does
not coincide with that given in the list of Esau's descendants
in 36: 2–3. That there should be such discrepancies in names
handed down in tradition across the centuries need hardly
surprise us. ✷

Jacob and Esau

THE STOLEN BLESSING

WHEN ISAAC GREW OLD and his eyes became so dim **27**
that he could not see, he called his elder son Esau and
said to him, 'My son', and he answered, 'Here I am.'
Isaac said, 'Listen now: I am old and I do not know when 2
I may die. Take your hunting gear, your quiver and your 3
bow, and go out into the country and get me some
venison. Then make me a savoury dish of the kind I like, 4

and bring it to me to eat so that I may give you my bles
5 ing before I die.' Now Rebecca was listening as Isa
talked to his son Esau. When Esau went off into th
6 country to find some venison and bring it home, she sai
to her son Jacob, 'I heard your father talking to you
7 brother Esau, and he said, "Bring me some venison an
make it into a savoury dish so that I may eat it and ble
8 you in the presence of the LORD before I die." Listen
9 me, my son, and do what I tell you. Go to the flock an
pick me out two fine young kids, and I will make the
into a savoury dish for your father, of the kind he like
10 Then take them in to your father, and he will eat them
11 that he may bless you before he dies.' Jacob said to h
mother Rebecca, 'But my brother Esau is a hairy mai
12 and my skin is smooth. Suppose my father feels me, I
will know I am tricking him and I shall bring a cur
13 upon myself instead of a blessing.' His mother answere
him, 'Let the curse fall on me, my son, but do as I say; g
14 and bring me the kids.' So Jacob fetched them and broug
them to his mother, who made them into a savoury dis
15 of the kind that his father liked. Then Rebecca took h
elder son's clothes, Esau's best clothes which she kept l
her in the house, and put them on her younger son Jacol
16 She put the goatskins on his hands and on the smoot
17 nape of his neck; and she handed her son Jacob th
18 savoury dish and the bread she had made. He came to h
father and said, 'Father.' He answered, 'Yes, my son; wh
19 are you?' Jacob answered his father, 'I am Esau, you
elder son. I have done as you told me. Come, sit up an
eat some of my venison, so that you may give me you
20 blessing.' Isaac said to his son, 'What is this that yc
found so quickly?', and Jacob answered, 'It is what th

LORD your God put in my way.' Isaac then said to Jacob, 21
'Come close and let me feel you, my son, to see whether
you are really my son Esau.' When Jacob came close to 22
his father, Isaac felt him and said, 'The voice is Jacob's
voice, but the hands are the hands of Esau.' He did not 23
recognize him because his hands were hairy like Esau's,
and that is why he blessed him. He said, 'Are you really 24
my son Esau?', and he answered, 'Yes.' Then Isaac said, 25
'Bring me some of your*a* venison to eat, my son, so that
I may give you my blessing.' Then Jacob brought it to
him, and he ate it; he brought wine also, and he drank it.
Then his father Isaac said to him, 'Come near, my son, 26
and kiss me.' So he came near and kissed him, and when 27
Isaac smelt the smell of his clothes, he blessed him and
said:

'Ah! The smell of my son is like the smell of open
    country
blessed by the LORD.
God give you dew from heaven   28
and the richness of the earth,
corn and new wine in plenty!
Peoples shall serve you,   29
nations bow down to you.
   Be lord over your brothers;
may your mother's sons bow down to you.
A curse upon those who curse you;
a blessing on those who bless you!'

Isaac finished blessing Jacob; and Jacob had scarcely left 30
his father Isaac's presence, when his brother Esau came in
from his hunting. He too made a savoury dish and brought 31

[a] *So Sept.: Heb. om.*

it to his father. He said, 'Come, father, and eat some o
32 my venison, so that you may give me your blessing.' H
father Isaac said, 'Who are you?' He said, 'I am Esau
33 your elder son.' Then Isaac became greatly agitated* an
said, 'Then who was it that hunted and brought m
venison? I ate it all before you came in and I blessed hin
34 and the blessing will stand.' When Esau heard what hi
father said, he gave a loud and bitter cry and said, 'Bles
35 me too, father.' But Isaac said, 'Your brother came trea
36 cherously and took away your blessing.' Esau said, 'He i
rightly called Jacob.* This is the second time he has sup
planted me. He took away my right as the first-born an
now he has taken away my blessing. Have you kept bac
37 any blessing for me?' Isaac answered, 'I have made hin
lord over you, and I have given him all his brothers a
slaves. I have bestowed upon him corn and new wine fo
his sustenance. What is there left that I can do for you, m
38 son?' Esau asked his father, 'Had you then only one bless
ing, father? Bless me too, my father.' And Esau crie
39 bitterly. Then his father Isaac answered:

'Your dwelling shall be far from the richness of the earth
far from the dew of heaven above.
40 By your sword shall you live,
and you shall serve your brother;
but the time will come when you grow restive
and break off his yoke from your neck.'

41 Esau bore a grudge against Jacob because of the blessing
which his father had given him, and he said to himself
'The time of mourning for my father will soon be here

[a] *Or* incensed.   [b] *That is* He supplanted.

then I will kill my brother Jacob.' When Rebecca was told 42
what her elder son Esau was saying, she called her younger
son Jacob, and she said to him, 'Esau your brother is
threatening to kill you. Now, my son, listen to me. Slip 43
away at once to my brother Laban in Harran. Stay with 44
him for a while until your brother's anger cools. When it 45
has subsided and he forgets what you have done to him,
I will send and fetch you back. Why should I lose you
both in one day?'

* This narrative continues the theme of the rivalry of
Jacob and Esau which was first touched upon in the story
of birthright in 25: 27–34. A general guide to the interpretation of the theme appears there (see pp. 123–4). Although
attempts have been made to find different sources woven
together in the narrative, it is best treated as a unity from the
J tradition. It is skilfully constructed. It begins (verses 1–4)
and ends (verses 30–40) with sharply contrasting conversa-
tions between father and son, Isaac and Esau. From the quiet
poignancy of the opening scene we move through the schem-
ing of a partisan mother and the shameless deceiving of an
old, blind father to words of consternation and bitter
recrimination.

Several motifs appear in the story. There are hints of
rivalry between two ways of life; Esau with his 'hunting
gear' (verse 3) stalking venison or game, Jacob with his
flocks and 'young kids' (verse 9). Shepherds may well have
chuckled as they listened to the story of how a smart young
shepherd outwitted the hunter. Likewise, particularly in the
blessings Isaac gives to Jacob (verses 27–9) and to Esau (verses
39–40) a community note is heard. What is at stake is the
future of the peoples descended from Jacob (i.e. the Israelites),
and from Esau (i.e. the Edomites). But central to the story is
again the future of the promise and the blessing given by

God to Abraham. Just as it was Isaac and not Ishmael wh
inherited the promise and the blessing from Abraham, so no
it is to Jacob and not to Esau that the fulness of the blessin
is given. And this almost in spite of what Jacob is.

Attempts have been made to draw something of the stin
from Jacob's despicable conduct by referring to ancient leg
ceremonies in which a goat is used to indicate new birth c
status, but the story, as it now stands, is not concerned t
defend Jacob. The only hint of extenuation is the role playe
by his mother Rebecca. Jacob cheats and deceives, and b
reaps a bitter harvest. Advised by Rebecca to flee to Harra
and there stay 'for a while until your brother's anger cools
(verse 44) that 'while' becomes twenty years (see 31: 41). H
never sees his mother again. At Harran the tables are turnec
the deceiver is deceived (see chapter 29). As the years pas
this favoured mother's son is to know the pain of losing h
own favoured son, Joseph, while Joseph's brothers lie t
him as surely as he had lied to his own father (see chapter
37–50). Looking back across his life Jacob can say 'har
years they have been and few, not equal to the years that m
fathers lived in their time' (47: 9). He schemes and cheats
he suffers the consequences of his own misdeeds. Yet this i
the man to whom the blessing is given. In the midst of al
the devious twists of his life God's purposes are being worke
out, even when Jacob is least aware of it.

1–4. Isaac is obviously totally unaware that Esau ha
renounced his birthright. As death approaches, he wishe
to give his blessing to his eldest son and rightful heir. Th
giving of the blessing marks the transferring from the fathe
to the son of all the vitality, the material prosperity, th
family aspirations and the spiritual hopes which have marke
the father's life. The meal may have been intended to strengthe
the vitality which has already begun to ebb from Isaac
witness his blindness, an affliction often associated with ol
age. Jacob himself is similarly blind when he gives his blessin
to the sons of Joseph (48: 10).

3. *venison:* better perhaps 'game', something hunted; it need not have been venison.

4. *a savoury dish:* the kind of dish or meal that Isaac liked, a particular delicacy.

5-17. Rebecca, the moving spirit in the incident, thinks of everything and anticipates her son's objections. A substitute meal of 'two fine young kids' (verse 9) from the flock is prepared. Jacob's smooth skin, on the hands and the neck which blind Isaac is likely to touch, is covered with hairy goatskin. Esau's best clothes are put on Jacob. To Jacob's anxious qualm that if things go wrong he will receive curse not blessing, Rebecca protests that she will take the curse upon herself.

7. The blessing is to be given *in the presence of the LORD*, a phrase which either stresses the solemnity and significance of the occasion or may equally well be translated 'with the LORD's approval'.

18-26. The tension in the narrative is underlined by the suspicions to which Isaac gives voice. How could the hunter have found the game 'so quickly'? In response Jacob has no hesitation in using God to further his own selfish purposes: It is what the LORD your God put in my way' (verse 20). The feel of the skin is all right, but the voice? 'The voice is Jacob's voice' (verse 22). The shameless exploitation of a father's blindness contrasts sharply with the concern expressed elsewhere in the Old Testament that blindness ought not to be exploited: 'A curse upon him who misdirects a blind man' (Deut. 27: 18).

25. *your venison:* see the N.E.B. footnote. The Septuagint simply makes explicit what the text implies.

26. *Come near, my son, and kiss me:* Isaac is suspicious to the last. The kiss brings Jacob so close to Isaac that, bereft of sight, he can call upon his sense of smell to confirm that it is indeed Esau. Esau's clothes will have about them the tang of the hunter and the open country.

27-9. The content of this blessing, which appears in

rhythmic, poetic form, is unusual in the patriarchal tradition. Instead of developing the themes of the giving of the lan or the promise of innumerable descendants it contains thre elements, only the last of which, the contrasting curse an blessing, is found in earlier blessing formulas in Genes (see 12: 3). The first element presupposes the giving of th land, and looks forward to material prosperity, *corn and ne wine in plenty*, the fruit of the *richness of the earth* and God providence. The second element is political, picking up th theme of the oracle given to Rebecca on the birth of h twins (25: 23). It points forward to, and perhaps presuppose the age of the empire of David and the early years of Solomor when the Edomites, among many other surrounding nation recognized the supremacy of Israel. Material prosperity an political greatness were long part of that fulness of life c *shalom* which Israel expected from God (see e.g. Ps. 72).

29. *Be lord over your brothers*: strictly speaking Jacob ha only one brother Esau. The plural *brothers* – the Septuagir logically reads the singular – underlines the future, nation element in the blessing.

30–40. The final scene between Isaac and Esau is deepl moving. The blessing given to Jacob is immediately followe by the bitter dénouement as Esau returns from the hunt.

32. Isaac is *greatly agitated* or, following the N.E.B. foot note, 'incensed'. The Hebrew word can denote stron emotion and its physical expression: 'trembled violently might catch the flavour of the word.

35–6. *He is rightly called Jacob*: here we are given anothe explanation of the name Jacob. Instead of being linked wit the word for 'heel' as in 25: 26, it is now linked with th similar sounding verb meaning 'to supplant' (see the N.E.F footnote) or 'cheat'. Just as the name Quisling has entere English as a synonym for traitor, so Jacob's name becam synonymous in Israel with supplanter or cheat (see the N.E.F footnote to Jer. 9: 4).

37–8. What is involved in a formal blessing is nowher

more clearly illustrated than in this section. The blessing is
no mere matter of words. Had it been so, Isaac presumably
would have cancelled what Jacob had obtained from him by
blatant deceit. But the blessing had been given; it was active.
It had set in train consequences which could not be revoked.

39-40. All that can be given to Esau is a secondary blessing
almost the opposite of what Jacob has received. The form of
Esau's blessing skilfully echoes the language and the thought
of the blessing given to Jacob. In verse 28 the Hebrew
preposition *min* is used before the words 'dew' and 'richness'
with the meaning 'some of' or 'a share in', though the
N.E.B. rightly sees that in English no word corresponding to
it is needed. In verse 39 the same preposition is used before
the word 'dew' meaning 'far from'. What Jacob receives,
Esau is denied.

40. The lordship promised to Jacob is re-emphasized, but
qualified by the claim that Esau will one day *break off his yoke*.
A Hebrew reader would no doubt think in national terms of
incidents such as that described in 1 Kings 11: 14-25 where,
after a period of subjection to David, the Edomites under
Hadad proved to be a thorn in the flesh of Solomon. *By your
sword shall you live:* the Edomites had an unsavoury reputation for savagery and cruelty. They are condemned in the
book of Amos

'because, sword in hand, they hunted their kinsmen down,
  stifling their natural affections' (Amos 1: 11).

41-5. The narrative ends by giving one reason why Jacob
left Canaan and resided for a while among his kinsfolk in
Harran. At this mother's instigation he slips away at once to
escape from a brother rightly intent on revenge. Another
explanation is offered in the following section. ✳

JACOB SENT TO PADDAN-ARAM

46 Rebecca said to Isaac, 'I am weary to death of Hittite women! If Jacob marries a Hittite woman like those who
28 live here, my life will not be worth living.' Isaac called Jacob, blessed him and gave him instructions. He said,
2 'You must not marry one of these women of Canaan. Go at once to the house of Bethuel, your mother's father, in Paddan-aram, and there find a wife, one of the daughters
3 of Laban, your mother's brother. God Almighty bless you, make you fruitful and increase your descendants
4 until they become a host of nations. May he bestow on you and your offspring the blessing of Abraham, and may you thus possess the country where you are now living,
5 the land which God gave to Abraham!' So Isaac sent Jacob away, and he went to Paddan-aram to Laban, son of Bethuel the Aramaean, and brother to Rebecca the mother
6 of Jacob and Esau. Esau discovered that Isaac had given Jacob his blessing and had sent him away to Paddan-aram to find a wife there; and that when he blessed him he had
7 forbidden him to marry a woman of Canaan, and that Jacob had obeyed his father and mother and gone to
8 Paddan-aram. Then Esau, seeing that his father disliked
9 the women of Canaan, went to Ishmael, and, in addition to his other wives, he married Mahalath sister of Nebaioth and daughter of Abraham's son Ishmael.

* This section from the P source looks back to the concluding verses of chapter 26 and in many ways is uneasily linked to the J narrative in chapter 27. Common to both traditions are Isaac's blessing of Jacob, and Jacob's departure to live among his kinsfolk in Mesopotamia. But there the resemblance stops. In this section Isaac's blessing of Jacob seems to be directly motivated by Esau's marrying Hittite women in Canaan. It is as if by so doing Esau had excluded himself from sharing in the promises made to Abraham. Jacob must therefore go to his Aramaean kinsfolk, not to escape Esau's revenge, but to get from among them a suitable wife, just as from them Rebecca had come to marry Isaac. Jacob is thus deliberately sent away by Isaac and given a blessing, described as 'the blessing of Abraham', a blessing which in its emphasis upon many 'descendants' and the possession of the land, fits in well with the tradition of the blessing given to Abraham and to Isaac (contrast 27: 28–9).

46. *I am weary to death of Hittite women!:* neither here nor in 26: 35 is any explanation given of Rebecca's and Isaac's aversion to these women; but see the comment on chapter 24.

28: 2. *the house of Bethuel:* see p. 110. *Paddan-aram:* see note on 25: 20 and map p. xiii.

3. *God Almighty:* see note on 17: 1. The language of the blessing given here closely echoes the promise made to Abraham in the P account of the covenant with Abraham in chapter 17.

6–9. Now that Jacob has been sent to seek a wife from among his mother's brother's family, Esau tries to restore his position in the family by marrying one of the daughters of his father's brother, Ishmael. From the point of view of the main religious theme of the patriarchal traditions, however, he is but marrying into a cul-de-sac. The outworking of God's purposes lies with Isaac, not with Ishmael. Esau's endeavour can no more ensure him a place within these purposes than Jacob's duplicity can exclude him from them.

9. *Mahalath sister of Nebaioth:* see note on 26: 34–5. *

JACOB AT BETHEL

10 Jacob set out from Beersheba and went on his way towards
11 Harran. He came to a certain place and stopped there for
the night, because the sun had set; and, taking one of the
stones there, he made it a pillow for his head and lay down
12 to sleep. He dreamt that he saw a ladder, which rested on
the ground with its top reaching to heaven, and angels of
13 God were going up and down upon it. The LORD was
standing beside him[a] and said, 'I am the LORD, the God of
your father Abraham and the God of Isaac. This land on
which you are lying I will give to you and your descend-
14 ants. They shall be countless as the dust upon the earth,
and you shall spread far and wide, to north and south, to
east and west. All the families of the earth shall pray to be
15 blessed as you and your descendants are blessed. I will be
with you, and I will protect you wherever you go and will
bring you back to this land; for I will not leave you until
16 I have done all that I have promised.' Jacob woke from
his sleep and said, 'Truly the LORD is in this place, and I did
17 not know it.' Then he was afraid and said, 'How fearsome
is this place! This is no other than the house of God, this is
18 the gate of heaven.' Jacob rose early in the morning, took
the stone on which he had laid his head, set it up as a sacred
19 pillar and poured oil on the top of it. He named that place
Beth-El;[b] but the earlier name of the city was Luz.

20   Thereupon Jacob made this vow: 'If God will be with
me, if he will protect me on my journey and give me
21 food to eat and clothes to wear, and I come back safely to
22 my father's house, then the LORD shall be my God, and

[a] *Or* on it *or* by it.   [b] *That is* House of God.

this stone which I have set up as a sacred pillar shall be a
house of God. And of all that thou givest me, I will without fail allot a tenth part to thee.'

* Most scholars recognize that this well-known story is
a blend of material from different traditions. The framework
of the story comes from the E source, verses 10-12 and 17-22:
note the emphasis upon the dream and the angels of God,
both characteristics of the E source. It explains why a certain
place was called Bethel and why the sanctuary at Bethel was
of continuing importance for worship in Israel. Within this
framework there is preserved in verses 13-16 from the J
source the account of how Jacob was made aware of his
place within the purposes of the LORD. The narrative has
several noteworthy features.

(i) There is the emphasis upon Bethel. Bethel had a long
and chequered religious history. It was an important religious
centre long before Jacob's time. The J tradition records how
Abraham in his early journeyings met the LORD near Bethel
and there built an altar (12: 7; 13: 3-4). Archaeology suggests
that Bethel was in fact an important Canaanite religious site
long before it passed into Hebrew hands. On the division of
the Hebrew kingdom subsequent to the death of Solomon,
Jeroboam made Bethel one of the centres of worship for the
northern kingdom (see I Kings 12: 25-32). In the eighth
century B.C. it was bitterly attacked by the prophets as an
illustration of false religion, the name Bethel, 'house of God'
being bitingly parodied as Beth-aven, 'house of trouble'
(Amos 4: 4; Hos. 5: 8). It owed its continuing importance as
a centre for worship in ancient Israel to its association in
tradition with Jacob. Even the Jacob tradition, however,
remains uncertain when the place was first called Bethel.
This narrative links it with Jacob's experience as he left home
to go to his Aramaean kinsfolk; the narrative in chapter 35
links it with his return home (see 35: 6-8, 15). As Jacob's

descendants went to worship at Bethel, with its large stone pillar or *maṣṣebah*, originally a Canaanite fertility symbol, as they offered their sacrifices in the morning and brought their tithes, they believed they were reliving the experience of their ancestor Jacob.

'Bethel', however, was not merely a place-name. There is evidence within the Old Testament, and from extra-biblical sources, that 'Bethel' was also the name of a deity. In the book of Jeremiah, in a passage attacking the Moabites, we read:

> 'and Moab shall be betrayed by Kemosh (i.e. the god of Moab),
> as Israel was betrayed by Bethel,
> a god in whom he trusted' (Jer. 48: 13).

What may well have been the original text of Gen. 31: 13 also points in the same direction (see the note there). The documents from the Jewish colony at Elephantiné in Egypt in the fifth century B.C. also mention Bethel as a god, the worship of whom may have been brought with them from Palestine.

(ii) The religious symbolism in the story is unusual. Dreams were a recognized form of revelation in Israel and elsewhere in the ancient world. Many stories are told of people resorting to temples or sacred sites at night in the expectation that there they would receive a dream vision. The content of Jacob's dream, however, is unparalleled in the Old Testament: 'a ladder, which rested on the ground with its top reaching to heaven' (verse 12). The word translated 'ladder' occurs only here in the Old Testament and is perhaps better translated 'ramp' or 'stairway'. Phrases such as 'with its top reaching to heaven' and 'this is the gate of heaven' (verse 17) suggest that the symbolism is taken from the great temple towers or ziggurats of Mesopotamia (see *Genesis 1–11*, pp. 105–7). Many of these ziggurats had names linking heaven and earth. A ramp or stairway led from the bottom to the top of the ziggurat.

At the foot the community gathered to offer worship; at the top there was a small shrine or 'house of god' where the god met with specially designated representatives of the people.

(iii) So far Jacob, with all his chicanery and deceit, has been the unwitting instrument in God's hands. At Bethel comes the moment when to Jacob, caught in a self-inflicted crisis, the LORD reveals himself. Jacob is now made aware that he stands within the promises made to Abraham. This is particularly the emphasis of the J section in verses 13–16, which pick up the language and thought of the promise to Abraham in 12: 2–3. There is added an emphasis peculiarly relevant to Jacob's immediate circumstances; the promise of the LORD's presence and protection to counter his loneliness and fears, the assurance that though he is leaving Canaan, it is still the promised land and to it he will return.

11. *a certain place*: in Hebrew there is an ambiguity in the word translated 'place'. It may mean either any spot or place or more specifically a holy place. By chance this *certain place* was to become in Jacob's experience a holy place. That Jacob, seeking a dream vision, deliberately chose to spend the night in what he knew to be a holy place, is another possible interpretation, but not one that fits so well with the character of Jacob as previously sketched nor with the surprise he expresses in verse 16.

12. *angels of God*: see note on 16: 7; the messengers *going up and down* signify that this is the moment and the place of communication between God and man.

13. *The LORD was standing beside him*: the relation between the LORD and the ladder in the vision is not at all clear. This is one reason for assuming that verse 13 marks the beginning of a different piece of tradition. If this verse is to be taken closely with what precedes it we might equally well translate 'the LORD was standing beside it', i.e. the ladder or stairway (see the N.E.B. footnote). *the God of your father Abraham and the God of Isaac*: see p. 12.

13–15. Behind the specific promises in this passage (for

147

which see above), there stands the faithfulness and the dependability of God: *for I will not leave you until I have done all that
I have promised* (verse 15). This dependability of God is often
depicted in the Old Testament in sharp contrast to the fickleness of men, and nowhere more so than in the Jacob traditions.

16. *Truly the LORD is in this place:* it is this, the presence
of the LORD, which makes the place peculiarly holy. Forced
to leave the security of his home, Jacob seems to stumble by
chance upon the LORD.

17. *How fearsome is this place!: fearsome* is not a particularly
happy translation; 'awesome' would be better. The natural
response to an encounter with the LORD is one of awe and
dread: cp. Moses' response to his encounter with the LORD
at the burning bush; he 'covered his face, for he was afraid
to gaze on God' (Exod. 3: 6).

18. The fact that the *sacred pillar* or *maṣṣebah* which Jacob
erects is nothing other than *the stone on which he had laid his
head*, robs it of any associations with Canaanite fertility
religion. It stands merely as a memorial to his experience.
poured oil on the top of it: thus signifying that it was a stone
consecrated to God. Anointing by oil as a sign of consecration
to a particular function or office was common practice in
Israel. So Samuel anointed Saul to be 'prince over his people
Israel' (1 Sam. 10: 1).

19. *He named that place Beth-El:* the name Bethel has been
deliberately divided here by the N.E.B. translators to make its
meaning clear: *Beth* = house, *El* is a name or title of God (see
the N.E.B. footnote and map p. xiv). The name of the place is
here said to derive from Jacob's experience. In verses 17 and
22, however, in the phrase 'house of God', the Hebrew text
uses not *El* but the more common plural form, *elohim*. The
name *Beth-El* in all probability goes back to the cult of the
Canaanite deity El or Beth-El. This narrative is a way of
baptizing that cult into the faith of Israel. *but the earlier name
of the city was Luz:* cp. 35: 6. On his death-bed Jacob, says
'God Almighty appeared to me at Luz in Canaan and blessed

me' (48: 3). Josh. 16: 2, however, clearly distinguishes Bethel
and Luz, implying that Luz lies somewhere west of Bethel.
Luz may have been the early Canaanite name for the district
in which the sacred shrine of Bethel was erected.

20–2. There is no need to read any cynical undertones into
Jacob's vow, as if he were attempting to bribe God – You
do this, then I in return will be prepared to accept you as my
God. What Jacob is doing is to grasp at the promise that God
has already made to him in verse 15. If God does prove in
experience to be thus dependable, then naturally Jacob will
worship him. Worship for the Old Testament is not an
attempt to bribe God but a response to God.

20. *food to eat and clothes to wear:* Jacob's request is modest,
the basic necessities of life and no more.

22. *this stone which I have set up as a sacred pillar shall be
a house of God:* the language here may well look back to
primitive ideas when the sacred pillar was identified with the
deity or the deity was thought to reside in the stone. In context in this narrative the sacred pillar marks the spot where
God's presence was, and can be, experienced. *a tenth part to
thee:* the custom of tithing appears in various forms in the
Old Testament (see e.g. Deut. 26: 12–15; Lev. 27: 30–2). In
human relationships a tithe is a form of tribute offered as a
mark of respect to a superior. So Abraham offers a tithe to
Melchizedek (14: 20). In religious terms it is a token acknowledgement by man that everything he possesses comes to him
from God.   ✳

JACOB MEETS RACHEL

Jacob continued his journey and came to the land of the **29**
eastern tribes. There he saw a well in the open country and ₂
three flocks of sheep lying beside it, because the flocks
were watered from that well. Over its mouth was a huge
stone, and all the herdsmen used to gather there and roll it ₃
off the mouth of the well and water the flocks; then they

4 would put it back in its place over the well. Jacob said to
them, 'Where are you from, my friends?' 'We are from
5 Harran', they replied. He asked them if they knew Laban
the grandson[a] of Nahor. They answered, 'Yes, we do.'
6 'Is he well?' Jacob asked; and they answered, 'Yes, he is
well, and here is his daughter Rachel coming with the
7 flock.' Jacob said, 'The sun is still high, and the time for
folding the sheep has not yet come. Water the flocks and
8 then go and graze them.' But they replied, 'We cannot
until all the herdsmen have gathered together and the
stone is rolled away from the mouth of the well; then we
9 can water our flocks.' While he was talking to them,
Rachel came up with her father's flock, for she was a
10 shepherdess. When Jacob saw Rachel, the daughter of
Laban his mother's brother, with Laban's flock, he
stepped forward, rolled the stone off the mouth of the well
11 and watered Laban's sheep. He kissed Rachel, and was
12 moved to tears. He told her that he was her father's kinsman and Rebecca's son; so she ran and told her father.
13 When Laban heard the news of his sister's son Jacob, he
ran to meet him, embraced him, kissed him warmly and
welcomed him to his home. Jacob told Laban everything,
14 and Laban said, 'Yes, you are my own flesh and blood.'
So Jacob stayed with him for a whole month.

* This charming story of Jacob's meeting with Rachel
invites comparison with chapter 24. There it was Laban's
sister Rebecca who was the centre of interest, now it is his
daughter Rachel. There it was an evening meeting at a well
outside the city, now it is earlier in the day – 'The sun is still
high' – at a well in the open country where the herdsmen

[a] *Lit.* son.

gather to water their flocks. There it was Abraham's servant coming with ten camels laden with gifts, now it is Jacob, apparently alone with nothing to offer but himself. There it is Rebecca who takes the initiative in watering the servant's camels, now it is Jacob who waters Rachel's flocks. Both stories are told in the same graphic style with a marked economy of words. The long journey is passed over without comment. Details such as precise place-names are conspicuously absent. They are irrelevant to the main interest. Jacob's animated questioning of the herdsmen leads quickly to his meeting with Rachel. Jacob the refugee from his own home finds himself welcomed among his own flesh and blood.

1. Jacob journeys to *the land of the eastern tribes*, literally 'the sons of the east', a vague and imprecise description which here must mean the people living in the general area of Paddan-aram.

2–3. Quarrels over watering rights were commonplace (cp. 26: 16–22 and Exod. 2: 16–17). Fair play is guaranteed by a local custom that the *huge stone* protecting the mouth of the well is not rolled away until all the local shepherds are present with their flocks. *all the herdsmen used to gather:* here and in verse 8 the Hebrew text reads 'flocks' instead of *herdsmen*. This leaves the verb *roll* awkwardly without a subject. The Samaritan text and some Greek manuscripts read *herdsmen*. Retaining the Hebrew text, however, we could translate 'All the flocks used to gather there and the stone would be rolled away'.

5. *Laban the grandson of Nahor:* as 24: 15 makes clear. The Hebrew 'son' (see the N.E.B. footnote) denotes a male member of the family and may equally well be translated *grandson*.

5–6. *Yes, we do... Yes, he is well:* Hebrew lacks any word for *Yes*. It answers a question by repeating the words of the question: *Is he well?...he is well*. All that is necessary in English is the simple answer 'Yes'.

9. *Rachel:* the name means 'ewe', an appropriate name for a girl in a shepherds' community.

10. Jacob apparently defies local custom. As the other shepherds sit, no doubt idly gossiping, he rolled away the stone and *watered Laban's sheep* which Rachel had brought to the well. That he did so single-handed is probably intended to stress his strength and energy. Compare the similar theme of a heroic deed by Moses in Exod. 2: 16–19.

11. *He kissed Rachel, and was moved to tears:* such a public embrace of a woman might have raised a few eyebrows in later Hebrew society, but Jacob's action may reflect the different and perhaps freer conventions of patriarchal times. Attempts have been made to explain Jacob's tears in terms of the formalized weeping associated with leaving and returning in certain primitive societies. This hardly seems necessary. The relief of the lonely refugee finding himself in contact with his own folk expresses itself in tears of joy.

14. The warmth of Laban's welcome to one who is his *own flesh and blood* (Hebrew 'bone and flesh'), contrasts sharply with the double-dealing that is soon to follow. ✷

JACOB DECEIVED

15 Laban said to Jacob, 'Why should you work for me for nothing simply because you are my kinsman? Tell me
16 what your wages ought to be.' Now Laban had two daughters: the elder was called Leah, and the younger
17 Rachel. Leah was dull-eyed, but Rachel was graceful and
18 beautiful. Jacob had fallen in love with Rachel and he said, 'I will work seven years for your younger daughter
19 Rachel.' Laban replied, 'It is better that I should give her
20 to you than to anyone else; stay with me. So Jacob worked seven years for Rachel, and they seemed like a few days
21 because he loved her. Then Jacob said to Laban, 'I have served my time. Give me my wife so that we may sleep
22 together.' So Laban gathered all the men of the place

together and gave a feast. In the evening he took his 23
daughter Leah and brought her to Jacob, and Jacob slept
with her. At the same time Laban gave his slave-girl 24
Zilpah to his daughter Leah. But when morning came, 25
Jacob saw that it was Leah and said to Laban, 'What have
you done to me? Did I not work for Rachel? Why have
you deceived me?' Laban answered, 'In our country it is 26
not right to give the younger sister in marriage before the
elder. Go through with the seven days' feast for the elder, 27
and the younger shall be given you in return for a further
seven years' work.' Jacob agreed, and completed the seven 28
days for Leah.

* Jacob's matrimonial problems raise interesting questions.
What lies behind the question about Jacob's 'wages' in verse
15? Was marriage in patriarchal society regarded as a form of
purchase, an agreed price being paid by the husband-to-be,
or his family, to the girl's father? If so, did Jacob, unable to
pay the accepted price, offer his services to Laban in lieu of
the price, as in later society a Hebrew enslaved for debt
could work off his debt by six years' labour (see Exod.
21: 1–2)? Or are Jacob's 'seven years' to be explained in the
light of a motif that occurs widely in folk-tale and legend, the
bride as the reward for some deed of valour or renown?
Caleb, in Josh. 15: 16, offers his daughter in marriage to
anyone who would attack and capture the town of Kiriath-
sepher. Until we know far more than we do about the
customs involved and the status which Jacob had in Laban's
household, we cannot be certain. Whatever the explanation,
the story of Jacob's marriage to two sisters must have caused
questioning frowns in later Israel. This practice is strictly
forbidden in the legislation in Leviticus: 'You shall not take
a woman who is your wife's sister to make her a rival-wife,
and to have intercourse with her during her sister's lifetime'

(Lev. 18: 18). This is one further illustration of the way in which the patriarchal narratives do not fit easily into the ethos of later Old Testament times.

There is a strong undercurrent of poetic justice in this story. Jacob the deceiver is himself deceived. The man who had shamelessly taken advantage of the blindness of his father, sees too late that he has been given the wrong bride. Laban is as smooth a double-dealer as Jacob. The stage is being set for the battle of wits between father-in-law and son-in-law in chapter 30. But unwittingly Laban in his double-dealing is serving the purposes of God. Leah, whom Laban foists upon Jacob, is destined to become the ancestress of some of Israel's most famous sons, including Moses and David.

16. *Leah:* the name may mean 'cow', a name which would be appropriate in a pastoral community, and probably expresses hoped-for fertility.

17. *Leah was dull-eyed:* the more traditional translations 'tender-' or 'weak-'eyed follow the Septuagint interpretation of a Hebrew word which nowhere else in the Old Testament refers to eyes. It is found used of 'tender' meat (Gen 18: 7) or 'soft words' (Job 41: 3). The N.E.B. translation assumes that it refers to eyes which lack fire or lustre. *Rachel was graceful and beautiful:* the same phrase is used of Joseph in 39: 7, where the N.E.B. translates 'handsome and good-looking'. Rachel is being singled out as the more physically attractive and desirable of the sisters.

19. *It is better that I should give her to you than to anyone else:* the marriage of first cousins is accepted practice in some Near Eastern societies. Either Laban's words to Jacob reflect this custom or he is merely expressing his pleasure that Rachel is marrying within the family.

20. The seven years Jacob worked *seemed like a few days because he loved her,* one of several romantic touches which enliven the narrative.

23. It was customary for the bride to be escorted to the bridal chamber by her parents; 24: 65 may suggest that her

face would be covered. It was this custom that enabled Laban to carry out his act of deceit, substituting Leah for Rachel.

24. *Laban gave his slave-girl Zilpah to his daughter Leah:* marriage documents from Nuzi (see pp. 13–14) provide extra-biblical evidence for a bride being provided with a slave-girl, as a maid, as part of the marriage contract. Rachel is similarly provided with a slave-girl, Bilhah (see verse 29).

26. Laban counters Jacob's angry protestations of being cheated by the claim that *In our country it is not right,* i.e. it is not the custom to marry the younger sister before the elder, a custom which is vouched for in many societies. But note the irony. Jacob, the younger son had cheated and supplanted his elder brother; now his desires are thwarted by a custom which insists that the younger shall not be married before the elder sister.

27. *Go through with the seven days' feast:* Hebrew simply 'complete seven'. This could be interpreted to mean 'seven years', a further seven years of work before marrying Rachel. The concluding words of verse 28 would then be translated 'and completed these seven more years'. In context, however, it seems better to see a reference to the customary seven days of the marriage festivities (cp. Judg. 14: 12). At the end of the festivities marking his marriage to Leah, Jacob is permitted to marry Rachel in return for the promise of *a further seven years' work.* ✲

RIVALRIES IN JACOB'S FAMILY

Then Laban gave Jacob his daughter Rachel as wife; and 28*b*, 29 he gave his slave-girl Bilhah to serve his daughter Rachel. Jacob slept with Rachel also; he loved her rather than 30 Leah, and he worked for Laban for a further seven years. When the LORD saw that Leah was not loved, he granted 31 her a child; but Rachel was childless. Leah conceived and 32 bore a son; and she called him Reuben,[a] for she said, 'The LORD has seen my humiliation; now my husband will

33 love me.' Again she conceived and bore a son and said, 'The LORD, hearing that I am not loved, has given me this

34 child also'; and she called him Simeon.[b] She conceived again and bore a son; and she said, 'Now that I have borne him three sons my husband and I will surely be united.'

35 So she called him Levi.[c] Once more she conceived and bore a son; and she said, 'Now I will praise the LORD'; therefore she named him Judah.[d] Then for a while she bore no more children.

30 When Rachel found that she bore Jacob no children, she became jealous of her sister and said to Jacob, 'Give

2 me sons, or I shall die.' Jacob said angrily to Rachel, 'Can I take the place of God, who has denied you children?'

3 She said, 'Here is my slave-girl Bilhah. Lie with her, so that she may bear sons to be laid upon my knees, and

4 through her I too may build up a family.' So she gave him her slave-girl Bilhah as a wife, and Jacob lay with her.

5,6 Bilhah conceived and bore Jacob a son. Then Rachel said, 'God has given judgement for me; he has indeed heard

7 me and given me a son', so she named him Dan.[e] Rachel's slave-girl Bilhah again conceived and bore Jacob another

8 son. Rachel said, 'I have played a fine trick on my sister

9 and it has succeeded'; so she named him Naphtali.[f] When Leah found that she was bearing no more children, she took her slave-girl Zilpah and gave her to Jacob as a wife,

10,11 and Zilpah bore Jacob a son. Leah said, 'Good fortune ha

[a] *That is* See, a son. [b] *That is* Hearing. [c] *That is* Union.
[d] *That is* Praise. [e] *That is* He has given judgement.
[f] *That is* Trickery.

come', and she named him Gad.*ᵃ* Zilpah, Leah's slave-girl, 12
bore Jacob another son, and Leah said, 'Happiness has 13
come,*ᵇ* for young women will call me happy.' So she
named him Asher.*ᶜ*

In the time of wheat-harvest Reuben went out and 14
found some mandrakes in the open country and brought
them to his mother Leah. Then Rachel asked Leah for
some of her son's mandrakes, but Leah said, 'Is it so small 15
a thing to have taken away my husband, that you should
take my son's mandrakes as well?' But Rachel said, 'Very
well, let him sleep with you tonight in exchange for your
son's mandrakes.' So when Jacob came in from the 16
country in the evening, Leah went out to meet him and
said, 'You are to sleep with me tonight; I have hired you
with my son's mandrakes.' That night he slept with her,
and God heard Leah's prayer, and she conceived and bore 17
a fifth son. Leah said, 'God has rewarded me, because 18
I gave my slave-girl to my husband.' So she named him
Issachar.*ᵈ* Leah again conceived and bore a sixth son. She 19, 20
said, 'God has endowed me with a noble dowry. Now
my husband will treat me in princely style, because I have
borne him six sons.' So she named him Zebulun.*ᵉ* Later 21
she bore a daughter and named her Dinah. Then God 22
thought of Rachel; he heard her prayer and gave her a
child; so she conceived and bore a son and said, 'God has 23
taken away my humiliation.' She named him Joseph,*ᶠ* 24
saying, 'May the LORD add another son!'

[*a*] *That is* Good Fortune.   [*b*] *So Targ.; Heb.* By my happiness.
[*c*] *That is* Happy.   [*d*] *That is* Reward.
[*e*] *That is* Prince.
[*f*] *The name may mean either* He takes away *or* May he add.

* This section records the birth of the eleven sons and the one daughter who were born to Jacob in Mesopotamia. No Hebrew reading this section could ever forget that the names of the eleven sons are the names of eleven out of the twelve tribes who later made up the nation of Israel. Attempts have been made to glean from this section something of the history of the tribes prior to the settlement in Canaan. The six sons of Leah have been taken to represent an older tribal confederacy with which the tribes represented by the sons of Rachel later united. The place of Reuben as the eldest son has been taken to indicate that the Reuben tribal group was originally the strongest element in such a confederacy. In many of the patriarchal traditions it is difficult to disentangle the individual from the group, but a comparison with 49: 1–27, Jacob's death-bed blessing of his twelve sons, suggests that whereas in chapter 49 it is the character and future destiny of the twelve tribes which is of central interest, here we are concerned more with personal, family tradition.

The names of the children are explained by reference to Jacob's two wives, Leah and Rachel, the rivalry between them and their desire for motherhood. The explanations cannot be regarded as scientific any more than in certain other incidents. We are moving in the realm of popular story-telling and tradition, with the names being explained by reference to words of similar sound. It is therefore hardly surprising that three of the names, Issachar, Zebulun and Joseph, are given not one, but two, different explanations. This is but one sign that the whole section is a mosaic of material from different sources, J and E; note in particular the concluding verses, 30: 22–4, where one explanation of the name Joseph, linking it with the Hebrew for 'take away' occurs in a sentence of which the subject is God (*'elohim*), while another, linking it with the Hebrew word meaning 'add', occurs in a sentence in which the subject is the LORD (YAHWEH).

Running through the section there is an underlying thematic pattern similar to that in chapter 27. There it was two brothers locked in rivalry for a father's blessing; here it is two sisters competing for a husband's affection and the joys of mother-hood. In each story the elder has prior legal status, and in each it is the younger who becomes the key link with the future. There is suspense and humour in the stratagems of the rival wives.

31. God's compassionate concern for the rejected and the unwanted is one of the recurring themes in the Old Testament. The fact that Jacob prefers Rachel to Leah and makes no attempt to conceal his preference, becomes the basis for God giving the desire of every wife in ancient society, a child. *Leah was not loved:* the Authorized Version and Revised Standard Version render 'hated'. This is too strong. In certain contexts the word means rather 'rejected', because of a preference being shown to someone else. Deut. 21: 15-17 legislates for a family situation where a man has two wives the 'one loved and the other unloved' and seeks to safeguard the rights of the children of the unloved wife. *Rachel was childless:* see note on 16: 1-2.

32. The birth of Leah's first son; *she called him Reuben.* Although the name Reuben is most reasonably explained, with the N.E.B. footnote, as 'See, a son', it is also likely to contain a play on the phrase *The LORD has seen my humilia-tion;* the Hebrew word for 'humiliation' containing the letters 'b' and 'n' which are part of Reuben.

33. Leah's second son, Simeon. This name sounds like the Hebrew verb *shama'*, to hear, which occurs in the phrase *The LORD, hearing that I am not loved* (see the N.E.B. footnote). The same word is used to explain the name Ishmael in 16: 11.

34. Leah's third son Levi. This name sounds like the Hebrew verb translated *united* (see the N.E.B. footnote).

35. Leah's fourth son Judah. This name sounds like the Hebrew verb to praise, used in the statement *Now I will praise the LORD* (see the N.E.B. footnote).

30: 1-2. *Give me sons, or I shall die:* Rachel bitterly gives voice to the frustration that gnaws at the heart of the childless wife, however much loved (cp. the story of Hannah in 1 Sam. 1). She had failed. The demand she makes upon Jacob seems to suggest that it is his fault. Jacob angrily retorts that her childlessness is inflicted by God.

3. For the custom of a childless wife giving her husband a slave-girl concubine, see the note on 16: 2. *sons to be laid upon my knees:* in some ancient societies the father acknowledged and claimed paternity by setting the child on his knees. In Gen. 50: 23 Joseph's grandchildren are said to have been 'born on his knees', which the N.E.B. correctly interprets as 'he also recognized as his'. A child of Bilhah's, therefore, laid on Rachel's knees, is being claimed as Rachel's own child.

6. Bilhah's first son Dan. This name sounds like the Hebrew verb translated *has given judgement* (see the N.E.B. footnote). The child is regarded as God's vindication of Rachel.

8. Bilhah's second son Naphtali. The name sounds like the Hebrew verb translated *I have played a trick* (see the N.E.B. footnote). *I have played a fine trick on my sister:* literally, 'with twisting of God I have twisted'. For the use of 'of God' in an adjectival sense, such as 'mighty' (Revised Standard Version) see *Genesis 1–11*, p. 16. Even the Authorized Version recognizes the usage here, translating 'with great wrestlings have I wrestled'. Perhaps 'I have had a desperate (or 'fateful'), struggle with my sister' would be better. The idea of wrestling or striving is not, however, certain for this Hebrew verb and the N.E.B. translation assumes that the basic idea is that of trickery. Rachel has successfully turned the tables on Leah by presenting Jacob with children by means of her slave-girl.

9–10. Rachel had complained of bearing Jacob no children, Leah now complains that her child-bearing days are over. She therefore plays Rachel at her own game, and her slave-girl Zilpah bears a son.

11. Zilpah's first son Gad; this name sounds like the Hebrew for *Good fortune* (see the N.E.B. footnote).

13. Zilpah's second son Asher: this name sounds like the Hebrew word for *Happiness* and the related verb to *call...* *happy*, both of which occur in this verse (see the N.E.B. footnote). The N.E.B. follows the Targum in making a minor alteration to the Hebrew text to read *Happiness has come*. The Hebrew 'By, or in, my happiness' (see the N.E.B. footnote) could be taken as an exclamation, 'How happy I am!'

14-18. The account of the birth of Issachar differs from that of the other children since it involves a short story, a humorous incident underlining the jealous rivalry between Leah and Rachel. There was a widespread belief in the ancient world that the mandrake – a fragrant plant which bears a small yellowish fruit about the size of a plum – was effective as a love potion and as an antidote to barrenness. The Greek goddess of love, Aphrodite, was sometimes referred to as 'Our Lady of the Mandrake'. The Hebrew word for man-drake is related to the word for love. The story here seems to be saying 'don't believe such nonsense'. Leah, who gives away her mandrakes to Rachel in return for the right to sleep with Jacob, bears two sons and a daughter, while Rachel, man-drakes and all, remains childless until 'God thought of (or 're-membered') Rachel' (verse 22). God alone gives life, just as he denies it.

14. *In the time of wheat-harvest:* from late April to early June. Rachel's request for the mandrakes, picked for Leah by her son Reuben, indicates her continuing and desperate desire for a child of her own womb.

15. *let him sleep with you tonight in exchange for your son's mandrakes:* this implies that Jacob, probably at Rachel's jealous prompting, had been denying Leah her conjugal rights.

18. Leah's fifth son Issachar. This name is similar in sound to the Hebrew word for 'reward' (see the N.E.B. footnote): *God has rewarded me*, literally, 'God has given my reward'. But it also echoes the verb translated 'hired' in verse 16.

20. Leah's sixth son Zebulun. This name is similar in

sound to the Hebrew verb translated *will treat me in princely style* (see the N.E.B. footnote). A cognate word in Ugaritic means 'Prince'. But it is also probably intended to echo the words translated 'endowed' and 'dowry'.

21. The birth of Leah's daughter Dinah is noted without comment or any attempt to explain the name. It prepares the way for the narrative in chapter 34.

22. Rachel's long frustrated desire is at last fulfilled, thanks to God's compassion: *God thought of Rachel; he heard her prayer.* For this use of *thought of* or remembered, looking towards the present as well as the past, see *Genesis 1–11*, p. 80.

24. Rachel's first son Joseph. This name is similar in sound both to the Hebrew verb translated 'taken away' in verse 23, and to that translated *add* (see the N.E.B. footnote). The name *Joseph*, therefore, looks in two directions; to the past, the trials and frustrations of which are now over, and to the future, which may mean hopes further fulfilled. ✳

A BATTLE OF WITS

25 When Rachel had given birth to Joseph, Jacob said to Laban, 'Let me go, for I wish to return to my own home
26 and country. Give me my wives and my children for whom I have served you, and I will go; for you know
27 what service I have done for you.' Laban said to him, 'Let me have my say, if you please. I have become prosperous
28 and the LORD has blessed me for your sake. So now tell me
29 what I owe you in wages, and I will give it you.' Jacob answered, 'You must know how I have served you, and
30 how your herds have prospered under my care. You had only a few when I came, but now they have increased beyond measure, and the LORD brought blessings to you wherever I went. But is it not time for me to provide for
31 my family?' Laban said, 'Then what shall I give you?',

but Jacob answered, 'Give me nothing; I will mind your
flocks*a* as before, if you will do what I suggest. Today I   32
will go over your flocks and pick out from them*b* every
black lamb, and all the brindled and the spotted goats, and
they shall be my wages. This is a fair offer, and it will be to   33
my own disadvantage later on, when we come to settling
my wages: every goat amongst mine that is not spotted or
brindled and every lamb that is not black will have been
stolen.' Laban said, 'Agreed; let it be as you have said.'   34
But that day he removed the he-goats that were striped   35
and brindled and all the spotted and brindled she-goats, all
that had any white on them, and every ram that was
black, and he handed them over to his own sons. Then he   36
put a distance of three days' journey between himself and
Jacob, while Jacob was left tending those of Laban's flocks
that remained. Thereupon Jacob took fresh rods of white   37
poplar, almond, and plane tree, and peeled off strips of
bark, exposing the white of the rods. Then he fixed the   38
peeled rods upright in the troughs at the watering-places
where the flocks came to drink; they faced the she-goats
that were on heat when they came to drink. They felt a   39
longing for the rods and they gave birth to young that
were striped and spotted and brindled. As for the rams,   40
Jacob divided them, and let the ewes run only with such
of the rams in Laban's flocks as were striped and black;
and thus he bred separate flocks for himself, which he did
not add to Laban's sheep. As for the goats, whenever the   41
more vigorous were on heat, he put the rods in front of
them at the troughs so that they would long for the rods;

[a] *Prob. rdg.; Heb. adds* I will watch.
[b] *So Sept.; Heb. adds* every spotted and brindled sheep and...

42 he did not put them there for the weaker goats. Thus the
43 weaker came to be Laban's and the stronger Jacob's. So Jacob increased in wealth more and more until he possessed great flocks, male and female slaves, camels, and asses.

* This story must have been told and retold with great delight. It is essentially a battle of wits between two wily shepherds each determined to further his own interests at the expense of the other. It has added piquancy inasmuch as it is a family quarrel between father-in-law and son-in-law, as well as a dispute between the ancestor of Israel and an Aramaean. There are some rough edges to the story. The text is difficult to interpret at points and the detail is far from clear, but it seems best to treat the passage as a unity from the J tradition. It begins with what reads like a typical piece of hard industrial bargaining. Jacob's request to Laban 'to return to my own home and country' (verse 25), is treated by Laban for what it probably was, the opening gambit in the search for a satisfactory wage settlement. Jacob, after stressing all the benefits he has brought to Laban (verses 29–30) makes an offer which must have seemed to Laban almost too good to be true. Flocks normally consisted of black goats and white sheep. Spotted or speckled goats and black sheep were rare. Yet these are the animals Jacob requests for his wages. Just to make doubly sure, Laban removes all such animals from the flocks, hands them over to his own sons, and keeps them at a safe distance from Jacob. But Jacob has the edge in oneupmanship. Working on the widely held view in the ancient world that what people or animals see at the moment of conception influences the appearance and character of the offspring, he has the black she-goats mating in sight of 'rods of white poplar, almond and plane tree' (verse 37) from which the bark has been stripped to expose the white of the wood; and the ewes are mated only with rams that are 'striped and

black' (verse 40). Jacob's multi-coloured flock, therefore, increases, and by skilful eugenics he breeds only the strongest animals. 'Thus the weaker came to be Laban's and the stronger Jacob's' (verse 42). The tables are well and truly turned.

A tale of two wily shepherds – but it is more. The one, Jacob, is the inheritor of God's promises; the LORD's blessing goes with him (verse 30). Laban's attempts, therefore, to down Jacob are doomed to failure by a higher providence which he serves, though he does not recognize it.

26. *Give me my wives and my children for whom I have served you:* in the legislation concerning debt-slavery in Exod. 21, and in certain texts from Nuzi (see pp. 13–14), it is stipulated that if a master gives his slave a wife and she bears him sons or daughters, the woman and her children belong to the master. It has been suggested that, in the light of this, Jacob may here be going beyond his legal rights, and that this lies behind Laban's complaint in 31:43: 'The daughters are my daughters, the children are my children.' But Jacob is not a slave, and little more than natural affection is needed to explain Laban's words.

27. *I have become prosperous:* it is hard to see why the N.E.B. has departed from the more usual meaning 'I have used divination', which it uses for the same Hebrew verb in 44: 5, 15. Just as Rebecca, in a perplexing situation 'went to seek guidance of the LORD' (25: 22), so Laban uses divination, a well-known method of ascertaining the mind or purpose of the deity, to discover that the reason for his increasing prosperity is Jacob's presence with him; *the LORD has blessed me for your sake.*

30. Jacob, in his reply, confirms this belief; *the LORD brought blessings to you wherever I went.* The expression *wherever I went* (literally, 'to my foot'), might also mean 'as a result of my presence (or 'my actions')'.

31. *I will mind your flocks as before:* the omission of 'I will watch' (see the N.E.B. footnote) is not strictly necessary.

The text is somewhat harsh, but it could be rendered 'I will mind and tend your flocks as before.'

32. As the words 'spotted' and 'brindled' are only applied to goats in the rest of the narrative, and as verse 33 makes clear it is only black lambs that are to belong to Jacob, it seems best to follow the Septuagint reading and omit the words 'every spotted and brindled sheep' from this verse (see the N.E.B. footnote).

35. *all that had any white on them:* the Hebrew word for 'white' is *laban*. Throughout the story there is a play on this word and the name Laban. We should get the same play in English by saying 'all that had any white on them belonged to Mr White'. Likewise in verse 37 there are three words that sound like Laban, the words translated 'white poplar', 'bark' and 'the white of the rods'. It is as if Jacob is white-washing Mr White, in the sense in which whitewashing is used in baseball, meaning to dismiss the opposing team for a duck. *he handed them over to his own sons:* this is the first mention in the narrative of Laban's sons. The reference to them has been used to support a somewhat dubious parallel between the Jacob–Laban story and the Nuzi texts (see below, pp. 172–3).

39. *They felt a longing for the rods:* better 'they mated beside the rods.' It was seeing the peeled rods at the moment of mating that was supposed to lead to the variegated off-spring.

40. This verse is not easy to reconcile with the rest of the story. If Laban had already removed the black rams from the flock, and given them to his sons three days' journey away (verse 36), how then did Jacob's ewes *run only with the rams in Laban's flocks as were striped and black?*

43. A very similar statement is made about Abraham's increasing wealth in 12: 16. In both cases the patriarch is in a potentially hazardous situation in a foreign land. ✻

JACOB PREPARES TO RETURN HOME

Jacob learnt that Laban's sons were saying, 'Jacob has **31** taken everything that was our father's, and all his wealth has come from our father's property.' He also noticed that 2 Laban was not so well disposed to him as he had once been. Then the LORD said to Jacob, 'Go back to the land 3 of your fathers and to your kindred. I will be with you.' So Jacob sent to fetch Rachel and Leah to his flocks out in 4 the country and said to them, 'I see that your father is not 5 as well disposed to me as once he was; yet the God of my father has been with me. You know how I have served 6 your father to the best of my power, but he has cheated 7 me and changed my wages ten times over. Yet God did not let him do me any harm. If Laban said, "The spotted 8 ones shall be your wages", then all the flock bore spotted young; and if he said, "The striped ones shall be your wages", then all the flock bore striped young. God has 9 taken away your father's property and has given it to me. In the season when the flocks were on heat, I had a 10 dream: I looked up and saw that the he-goats mounting the flock were striped and spotted and dappled. The angel 11 of God said to me in my dream, "Jacob", and I replied, "Here I am", and he said, "Look up and see: all the he- 12 goats mounting the flock are striped and spotted and dappled. I have seen all that Laban is doing to you. I am 13 the God who appeared to you at*[a]* Bethel where you anointed a sacred pillar and where you made your vow. Now leave this country at once and return to the land of your birth."' Rachel and Leah answered him, 'We no 14

[a] who...at: *so Sept.; Heb. om.*

15 longer have any part or lot in our father's house. Does he
not look on us as foreigners, now that he has sold us and
16 spent on himself the whole of the money paid for us? But
all the wealth which God has saved from our father's
clutches is ours and our children's. Now do everything
17 that God has said.' Jacob at once set his sons and his wives
18 on camels, and drove off all the herds and livestock*a* which
he had acquired in Paddan-aram, to go to his father Isaac
in Canaan.

✻ This section in part covers the same ground as the previous
section, but it comes mainly from the E tradition and presupposes a rather different relationship between Laban and
Jacob. The religious element in the story is much more explicit,
and every opportunity is taken to justify Jacob's character
(compare the comment on the relationship between the J and
the E traditions in chapters 12 and 20 on p. 5). In chapter 30
no reason is given for Jacob's decision to leave Laban's
household and return to his own country, except that it is
his 'wish' (30: 25). Here the interweaving of the human and
the divine strands in Israel's experience is neatly underlined
by a twofold explanation in terms of human relationships –
the envy of Laban's sons (verse 1), and Laban's increasing
unfriendliness (verse 2) – and a twofold explanation in terms
of God's initiative – the LORD says to Jacob, 'Go back'
(verse 3) and God says 'leave this country at once and return
to the land of your birth' (verse 13). Characteristic of the E
tradition is the fact that central to the narrative is a dream in
which God makes himself and his purpose known to Jacob.
Jacob is no longer the wily shepherd outsmarting his rival.
He is the aggrieved, innocent party in all that happens. Each
move that Laban makes is countered by God. When Laban
turns unfriendly, 'yet the God of my father has been with

[a] *So Pesh.; Heb. adds* which he had acquired, the herds he had
purchased.

ne' (verse 5). Laban fails again and again to cheat Jacob over
his wages because 'God did not let him do me any harm'
(verse 7). Jacob is thus presented to us not for our admiring
chuckles, but for our wonder and approval as a man whose
every step is led and guarded by God.

3. *I will be with you*: repeating, at the moment of return
from exile, the promise made to Jacob by the LORD at the
moment of his leaving home to go into exile (28: 15). All
the Jacob stories illustrate the truth in this promise.

4. *So Jacob sent to fetch Rachel and Leah*: the ensuing family
council recalls the way in which Rebecca was asked to give
her consent to her marriage with Isaac (see 24: 58). It seems to
presuppose that Laban still has some legal hold over his
married daughters, a claim Rachel and Leah deny (verses
14–16) on the grounds that he has forfeited any such right
by his conduct towards them. The family council serves to
vindicate Jacob's proposed course of action. Not only does he
act in response to God's command, but Laban's own daughters
connive in the plan to flee from their father's house.

7. *he has cheated me and changed my wages ten times over*:
although *ten times over* means no more than 'several times'
or 'time and again', this goes far beyond what has been
recorded in the previous section. Verse 8 gives two illustrations
of such cheating, neither of which can be easily reconciled
with the previous narrative in which there is no suggestion
that 'spotted' or 'striped' animals were born on different
occasions to nullify Laban's attempts to cheat Jacob.

9–13. Dreams as a means of communication between God
and man are common in the E source. The content of this
dream, however, is curious. It is not clear how the 'striped
and spotted and dappled' he-goats mounting the flock
frustrate Laban's double-dealing. The contrast with chapter
30, however, is marked. There Jacob comes out on top very
much because of his native wit and shrewdness, here the
dream makes him aware of God's guiding providence.

11. *The angel of God*: see 16: 7.

13. *I am the God who appeared to you at Bethel:* this, the reading of the Septuagint (see the N.E.B. footnote), reflects the way in which the phrase was understood in Israel. The Hebrew text 'I am the God Bethel' may well preserve the memory of the fact that Bethel is not merely the name of a place but the name of a God (see p. 146). Such a phrase, in which the deity identifies himself, usually occurs at the beginning of a dream not, as here, near the end (cp. 28: 13). The position here is probably quite deliberate. The first half of the dream looks backwards to what is now the past; the end of the dream points to the future, to the fulfilment of the promise made to Jacob by the God who had met him at Bethel when he left home (28: 15).

15. *spent on himself the whole of the money paid for us:* this presupposes that Jacob paid Laban a bride-price or *mohar* for his daughters, a fact nowhere previously stated. In many societies part of the *mohar* was reserved inalienably for the woman. This is the basis for Rachel and Leah's complaint. Laban has pocketed for himself what was theirs by right.

18. The longer Hebrew text (see the N.E.B. footnote) seems needlessly repetitive, but such repetition is not uncommon in Hebrew narrative style.   ✳

THEFT AND RECRIMINATION

19 When Laban the Aramaean had gone to shear his sheep,
20 Rachel stole her father's household gods,*a* and Jacob
21 deceived Laban, keeping his departure secret. So Jacob
ran away with all that he had, crossed the River and made
22 for the hill-country of Gilead. Three days later, when
23 Laban heard that Jacob had run away, he took his kinsmen with him, pursued Jacob for seven days and caught
24 up with him in the hill-country of Gilead. But God came to Laban in a dream by night and said to him, 'Be careful to say nothing to Jacob, either good or bad.'

[a] Heb. teraphim.

When Laban overtook him, Jacob had pitched his tent 25
in the hill-country of Gilead, and Laban pitched his in the
company of his kinsmen in the same hill-country. Laban 26
said to Jacob, 'What have you done? You have deceived me
and carried off my daughters as though they were captives
taken in war. Why did you slip away secretly without 27
telling me? I would have set you on your way with songs
and the music of tambourines and harps. You did not even 28
let me kiss my daughters and their children. In this you
were at fault. It is in my power to do you an injury, but 29
yesterday the God of your father spoke to me; he told me
to be careful to say nothing to you, either good or bad.
I know that you went away because you were homesick 30
and pining for your father's house, but why did you steal
my gods?'

Jacob answered, 'I was afraid; I thought you would 31
take your daughters from me by force. Whoever is found 32
in possession of your gods shall die for it. Let our kinsmen
here be witnesses: point out anything I have that is yours,
and take it back.' Jacob did not know that Rachel had
stolen the gods. So Laban went into Jacob's tent and 33
Leah's tent and that of the two slave-girls, but he found
nothing. When he came out of Leah's tent he went into
Rachel's. Now she had taken the household gods and put 34
them in the camel-bag and was sitting on them. Laban
went through everything in the tent and found nothing.
Rachel said to her father, 'Do not take it amiss, sir, that 35
I cannot rise in your presence: the common lot of woman
is upon me.' So for all his search Laban did not find his
household gods.

Jacob was angry, and he expostulated with Laban, 36
exclaiming, 'What have I done wrong? What is my

37 offence, that you have come after me in hot pursuit and
gone through all my possessions? Have you found anything belonging to your household? If so, set it here in
front of my kinsmen and yours, and let them judge
38 between the two of us. In all the twenty years I have been
with you, your ewes and she-goats have never mis-
39 carried; I have not eaten the rams of your flocks; I have
never brought to you the body of any animal mangled by
wild beasts, but I bore the loss myself; you claimed compensation from me for anything stolen by day or by night.
40 This was the way of it: by day the heat consumed me and
41 the frost by night, and sleep deserted me. For twenty
years I have been in your household. I worked for you
fourteen years to win your two daughters and six years
for your flocks, and you changed my wages ten times
42 over. If the God of my father, the God of Abraham and
the Fear of Isaac, had not been with me, you would have
sent me away empty-handed. But God saw my labour
and my hardships, and last night he rebuked you.'

✻ As Jacob and his family secretly leave for Canaan interest
centres on Rachel's theft of her father's household gods or
teraphim. Whatever *teraphim* may mean in other Old Testament passages – in Ezek. 21: 21 and Zech. 10: 2 they are
associated with divination – they seem in this narrative to be
small figurines of the family gods. Laban indeed calls them,
in verse 30, 'my gods'. But why did Rachel steal them?
Among the Nuzi texts (see pp. 13–14) there is a tablet of
adoption, concerning the adoption of Wullu by Nashwi,
which among other things stipulates: 'If Nashwi has a son of
his own, he will divide the inheritance equally with Wullu,
but it is the son of Nashwi who will take the gods of Nashwi.
If Nashwi has no son of his own then Wullu will take the gods

of Nashwi.' Possession of the family gods, therefore, seems to be the *prima facie* credentials of the chief heir to the family estate. Against this background it is tempting to suggest that, in stealing the family gods, Rachel is trying to ensure for Jacob what she regards as his rightful claim to Laban's estate, a claim unlikely to be recognized given the tense relationship between Jacob and Laban and the fact that Laban has sons of his own. But we ought to hesitate before pressing the analogy too far. There is nothing in the story to suggest that Jacob is to be regarded as the adopted son of Laban. Moreover, the possession of the household gods only seems to be of legal significance at Nuzi subsequent to the death of the father of the family. There is no hint that possession of them during a man's lifetime conferred any legal claim to that man's estate. Jacob himself seems to be totally unaware of any such legal significance attaching to the household gods, when he takes a solemn oath which unwittingly places Rachel's life in jeopardy (verse 32).

If customs at Nuzi lie in the background to this narrative – a blend of J and E material not always easily separable – it can only be in the very distant background. The story, as it now lies before us, is told with a great deal of humour and seems primarily concerned to hold Laban and his religion up to ridicule. His gods are small objects which can be hidden in a camel-bag. He mounts a futile search for them. Rachel is sitting on the camel-bag. She refuses to get up, claiming an awkward moment during her menstrual period. The law in Lev. 15 declares that during such a period a woman is ritually unclean, and 'Everything on which she lies or sits during her impurity shall be unclean' (Lev. 15: 20). So much for the gods of Laban. On the contrary, the God of Jacob had all along been with him, and was protecting him even in the midst of this last unfriendly act, the accusation of theft. The Nuzi parallel hardly seems necessary to account for Rachel's action. She may well have stolen the household gods either to spite her father or because she wished to take with her into a foreign land something that would be a constant reminder of the home she was leaving.

19. *Laban the Aramaean:* Old Testament tradition frequently links the patriarchs with the Aramaean district of north-west Mesopotamia (see Deut. 26: 5 and p. 110 of *Genesis 1–11*). Cp. 25: 20. *had gone to shear his sheep:* the spring sheep-shearing was a time not only of hard work but of joyful celebration (cp. 1 Sam. 25). This, plus the distance that Laban himself had put between his own flocks and Jacob's, provided Jacob with the opportunity to steal away.

20. *Jacob deceived Laban:* literally, 'stole the heart of Laban', using the same verb as in verse 19 where Rachel stole the household gods. The word 'steal' with various shades of meaning echoes across the story. In the literal sense of steal it occurs again in verse 30, and twice in verse 39 (see the Revised Standard Version 'stolen by day or stolen by night'); with the meaning 'deceive' it occurs again in verse 26, and in verse 27 it is translated 'secretly', perhaps better 'stealthily'.

21. *the River:* the Euphrates; see the note on 15: 18. *the hill-country of Gilead:* the mountainous region east of the river Jordan and south of the Sea of Galilee (see map p. xiv). In later Old Testament times it was very much disputed territory between the Israelites and their northern Aramaean neighbours (cp. Amos 1: 3–5), a conflict which may be reflected in the story of the boundary mark in verses 43–54. A large, slow-moving caravan such as Jacob was leading would hardly have reached this district from Paddan-aram in ten days, as is implied in verses 22–3, but the numbers may simply be intended to indicate a considerable time.

24. Typically, for the E narrative, God intervenes through a dream in which Laban is warned *to say nothing to Jacob, either good or bad,* i.e. to make no threats against Jacob of any kind. For this idiomatic use of *good or bad,* conveying the idea of 'everything', cp. Gen. 2: 9 (see *Genesis 1–11*, p. 35).

25–32. Laban may make no threats, but he has a twofold

complaint; his daughters and families have gone without the chance to say farewell, and his household gods have been stolen. Jacob replies briefly to each charge in verses 31–2.

32. *Jacob did not know that Rachel had stolen the gods:* again the stress upon Jacob's innocence. Only this could justify the oath which puts Rachel's life in jeopardy.

36–42. Laban's futile search provides Jacob with the opportunity to give vent to righteous indignation. He protests that

(i) he has been a skilful shepherd: 'your ewes and she-goats have never miscarried' (verse 38);

(ii) he has been a responsible shepherd, never using his position of trust for his own advantage; not even insisting upon his legal rights. No shepherd could be expected to guarantee that the flock would not be attacked by wild beasts, but he could be expected to take steps to defend the flock. The law in Exod. 22: 13 stipulates, 'If it (e.g. a sheep) has been mauled by a wild beast, he shall bring it in as evidence; he shall not make restitution for what has been mauled.' Even in such cases, claims Jacob, 'I bore the loss myself' (verse 39);

(iii) he had worked long and unstintingly for Laban, twenty years in all, fourteen for his daughters and six for the flocks;

(iv) only God's presence and protection had prevented him from being swindled and 'sent...away empty-handed' (verse 42).

This picture of injured, outraged innocence does not easily square with the portrait of Jacob in chapter 30.

41. *six years for your flocks:* the first mention of a fixed period of time during which Jacob worked in return for flocks.

42. *the Fear of Isaac:* only here and in verse 53 does this title of God occur. It has been argued that it ought to be translated 'the kinsman of Isaac', a title stressing the relationship which links God with one of the patriarchs, but this is

doubtful. It may mean no more than the God who inspired awe in Isaac. It does not seem to have survived as a cultic title in later Israel.   ✳

THE AGREEMENT

43 Laban answered Jacob, 'The daughters are my daughters, the children are my children, the flocks are my flocks; all that you see is mine. But as for my daughters, what can I do today about them and the children they have borne?
44 Come now, we will make an agreement, you and I, and
45 let it stand as a witness between us.' So Jacob chose a great
46 stone and set it upright as a sacred pillar. Then he told his kinsmen to gather stones, and they took them and built a cairn, and there beside the cairn they ate together.
47 Laban called it Jegar-sahadutha,*a* and Jacob called it Gal-
48 ed.*b* Laban said, 'This cairn is witness today between you
49 and me.' For this reason it was named Gal-ed; it was also named Mizpah,*c* for Laban said, 'May the LORD watch between you and me, when we are parted from each
50 other's sight. If you ill-treat my daughters or take other wives beside them when no one is there to see, then God
51 be witness between us.' Laban said further to Jacob, 'Here is this cairn, and here the pillar which I have set up
52 between us. This cairn is witness and the pillar is witness: I for my part will not pass beyond this cairn to your side, and you for your part shall not pass beyond this cairn and
53 this pillar to my side to do any injury, otherwise the God of Abraham and the God of Nahor will judge between us.'*d* And Jacob swore this oath in the name of the Fear of

[a] *Aramaic for* Cairn of Witness.   [b] *Hebrew for* Cairn of Witness.
[c] *That is* Watchtower.
[d] *So Sept.; Heb. adds* the God of their father.

Isaac his father. He slaughtered an animal for sacrifice, 54
there in the hill-country, and summoned his kinsmen to
the feast. So they ate together and spent the night there.

Laban rose early in the morning, kissed his daughters and 55[a]
their children, blessed them and went home again.

* This section, a blend of the J and E traditions, has many
rough edges. The one tradition, E, seems to have its roots in
an old cult legend centring on the sacred pillar, *maṣṣebah* at
Mizpah – note the play on similar sounding words. The other
tradition, J, preserves the memory of an early non-aggression
pact, specifying the boundary between an Aramaean and an
Israelite group, in the disputed region of Gilead, east of the
Jordan. It gives the reason for a certain cairn, *gal*, in Gilead –
we might say a cairn in the Cairngorms – with twin Aramaic
and Hebrew names. These traditions have been used to tell
the story of the agreement or covenant (see the note on 15: 18)
which ends the family dispute between Jacob and Laban. In
spite of all that has gone before, the initiative comes from
Laban and perhaps even more strongly than is apparent in the
present text. In the light of verse 51 where Laban speaks of
'the pillar which I have set up', it is possible that an earlier
form of the story spoke of Laban, rather than Jacob, choosing
the great stone in verse 45. The old Latin text reads 'Laban'
at the beginning of verse 46.

44. *let it stand as a witness between us:* the text here, which
makes the agreement the witness, is awkward. Elsewhere the
witness is the cairn (verse 48) and/or the pillar (verse 52) or
God (verse 50). It would be preferable to read here, as at the
end of verse 50 'let God be witness between us'.

45. *sacred pillar:* Hebrew *maṣṣebah*, see p. 148.

47. *Laban called it Jegar-sahadutha and Jacob called it Gal-ed:*
Jegar-sahadutha, the only Aramaic word in Genesis, means
'Cairn of Witness', and is equivalent in meaning to the Hebrew

[a] *32: 1 in Heb.*

Gal-ed (see the N.E.B. footnote). *Gal-ed* provides a further play on the word *gal*, cairn.

48. The cairn takes the place of any written contractual document. It is visible witness to the solemnly undertaken agreement.

49. This whole verse is best taken as an explanatory comment which seeks to account both for the name of a cairn called *Gal-ed*, and also for the name *Mizpah*, 'Watchtower', (see the N.E.B. footnote) which is here linked by sound to the Hebrew verb 'to watch': *May the LORD watch between you and me*. If it is an explanatory comment, this may be the reason for the sole mention of the LORD in this passage, strangely on the lips of Laban. *Mizpah* appears as the name of a tower east of the Jordan in the narrative in Judg. 10 and 11. Its precise location is uncertain.

50. In a polygamous society the position of a wife may be precarious. She may be replaced by another wife, more favoured, and either ignored or ill-treated. Laban, in terms of the agreement, seeks to safeguard his daughters from such a fate. Such a provision is not infrequently written into marriage documents in the ancient Near East. The Nuzi text quoted above, in the context of Rachel's theft of the household gods, stipulates that 'if Wullu takes another wife, he loses all right to Nashwi's land and property' (see pp. 172-3).

53. *otherwise the God of Abraham and the God of Nahor will judge between us*: this is the reading of the Septuagint. The Hebrew text adds 'the God of their father' (see the N.E.B. footnote) or 'their ancestral gods'. Interpreting the Hebrew addition as 'their ancestral gods' underlines what is clearly intended. The *God of Abraham* and the *God of Nahor* are different deities, the gods respectively of Jacob, grandson of *Abraham*, and Laban, grandson of *Nahor*. As in similar agreements and treaties from the ancient Near East, the gods of the contracting parties are invoked to guarantee the keeping of the terms of the agreement. *Fear of Isaac*: see above on verse 42.

54. *He slaughtered an animal for sacrifice:* the agreement is solemnized by a sacrifice, which takes the form of a shared meal, in which parts of the animal are offered to God and parts eaten by the worshippers (cp. Lev. 7: 11–21). This symbolizes and cements the bond which unites the contracting parties to one another and to their gods.

55. The N.E.B. joins this verse to what follows (as in the Hebrew text's division of the chapters; see footnote); but in reality it rounds off the narrative which has just reached its climax. Laban courteously bids his daughters farewell and returns home. ✲

THE ENCOUNTER AT MAHANAIM

Then Jacob continued his journey and was met by angels **32** of God. When he saw them, Jacob said, 'This is the com- 2 pany of God', and he called that place Mahanaim.[a]

✲ This tantalizingly brief episode provides, on one level, an explanation of the place-name, Mahanaim (see map p. xiv), later destined to be an important fortress town east of the Jordan. David retreated to it in face of his son Absalom's revolt (2 Sam. 17: 24, 27). The name, which means 'Two Companies' (see the N.E.B. footnote) is explained in terms of 'the company of God', the angels or messengers of God whom Jacob encounters there. But there is more to it than that. As Jacob was about to go into exile from the promised land, he had a vision at Bethel, a vision centring upon angels of God (see 28: 11–19); so now, returned from exile and on the point of re-entering the promised land, he again encounters the angels of God. His departure was a crisis point marked by an encounter which assured him of God's protecting presence; his return is another crisis point marked by a further encounter with God, though we are given no hint as to

[a] *That is* Two Companies.

the nature of this encounter. These verses probably contain the E parallel to the fuller and more mysterious J story of Jacob's encounter at the ford of Jabbok described in 32: 22–32. ✳

PREPARING TO MEET ESAU

3 Jacob sent messengers on ahead to his brother Esau to the
4 district of Seir in the Edomite country, and this is what he told them to say to Esau, 'My lord, your servant Jacob says, I have been living with Laban and have stayed there
5 till now. I have oxen, asses, and sheep, and male and female slaves, and I have sent to tell you this, my lord, so
6 that I may win your favour.' The messengers returned to Jacob and said, 'We met your brother Esau already on the
7 way to meet you with four hundred men.' Jacob, much afraid and distressed, divided the people with him, as well as the sheep, cattle, and camels, into two companies,
8 thinking that, if Esau should come upon one company
9 and destroy it, the other company would survive. Jacob said, 'O God of my father Abraham, God of my father Isaac, O LORD at whose bidding I came back to my own country and to my kindred, and who didst promise me
10 prosperity, I am not worthy of all the true and steadfast love which thou hast shown to me thy servant. When I crossed the Jordan, I had nothing but the staff in my
11 hand; now I have two companies. Save me, I pray, from my brother Esau, for I am afraid that he may come
12 and destroy me, sparing neither mother nor child. But thou didst say, I will prosper you and will make your descendants like the sand of the sea, which is beyond all counting.'

13 Jacob spent that night there; and as a present for his

brother Esau he chose from the herds he had with him two 14
hundred she-goats, twenty he-goats, two hundred ewes
and twenty rams, thirty milch-camels with their young, 15
forty cows and ten young bulls, twenty she-asses and ten
he-asses. He put each herd separately into the care of a 16
servant and said to each, 'Go on ahead of me, and leave
gaps between the herds.' Then he gave these instructions 17
to the first: 'When my brother Esau meets you and asks
you to whom you belong and where you are going and
who owns these beasts you are driving, you are to say, 18
"They belong to your servant Jacob; he sends them as a
present to my lord Esau, and he is behind us."' He gave 19
the same instructions to the second, to the third, and all
the drovers, telling them to say the same thing to Esau
when they met him. And they were to add, 'Your servant 20
Jacob is behind us'; for he thought, 'I will appease him
with the present that I have sent on ahead, and afterwards, when I come into his presence, he will perhaps
receive me kindly.' So Jacob's present went on ahead of 21
him, but he himself spent that night at Mahaneh.

* Jacob's homecoming is fraught with anxiety. He dreads
a meeting with Esau. A brother's grudge may have intensified during the twenty years of their separation. A conciliatory
message sent to Esau elicits the information that Esau is on
his way to meet him with a threateningly large force of
400 men. Jacob deals with the situation in three ways:

(i) he takes sensible military precautions, dividing his
people into two companies so that if one is attacked the other
may escape (verses 7–8);

(ii) he prays (verses 9–12);

(iii) he sends lavish presents in an attempt to appease Esau
(verses 13–21).

.Although attempts have been made to divide this narrative into two parallel stories, verses 3–12 and verses 13–21, it is better to treat the whole as a unity from the J source.

3. *messengers:* the word is the same as that rendered 'angels' in verse 1. God's messengers to Jacob have their counterpart in the messengers of a rather different kind whom Jacob now sends to Esau. *the district of Seir in the Edomite country:* Seir is a mountainous region south of the Dead Sea which was settled by the Edomites, who traced their ancestry to Esau (see note on 25: 22–6 and chapter 36).

4–5. This is an excellent example of the typical ancient Near Eastern equivalent of a letter. A brief message from x to y is entrusted orally to a messenger. The messenger goes to y and delivers the message in the form 'Thus says x' repeating the exact words spoken to him by x. The prophets of Israel, prefacing their words with 'Thus says the LORD' seem to have thought of themselves as God's messengers to Israel.

7. *into two companies:* words recalling the place-name Mahanaim echo across the story – 'one company' (verse 8), 'two companies' (verse 10), and the place-name Mahaneh which means 'camp' or 'company' (verse 21).

9–12. Jacob's prayer may be taken as a typical expression of the personal faith of many devout people in Israel. It begins with an invocation of the God who is known and worshipped, in this case the 'God of my father Abraham, God of my father Isaac' (verse 9), identified with the LORD. It continues with thanksgiving that the promises made by this God in the past have been fulfilled, beyond the worshipper's deserving, because of the dependability, 'the true and steadfast love' (verse 10) of God. It moves from thanksgiving into an urgent plea for help: 'Save me' (verse 11). One note conspicuously absent is confession. Jacob's whole attitude in this section, however, recognizes that he has offended against Esau and that Esau may be expected to be justifiably angry.

9. *at whose bidding I came back:* picking up the LORD's words to Jacob in 31: 3.

12. The promise here recalls the general theme of the promise made to Jacob at Bethel (28: 13–15); the specific language, *your descendants like the sand of the sea, which is beyond all counting*, is more reminiscent of the promise made to Abraham when he had proved willing to sacrifice Isaac (22: 17).

14–21. There is an element of wry humour in the narrative here. As each herd, led by a drover, comes to Esau, we can imagine him standing there and thinking 'What, another present?' The purpose of the lavish gifts, however, is deadly serious. The anger of a wronged brother must be assuaged.

14. *two hundred she-goats, twenty he-goats:* in each case the value of the gift is enhanced by including male and female animals, thus ensuring future breeding.

21. *at Mahaneh:* this translation assumes that *Mahaneh* is a place-name, presumably a variant of Mahanaim. It would be equally possible to translate 'in camp'.

Although no English translation can convey it, the Hebrew word for 'face', *panim*, occurs five times in verses 20–1. In one form or another, it lies behind the renderings 'appease', 'ahead', 'presence' and 'receive' in verse 20, and 'ahead of him' in verse 21. This prepares the way for the strange episode at Penuel, where Jacob encounters God 'face to face' (32: 30). *

JACOB AT PENUEL

During the night Jacob rose, took his two wives, his two 22
slave-girls, and his eleven sons, and crossed the ford of
Jabbok. He took them and sent them across the gorge 23
with all that he had. So Jacob was left alone, and a man 24
wrestled with him there till*ᵃ* daybreak. When the man saw 25
that he could not throw Jacob, he struck him in the
hollow of his thigh, so that Jacob's hip was dislocated as

[a] *Or* at.

26 they wrestled. The man said, 'Let me go, for day is breaking', but Jacob replied, 'I will not let you go unless

27 you bless me.' He said to Jacob, 'What is your name?',

28 and he answered, 'Jacob.' The man said, 'Your name shall no longer be Jacob, but Israel,*a* because you strove with

29 God and with men, and prevailed.' Jacob said, 'Tell me, I pray, your name.' He replied, 'Why do you ask my

30 name?', but he gave him his blessing there. Jacob called the place Peniel,*b* 'because', he said, 'I have seen God face

31 to face and my life is spared.' The sun rose as Jacob passed

32 through Penuel, limping because of his hip. This is why the Israelites to this day do not eat the sinew of the nerve that runs in the hollow of the thigh; for the man had struck Jacob on that nerve in the hollow of the thigh.

* There is no more strange or perplexing narrative than this in the whole of the Old Testament. The boldness of the language and the symbolism in the story is startling. It is not recounted as a dream or vision, but as an incident which happened one night. Jacob wrestled with an unidentified 'man' who turned out to be God, wrestled and lived to tell the tale. Gathered into the story are so many curious elements that we can only assume that here is a story which has taken many centuries to reach its present form, and which has assimilated material, some of it very primitive, which goes back long before the time of Jacob. It is like an old house which has had additions built on to it, and has been restored and renovated more than once during the passing years. Within the present story we may find:

(i) an explanation of the name given to the ford of Jabbok (see map p. xiv). This links the name Jabbok with the Hebrew verb translated 'wrestled' in verses 24–5, a verb

[a] *That is* God strove.   [b] *That is* Face of God (*elsewhere* Penuel)

found only here in the Old Testament. This is 'Wrestling' ford, for here a man wrestled with Jacob;

(ii) an unidentified man who disputes Jacob's crossing of the river. This may have its roots in stories, widespread in many cultures, of the river spirit who has to be placated or defeated before he will allow the traveller to cross. The unidentified man may originally have been the river spirit of the Jabbok;

(iii) the belief that spirits and ghosts who haunt the night are doomed to disappear before daybreak. 'Let me go', says the man, 'for day is breaking' (verse 26). Thus the ghost of Hamlet's father 'faded on the crowing of the cock' (*Hamlet*, I. i. 157);

(iv) an explanation of the name Israel (verse 28), and of the occasion on which Jacob's name was changed to Israel (35: 10 attributes this name change to another occasion and to a different place);

(v) an explanation as to why a certain place or sanctuary was called Penuel (verse 30). It is even possible that worship at Penuel involved some form of limping ritual dance, and that this was traced back to Jacob passing through Penuel, limping;

(vi) an explanation of the origin of a food taboo, the Israelite refusal to eat 'the sinew of the nerve that runs in the hollow of the thigh' (verse 32), a food taboo not otherwise mentioned in the laws in the Old Testament. It may go back to the association of the thigh with procreation.

Once we have looked at all these elements, however, they hardly tell us what the incident as a whole means in its present context. The J source is not interested in collecting and preserving primitive or popular religious ideas; it has a serious theological purpose, not least in this passage. We can begin by asking, why does this passage come between the description of Jacob's preparations to meet Esau and the account of the meeting in chapter 33? We left Jacob anticipating his meeting with Esau with anxious fear. He prays to

God, 'Save me' (verse 11). His prayer is answered in the struggle, in the darkness of the eerie gorge of Jabbok, with someone who turns out to be God. Jacob's greatest need is not how to come to terms with Esau, but how to come to terms with God. God was not there merely to answer a selfish cry. This was to be a costly experience, the cost symbolized by the dislocating of Jacob's hip. Yet he persevered, struggled, refused to let his unknown assailant go, until he finds that he has seen God face to face. The history of the people of Israel was often to be the tale of just such an encounter with God; a costly, turbulent struggle in the darkness of tragedy, exile and persecution, but an authentic experience in which they came face to face with God. There is a further point. The change of name from Jacob to Israel is of central importance to the story. Out of the struggle comes a new Jacob, symbolized by the new name; no longer the deceiver or the twister (27: 36), but now Israel, one who has striven with God (see verse 28). It is this new Jacob, new not only in name but in character – the name being the indicator of character and destiny (see the note on 17: 4–5) – who now goes to meet Esau.

22. *his two wives, his two slave-girls, and his eleven sons:* curiously no mention of his one daughter Dinah who features prominently in the following chapter. *Jabbok:* a river now known as the Nahr ez Zerka. It rises in the Jordanian uplands and cuts a deep gorge as it flows down to enter the river Jordan some 40 miles (64 km) south of the Sea of Galilee.

24. *a man wrestled with him:* for this mysterious man who turns out to be God or a divine being, compare the story of the three men who appeared before Abraham's tent (18: 1) and are later identified as angels or divine messengers (19: 1). The prophet Hosea, who seems to have known this story in a slightly different form, talks of the man as an angel.

'Even in the womb Jacob overreached his brother,
and in manhood he strove with God.

The divine angel stood firm and held his own;
Jacob wept and begged favour for himself'

(Hos. 12: 3–4).

till daybreak: this is preferable to the alternative rendering 'at daybreak' (see the N.E.B. footnote), since, after the wrestling has gone on for some time, the man asks to depart 'for day is breaking' (verse 26).

26. *I will not let you go unless you bless me:* Jacob wishes to possess the vitality and the energy so evidently displayed by his assailant. The theme of blessing here echoes the story told in chapter 27 (and its parallel in 28: 2–4). There Jacob obtained his father's blessing by deceit; here he obtains God's blessing in a costly struggle.

28. *Your name shall no longer be Jacob, but Israel:* linguistically the name Israel may mean either 'God strove' (see the N.E.B. footnote) or 'May God strive'. Here it is popularly explained in a different way, with God as the object, not the subject, of the verb strive. It is thus said to reflect Jacob's experience, *you strove with God and with men* or 'you strove with beings divine and human'. *with men:* does this refer to Jacob's successful outwitting of Esau and Laban, or is there an echo here of an old Hebrew folk legend about the exploits of a great hero like the Greek Hercules? (cp. the story of the 'huge stone' in 29: 1–10).

29. Jacob's request to know his adversary's *name* springs from the belief that to know the name of a deity is to possess the secret of his character and therefore to have access to the power which the deity possesses (cp. Exod. 3: 13–14). Here God does not reveal his name (cp. Judg. 13: 18); he remains mysterious.

30. The name Peniel, a linguistic variant of the more usual Penuel (verse 31; Judg. 8: 8–9, 17), is taken to mean 'Face of God' (see the N.E.B. footnote), and to reflect Jacob's experience of seeing God *face to face*. Of Moses alone, elsewhere in the Old Testament, is it claimed that the LORD spoke to him

or knew him face to face (Exod. 33: 11; Deut. 34: 10).
Otherwise it was believed that to see God was a fatal experience (see the note on 16: 13). Thus the exceptional nature of
what happened is underlined in the words *and my life is spared.* *

THE MEETING WITH ESAU

33 Jacob raised his eyes and saw Esau coming towards him
with four hundred men; so he divided the children
2 between Leah and Rachel and the two slave-girls. He put
the slave-girls with their children in front, Leah with her
3 children next, and Rachel with Joseph last. He then went
on ahead of them, bowing low to the ground seven times
4 as he approached his brother. Esau ran to meet him and
embraced him; he threw his arms round him and kissed
5 him, and they wept. When Esau looked up and saw the
women and children, he said, 'Who are these with you?'
Jacob replied, 'The children whom God has graciously
6 given to your servant.' The slave-girls came near, each
7 with her children, and they bowed low. Then Leah with
her children came near and bowed low, and afterwards
8 Joseph and Rachel came near and bowed low also. Esau
said, 'What was all that company of yours that I met?'
And he answered, 'It was meant to win favour with you,
9 my lord.' Esau answered, 'I have more than enough.
10 Keep what is yours, my brother.' But Jacob said, 'On no
account: if I have won your favour, then, I pray, accept
this gift from me; for, you see, I come into your presence
as into that of a god, and you receive me favourably.
11 Accept this gift which I bring you; for God has been
gracious to me, and I have all I want.' So he urged him,
and he accepted it.

Then Esau said, 'Let us set out, and I will go at your 12
pace.' But Jacob answered him, 'You must know, my 13
lord, that the children are small; the flocks and herds are
suckling their young and I am concerned for them, and if
the men overdrive them for a single day, all my beasts
will die. I beg you, my lord, to go on ahead, and I will go 14
by easy stages at the pace of the children and of the livestock that I am driving, until I come to my lord in Seir.'
Esau said, 'Let me detail some of my own men to escort 15
you', but he replied, 'Why should my lord be so kind to
me?' That day Esau turned back towards Seir, but Jacob 16, 17
set out for Succoth; and there he built himself a house and
made shelters for his cattle. Therefore he named that
place Succoth.[a]

On his journey from Paddan-aram, Jacob came safely 18
to the city of Shechem in Canaan and pitched his tent to
the east of it. The strip of country where he had pitched his 19
tent he bought from the sons of Hamor father of Shechem for a hundred sheep.[b] There he set up an altar and 20
called it El-Elohey-Israel.[c]

✲ The long-feared meeting with Esau now takes place.
Jacob's apprehensiveness is evident in the way he divides his
people, keeping Rachel his favourite wife and her son Joseph
at the rear. He is humbly submissive. The tension is broken as
Esau, who is depicted in a very favourable light, warmly
embraces his brother. Courtesy demands that Esau should
initially decline Jacob's gifts; courtesy equally demands that
Jacob should insist and that Esau should finally accept. But
old suspicions remain. Jacob finds an excuse to refuse to

[a] *That is* Shelters.
[b] *Or* pieces of money (*cp. Josh. 24: 32; Job 42: 11*).
[c] *That is* God the God of Israel.

accompany Esau to Seir, or to accept an escort from him. The reconciled brothers part. Esau has no further role in the Genesis narrative.

3. *bowing low to the ground seven times as he approached his brother:* a parallel to this seven times is found in many of the Amarna documents from the fourteenth century B.C. Thus Abdiheba of Jerusalem prefaces his letters to his Egyptian imperial overlord with the words: 'At the feet of the king, my lord, seven times and seven times I fall' (see *Documents from Old Testament Times* (see p. 317), p. 43). In such contexts *seven times* means 'over and over again'.

10. *I come into your presence as into that of a god:* more literally, 'to see your face is like seeing the face of God' (Revised Standard Version). The phrase 'seeing the face of God' seems to be a deliberate echo of Jacob's encounter at Penuel. Perhaps Jacob is implying that he sees Esau in a new light after his encounter with God.

16. The brothers part, Esau going towards Seir (see the note on 32: 3), while Jacob sets out for Succoth, possibly but by no means certainly modern Deir 'Alla, near the Jabbok, west of Penuel. Succoth was an important settlement in the early days of the Hebrew occupation of Canaan (Judg. 8: 5–16).

17. The J narrative ends with a brief explanation of the name *Succoth*, which means 'Shelters' (see the N.E.B. footnote), linking it with the temporary *shelters* which Jacob made there *for his cattle*.

Jacob *built himself a house;* this is the first mention of any of the patriarchs constructing a house. It cannot have been intended to be a very permanent structure, since Jacob is soon on the move again, and reverting, like his ancestors, to living in tents.

18. In a brief note the P tradition brings Jacob back from Paddan-aram, across the Jordan to Shechem, the first important site visited by Abraham in Canaan (12: 6). At Shechem Abraham was promised the land. It is natural that Jacob should return to the scene of this promise.

19. For the significance of the purchase of land see the notes on chapter 23. *for a hundred sheep:* this translation follows the Septuagint and the Targum Onkelos. The Hebrew word rendered 'sheep' occurs only twice elsewhere in the Old Testament (Josh. 24: 32; Job 42: 11). It is as likely that we should render 'pieces of money' (see the N.E.B. footnote), though the precise weight or value of such pieces of money is unknown. In chapter 23 Abraham is involved in a money transaction in the purchase of the plot at Machpelah.

20. As Abraham built an altar to the LORD at Shechem, so Jacob builds an altar to El-Elohey-Israel, 'God the God of Israel' (see the N.E.B. footnote), thus claiming for the religion of Israel a site which the narrative in Judges suggests was dedicated to the worship of a local deity called El-berith, 'god of the covenant' (Judg. 9: 46) or Baal-berith, 'Baal (or 'lord') of the covenant' (Judg. 8: 33; 9: 4).

In the concluding verses of this chapter, which come from the E source, Shechem is the name not of a city, but of a man, the son of Hamor. The name Hamor means 'ass'. In the light of the texts from Mari (see *The Making of the Old Testament*, p. 9, in this series), in which an ass is slain to institute a covenant, there has been speculation that the sons of Hamor could mean something like confederates, allies, people bound together by a covenant. In the present narrative, however, Hamor cannot be anything other than a personal name. ✳

THE RAPE OF DINAH

Dinah, the daughter whom Leah had borne to Jacob, went **34** out to visit the women of the country, and Shechem, son 2 of Hamor the Hivite the local prince, saw her; he took her, lay with her and dishonoured her. But he remained 3 true to Jacob's daughter Dinah; he loved the girl and comforted her. So Shechem said to his father Hamor, 4 'Get me this girl for a wife.' When Jacob heard that 5 Shechem had violated his daughter Dinah, his sons were

with the herds in the open country, so he said nothing
6 until they came home. Meanwhile Shechem's father
7 Hamor came out to Jacob to discuss it with him. When
Jacob's sons came in from the country and heard, they
were grieved and angry, because in lying with Jacob's
daughter he had done what the Israelites held to be an
8 outrage, an intolerable thing. Hamor appealed to them in
these terms: 'My son Shechem is in love with this girl;
9 I beg you to let him have her as his wife. Let us ally ourselves in marriage; you shall give us your daughters, and
10 you shall take ours in exchange. You must settle among
us. The country is open to you; make your home in it,
11 move about freely and acquire land of your own.' And
Shechem said to the girl's father and brothers, 'I am eager
12 to win your favour and I will give whatever you ask. Fix
the bride-price and the gift as high as you like, and I will
give whatever you ask; but you must give me the girl in
marriage.'

13 Jacob's sons gave a dishonest reply to Shechem and his
father Hamor, laying a trap for them because Shechem
14 had violated their sister Dinah: 'We cannot do this,' they
said; 'we cannot give our sister to a man who is uncircum-
15 cised; for we look on that as a disgrace. There is one condition on which we will consent: if you will follow our
16 example and have every male among you circumcised, we
will give you our daughters and take yours for ourselves.
Then we can live among you, and we shall all become
17 one people. But if you refuse to listen to us and be circum-
18 cised, we will take the girl and go away.' Their proposal
19 pleased Hamor and his son Shechem; and the young man,
who was held in respect above anyone in his father's

house, did not hesitate to do what they had said, because his heart was taken by Jacob's daughter.

So Hamor and Shechem went back to the city gate and 20 addressed their fellow-citizens: 'These men are friendly 21 to us; let them live in our country and move freely in it. The land has room enough for them. Let us marry their daughters and give them ours. But these men will agree to 22 live with us and become one people on this one condition only: every male among us must be circumcised as they have been. Will not their herds, their livestock, and all 23 their chattels then be ours? We need only consent to their condition, and then they are free to live with us.' All the 24 able-bodied[a] men agreed with Hamor and Shechem, and every single one of them was circumcised, every able-bodied male. Then two days later, while they were still in 25 great pain, Jacob's two sons Simeon and Levi, full brothers to Dinah, armed themselves with swords, boldly entered the city and killed every male. They cut down Hamor and 26 his son Shechem and took Dinah from Shechem's house and went off with her. Then Jacob's other[b] sons came in 27 over the dead bodies and plundered the city, to avenge their sister's dishonour. They seized flocks, cattle, asses, 28 and everything, both inside the city and outside in the open country; they also carried off all their possessions, 29 their dependants, and their women, and plundered everything in the houses.

Jacob said to Simeon and Levi, 'You have brought 30 trouble on me, you have made my name stink among the people of the country, the Canaanites and the Perizzites. My numbers are few; if they muster against me and

[a] *Lit.* going out of the city gate.   [b] *So Vulg.; Heb. om.*

attack me, I shall be destroyed, I and my household with
31 me.' They answered, 'Is our sister to be treated as a
common whore?'

* This is the only story which tradition has preserved concerning Dinah, the daughter of Jacob. She is raped by Shechem
the son of Hamor. In spite of Shechem's family's attempt to
remedy the situation, a grim revenge is exacted by her
brothers, led by Simeon and Levi. Brothers had the responsibility of defending the honour of the family. The story comes
to us now as a piece of personalized history, but it is reasonable to assume that it preserves the memory of some incident
during the settlement of some Hebrew group or groups in
Canaan. It involves the city of Shechem, an important
Canaanite communication centre in the central highlands,
lying in the valley between Mount Ebal and Mount Gerizim,
not far from modern Nablus. When we try to get back beyond
the present personalized form of the story to a historical
kernel, we can do little more than speculate, except to say
that it must have concerned a violent seizure of Shechem. It
seems to be an old story since in later Israel Simeon and Levi
appear in very different roles, Levi ceasing to be a tribal group
and becoming a priestly caste, Simeon fading into insigni-
ficance and occupying territory much further south than the
locality of the present narrative (see Josh. 19: 1–9 and 21:
1–42). The comment on Simeon and Levi in 49: 5–7 relates
their subsequent fortunes to this incident (see p. 303). In its
present form, however, the story touches upon themes which
we find elsewhere in the patriarchal narratives. There are
dangers involved in settling in Canaan. Canaan may be the
promised land, but the promise cannot be realized by going
native, by assimilating with other peoples already settled
there. Lot chose to settle among the cities of the plain with
tragic consequences (chapter 18); both Abraham and Isaac
had trouble with the inhabitants of Gerar (chapters 20 and

26). In particular any form of inter-marriage is dangerous (see p. 108), not for racial so much as for religious reasons. Circumcision is the visible mark of covenant relationship (see pp. 58–9); any marriage with the uncircumcised is therefore impossible. There is a gruesome humour in the way in which the story relates how Shechem's family agree to the demand for circumcision, and, in their temporary physical discomfiture, are massacred.

Then there is Jacob, the new man bearing the new name Israel. He has made his peace with both Laban and Esau. But the past is not so easily buried. The man who caused sorrow to others is now to find sorrow in his own family. His only daughter is raped; his sons act in a way which, however justifiable, threatens the future (see verse 30). Later, this once favoured son is to lose his own favoured son (37: 33–5).

There have been many attempts to disentangle the present narrative into two more-or-less parallel stories from the J and E sources, with Shechem playing the leading role in one, Hamor in the other; with one featuring the circumcision incident, the other knowing nothing about it. It is better to read the chapter as a unity from the J source.

2. *Hamor the Hivite:* the Septuagint reads 'Horite' instead of *Hivite* (see note on 15: 21). *Hivite* may be used here, however, as a general name for the local inhabitants of Canaan. *lay with her and dishonoured her:* a somewhat literal translation which might be better rendered 'forcibly raped her'.

3. *he loved the girl and comforted her: comforted* is literally, 'spoke to the heart of', an idiom which might equally well mean 'spoke tenderly to'. Trying to win her affection seems better in context than comforting.

7. *he had done what the Israelites held to be an outrage, an intolerable thing:* here 'Israel' – the word translated *Israelites* is literally 'in Israel' – is used to refer to the nation which traced its ancestry back to Jacob/Israel. *an outrage:* this word frequently describes unacceptable sexual practices, including the

rape of a virgin (2 Sam. 13: 12 where the text means literally 'do not commit this outrage') and homosexuality (Judg. 19: 23).

8-10. The discussion is conducted on a family basis, the initiative being taken by Shechem's father, Hamor. Hamor proposes to rectify the situation by a general policy of inter-marriage, which will unite the landless semi-nomads with the local inhabitants. Such a policy would guarantee the incomers land. Behind the general disapproval of the suggested arrangement which is implied in the narrative, may lie the thought that land can only come to the descendants of Abraham as God's gift in fulfilment of his promises.

12. *Fix the bride-price and the gift as high as you like:* the *bride-price and the gift* are one and the same thing, the payment which the intending groom makes to the bride's father to secure his daughter.

13. *Jacob's sons gave a dishonest reply:* this is one of the few places in the patriarchal stories where the writer makes a specific moral comment on what is happening. Granted the initial incident, Shechem and his family appear in the narrative in a conciliatory and favourable light. Jacob's sons are worthy of their father at his worst.

13-25. The attitude to circumcision in this passage is interesting. The profound religious significance of circumcision has been stressed in 17: 9-14, yet the brothers are prepared to use circumcision as a means of temporarily incapacitating Shechem and his fellow-citizens in order to pave the way for revenge. Shechem and his fellow-citizens, on the other hand, regard circumcision as a trivial price to pay for an alliance which will potentially increase their own power and wealth. The Old Testament repeatedly draws attention to the way in which men can misunderstand or use for their own selfish purposes the most significant religious ideas and practices.

24. *All the able-bodied men:* literally, 'all going out of the city gate' (see the N.E.B. footnote and the note on 23: 10).

27. *Jacob's other sons:* the Vulgate addition of *other* (see the
N.E.B. footnote) does no more than bring out the meaning
which the context implies. Simeon and Levi, who throughout
played the leading roles, complete the massacre, then the
other brothers *came in over the dead bodies* to follow up the
slaughter by sacking and pillaging.

28-9. *They seized flocks, cattle, asses, and everything:* an ironic
touch. Hamor and Shechem had persuaded their fellow
citizens to accept circumcision to pave the way for an alliance
which would put at their disposal the herds, the livestock, and
all the possessions of the incomers (verse 23). The tables are
now turned. The sons of Jacob make off with all they possess,
including – and this is typical of military conquest in the
ancient world – *their dependants, and their women.*

30. Jacob, who has played a minor role in the story, has
no objection to what has happened on religious or moral
grounds. His comment is purely pragmatic. If he and his
family are to settle in Canaan, any needless provocation of
the local inhabitants should be avoided, especially where the
locals are obviously more powerful than the incomers.
Inter-marriage may be disapproved, but peaceful coexistence
is desirable.

31. The brothers' retort is unanswerable. The family
honour was at stake. It had to be avenged. The narrative
leaves us asking on what conditions peaceful coexistence
would be possible. This question more than once perplexed
ancient Israel, and it has been part of Jewish experience ever
since. ✻

JACOB RETURNS TO BETHEL

God said to Jacob, 'Go up to Bethel and settle there; build **35**
an altar there to the God who appeared to you when you
were running away from your brother Esau.' So Jacob 2
said to his household and to all who were with him, 'Rid
yourselves of the foreign gods which you have among

you, purify yourselves, and see your clothes are mended.[a]

3 We are going to Bethel, so that I can set up an altar there to the God who answered me in the day of my distress, and who has been with me all the way that I have come.'

4 So they handed over to Jacob all the foreign gods in their possession and the rings from their ears, and he buried

5 them under the terebinth-tree near Shechem. Then they set out, and the cities round about were panic-stricken, and the inhabitants dared not pursue the sons of Jacob.

6 Jacob and all the people with him came to Luz, that is

7 Bethel, in Canaan. There he built an altar, and he called the place El-bethel, because it was there that God had revealed himself to him when he was running away from

8 his brother. Rebecca's nurse Deborah died and was buried under the oak below Bethel, and he named it Allon-bakuth.[b]

9 God appeared again to Jacob when he came back from

10 Paddan-aram and blessed him. God said to him:

> 'Jacob is your name,
>   but your name shall no longer be Jacob:
>   Israel shall be your name.'

11 So he named him Israel. And God said to him:

> 'I am God Almighty.
>   Be fruitful and increase as a nation;
>   a host of nations shall come from you,
>   and kings shall spring from your body.
12   The land which I gave to Abraham and Isaac
>   I give to you;
>   and to your descendants after you I give this land.'

[a] *Or* change your clothes.   [b] *That is* Oak of Weeping.

God then left him,[a] and Jacob erected a sacred pillar in the 13, 14
place where God had spoken with him, a pillar of stone,
and he offered a drink-offering over it and poured oil on
it. Jacob called the place where God had spoken with him 15
Bethel.

※ Bethel is of central significance in the Jacob traditions
(see the introductory comments on chapter 28: 10-22). The
narrative naturally brings Jacob, after his exile, back to Bethel
where again God appears to him, and a promise is repeated.

The main narrative material in this section, verses 1-8,
14-15, comes from the E source. In between, in verses 9-13,
there is to be found almost everything that the P source has
to say about Jacob. The material here is very disjointed, and
contains a considerable amount of overlap with material
found elsewhere. Thus if we take first the P material in verses
9-13, verse 10 contains another account of the name-change
from Jacob to Israel (cp. 32: 28); verses 11-12 reaffirm the
basic promise made to Abraham in the P account of the
covenant in chapter 17: 1-8 (see the notes on chapter 17),
with some of the language sounding rather curious in this
context. It is odd to command a man who already has a
large family to 'Be fruitful and increase'. It is important to
this tradition, however, that having brought Jacob safely
back to Canaan, the promises once made to Abraham should
be unequivocally confirmed to Jacob. Verses 1-8, 14-15
contain two further explanations of the place-name Bethel
(in verses 7 and 15) in addition to that already given at 28:
18-19. Verse 8 refers to the death of Rebecca's nurse Deborah.

We cannot fully understand this section unless we remember
the long-continuing importance of Bethel as a place of worship and pilgrimage in ancient Israel. The language of verses
1-4 seems to echo the invitation to pilgrims, 'Go up to
Bethel', and to lay down the conditions for true pilgrimage;
an act of renunciation (' Rid yourselves of the foreign gods'),

[a] *So Vulg.; Heb. adds* in the place where he had spoken with him.

and an act of purification. It has indeed been argued that Jacob's journey from Shechem to Bethel reflects an annual pilgrimage in early Israel commemorating the transfer of the centre of worship for the Hebrew tribes from Shechem to Bethel. This, however, is highly speculative.

1. *build an altar there:* see the note on 12:8. The E tradition in chapter 28 made Jacob erect a sacred pillar at Bethel; now comes the command to *build an altar*, a more legitimate expression of Israel's faith.

2. *Rid yourselves of the foreign gods:* the foreign gods may be the *teraphim* Rachel brought with her, and doubtless any other objects of religious significance brought by Jacob's family from Mesopotamia. The lack of precise reference suggests that the injunction has a much wider application to the total repudiation of other gods. Verse 4 adds 'the rings from their ears'; earrings being commonly worn in the ancient Near East, some of them, crescent-shaped, having associations with the worship of the moon-god. *purify yourselves:* a cultic commandment designed to ensure that all who approached the holy place of God would be in an appropriate condition of holiness. Lev. 11–16 contain laws concerned with such purification. *see your clothes are mended:* it is better to follow the N.E.B. footnote translation and see here a reference not to mending, but to 'changing' clothes. The putting on of fresh garments is, in many religions, symbolic of the new life which is offered to the worshipper.

4. *the terebinth-tree near Shechem:* see the note on 12:6. The custom of burying sacred objects at certain holy spots was common in the ancient world. The move from Shechem to Bethel, however, marks for the E source an important transition in Jacob's life. The symbols of the old life are buried. He goes to Bethel to a new future centred solely upon the one God whose providence, often unrecognized, had over-arched his life.

5. *the cities round about were panic-stricken:* literally, 'a terror of God was upon the cities'. The N.E.B. translation

assumes that 'of God' is here used adjectivally (see the note on 30: 8). A more literal translation may be defended here on the grounds that what Jacob feared, the revenge of the local inhabitants, was prevented by God, the God who was later believed to fight on behalf of Israel and throw their enemies into confusion (e.g. Josh. 10: 10).

6. *Luz, that is Bethel:* see the note on 28: 19.

7. *he called the place El-bethel: place* probably means 'sacred place', the altar or the shrine. Just as at Shechem the local deity was to be identified with Israel's God and called El-Elohey-Israel (33: 20), so the local deity at Bethel is identified with the God of Jacob's experience and named *El-bethel.*

8. It is difficult to know what gave rise to this brief reference to the death and burial of *Rebecca's nurse Deborah.* Rebecca herself was last mentioned at 27: 46, while her nurse, referred to in 24: 59, has not hitherto been named. An attempt is obviously being made to explain why a certain oak near Bethel was called *Allon-bakuth,* 'Oak of Weeping' (see the N.E.B. footnote). Judg. 4: 5 refers to another Deborah, a prophetess, who sat 'beneath the Palm-tree of Deborah between Ramah and Bethel'. Perhaps with the passing of time the two names and trees became confused.

10–12. On these verses, see above p. 199. The P source here gives the change without explanation, but simply associates it with the blessing in verses 11–12. *I am God Almighty* (verse 11): see note on 17: 1. The blessing repeats that of 17: 1–8, thus affirming the continuing validity of the promise to Abraham.

13. The words at the end of this verse which the N.E.B. omits, following the Vulgate, may be an accidental anticipitation of what occurs more naturally at the end of the next verse. Deliberate repetition, however, is characterististic of Hebrew narrative style, and the longer text may be retained here.

14. *a sacred pillar…and poured oil on it:* see the note on 28: 18. The additional phrase *he offered a drink-offering over it*

emphasizes that the sacred pillar is no mere memorial stone, but a place of worship. Regulations concerning the libation or drink-offering, which was usually offered together with another type of sacrifice, are to be found in Num. 28 and 29. ✻

FAMILY MATTERS

16 They set out from Bethel, and when there was still some distance to go to Ephrathah, Rachel was in labour and her
17 pains were severe. While her pains were upon her, the midwife said, 'Do not be afraid, this is another son for
18 you.' Then with her last breath, as she was dying, she named him Ben-oni,*a* but his father called him Benjamin.*b*
19 So Rachel died and was buried by the side of the road to
20 Ephrathah, that is Bethlehem. Jacob set up a sacred pillar over her grave; it is known to this day as the Pillar of
21 Rachel's Grave. Then Israel journeyed on and pitched his
22 tent on the other side of Migdal-eder. While Israel was living in that district, Reuben went and lay with his father's concubine Bilhah, and Israel came to hear of it.

23 The sons of Jacob were twelve. The sons of Leah: Jacob's first-born Reuben, then Simeon, Levi, Judah,
24 Issachar and Zebulun. The sons of Rachel: Joseph and
25 Benjamin. The sons of Rachel's slave-girl Bilhah: Dan
26 and Naphtali. The sons of Leah's slave-girl Zilpah: Gad and Asher. These were Jacob's sons, born to him in
27 Paddan-aram. Jacob came to his father Isaac at Mamre by Kiriath-arba, that is Hebron, where Abraham and Isaac
28 had dwelt. Isaac had lived for a hundred and eighty years when he breathed his last. He died and was gathered to his

[a] *That is* Son of my ill luck.
[b] *That is* Son of good luck *or* Son of the right hand.

father's kin at a very great age, and his sons Esau and   29
Jacob buried him.

✻ The Jacob traditions are rounded off by a series of brief
notes on family matters drawn from the three major sources
in Genesis:

verses 16–20, from the E source, describe the death of
Rachel in child-birth;

verses 21–2, from the J source – note the change of name
from Jacob in verse 20 to Israel in verse 21 – make brief
reference to an unsavoury incident involving Reuben, Jacob's
eldest son;

verses 23–9, from the P source, list Jacob's sons. The names
are the same as those found in the J and E narratives in 29:
29–30: 24, and 46: 8–27, but there is one major discrepancy.
The narrative in 35: 16–21 has just stated that Benjamin was
born not far from Bethel in Canaan, yet verse 27 lists him
among the sons born to Jacob in Paddan-aram. Likewise the
note about Isaac's death at 180 years old, in verse 28, raises
difficulties. When, according to P, Esau married his Hittite
wives, Isaac must have been 100 years old (see the chronology
implied in 25: 26 and 26: 34). Chapter 27, immediately
following the note of Esau's marriages, seems to presuppose
that Isaac is on his death-bed. How then did he survive for
another eighty years? The weaving together of different
sources and traditions gives the easiest explanation of such
discrepancies.

16–21. This section contains two aetiologies, one (verses
16–18) explaining why Jacob's youngest son was called
Benjamin, the other (verses 19–21) telling why a pillar was
known as 'the Pillar of Rachel's Grave'.

16. *Ephrathah*: both here, and in verse 19, the name of this
place would be better rendered 'Ephrath'. Its location is
uncertain. Rachel's grave, according to 1 Sam. 10: 2, was
located in the territory of Benjamin to the north of Jerusalem.

This fits the assumption in this passage that Ephrath cannot have been too far from Bethel. If this be so, then the comment in verse 19, 'that is Bethlehem', must be a later, erroneous comment since Bethlehem lies to the south of Jerusalem. An Ephrath associated with Bethlehem is mentioned in Micah 5: 2. There may have been more than one village with this name. The Rachel's tomb, near Bethlehem, shown to tourists today, is of Crusader construction, though an earlier structure is known from about the fourth century A.D.

18. *she named him Ben-oni:* with her dying breath Rachel gives her son a name, *Ben-oni*, which could mean 'Son of my strength', but which could also mean 'Son of my ill luck' (see the N.E.B. footnote). Since a name is supposed to indicate a child's future or destiny, and this is a name potentially of ill omen, Jacob takes immediate steps to counteract it, calling the child *Benjamin*; *jamin* in Hebrew means 'the right hand or side' or 'the south' (see p. 13 for the *Beni-iamina* of the Mari texts and p. 9 of *The Making of the Old Testament* in this series). In many languages the right hand is associated with skill or good luck. In English we have 'dextrous' from the Latin word for the right hand, and its opposite 'sinister' from the Latin word for the left hand. *Benjamin*, therefore, means 'Son of good luck' or 'Son of the right hand' (see the N.E.B. footnote). Either way, since the right hand is the place of honour, the name indicates a fortunate future for the child.

20. the *sacred pillar* or *maṣṣebah* is obviously devoid of any religious significance. It is purely a memorial stone marking the spot of Rachel's death. Unlike certain other religions in the ancient Near East, the religion of Israel did not encourage the cult of the dead.

21. *Migdal-eder:* location unknown. The name means 'tower of the flock', and could be applied to many places which had animal enclosures.

22. Reuben's conduct in having intercourse *with his father's concubine Bilhah* is noted without comment. The Septuagint text adds 'and he (i.e. Israel) disapproved of it'.

Reuben is condemned for this act in 49: 4. The fact that Reuben was the eldest son suggests that this may reflect a tradition that once the tribe of Reuben had a position of political pre-eminence. During the Old Testament period, however, it is politically insignificant, as indeed are the two next sons, Simeon and Levi. We do not know why or how this happened.

27. Isaac was last mentioned in P at 25: 9–11 where he buries his father Abraham near Mamre. It is natural that P now brings Jacob back to his father at *Mamre by Kiriath-arba, that is Hebron* (see the note on 23: 2).

29. Although it is not stated here, Isaac, according to 49: 31, is buried in the family burial place at the cave of Machpelah. Just as Abraham's sons Isaac and Ishmael were present at his burial, so Jacob and Esau are present at Isaac's burial. *gathered to his father's kin:* see the note on 25: 8. ✶

THE DESCENDANTS OF ESAU

This is the table of the descendants of Esau: that is Edom. **36** Esau took Canaanite women in marriage, Adah daughter 2 of Elon the Hittite and Oholibamah daughter of Anah son[a] of Zibeon the Horite,[b] and Basemath, Ishmael's 3 daughter, sister of Nebaioth.

Adah bore Eliphaz to Esau; Basemath bore Reuel, and 4[c], 5 Oholibamah bore Jeush, Jalam and Korah. These were Esau's sons, born to him in Canaan. Esau took his wives, his 6 sons and daughters and everyone in his household, his herds, his cattle, and all the chattels that he had acquired in Canaan, and went to the district of Seir[d] out of the way

[a] *So Sam.; Heb.* daughter.
[b] *Prob. rdg. (cp. verses 20, 21); Heb.* Hivite.
[c] *Verses 4, 5, 9–13: cp. 1 Chron. 1: 35–7.*
[d] Seir: *so Pesh.; Heb. om.*

7 of his brother Jacob, because they had so much stock that
   they could not live together; the land where they were
8 staying could not support them because of their herds. So
   Esau lived in the hill-country of Seir. Esau is Edom.

9   This is the table of the descendants of Esau father of the
   Edomites in the hill-country of Seir.

10   These are the names of the sons of Esau: Eliphaz was
   the son of Esau's wife Adah. Reuel was the son of Esau's
11 wife Basemath. The sons of Eliphaz were Teman, Omar,
12 Zepho, Gatam and Kenaz. Timna was concubine to
   Esau's son Eliphaz, and she bore Amalek to him. These
13 are the descendants of Esau's wife Adah. These are the
   sons of Reuel: Nahath, Zerah, Shammah and Mizzah.
   These were the descendants of Esau's wife Basemath.
14 These were the sons of Esau's wife Oholibamah daughter
   of Anah son[a] of Zibeon. She bore him Jeush, Jalam and
   Korah.

15   These are the chiefs descended from Esau. The sons of
   Esau's eldest son Eliphaz: chief Teman, chief Omar, chief
16 Zepho, chief Kenaz, chief Korah, chief Gatam, chief
   Amalek. These are the chiefs descended from Eliphaz in
   Edom. These are the descendants of Adah.

17   These are the sons of Esau's son Reuel: chief Nahath,
   chief Zerah, chief Shammah, chief Mizzah. These are the
   chiefs descended from Reuel in Edom. These are the
   descendants of Esau's wife Basemath.

18   These are the sons of Esau's wife Oholibamah: chief
   Jeush, chief Jalam, chief Korah. These are the chiefs born
   to Oholibamah daughter of Anah wife of Esau.

19   These are the sons of Esau, that is Edom, and these are
   their chiefs.

[a] *So Sam.; Heb.* daughter.

These are the sons of Seir the Horite, the original in- 20[a]
habitants of the land: Lotan, Shobal, Zibeon, Anah,
Dishon, Ezer and Dishan. These are the chiefs of the 21
Horites, the sons of Seir in Edom. The sons of Lotan were 22
Hori and Hemam, and Lotan had a sister named
Timna.

These are the sons of Shobal: Alvan, Manahath, Ebal, 23
Shepho and Onam.

These are the sons of Zibeon: Aiah and Anah. This is 24
the Anah who found some mules[b] in the wilderness while
he was tending the asses of his father Zibeon. These are the 25
children of Anah: Dishon and Oholibamah daughter of
Anah.

These are the children of Dishon:[c] Hemdan, Eshban, 26
Ithran and Cheran. These are the sons of Ezer: Bilhan, 27
Zavan and Akan. These are the sons of Dishan: Uz and 28
Aran.

These are the chiefs descended from the Horites: chief 29
Lotan, chief Shobal, chief Zibeon, chief Anah, chief 30
Dishon, chief Ezer, chief Dishan. These are the chiefs that
were descended from the Horites according to their clans
in the district of Seir.

These are the kings who ruled over Edom before there 31[d]
were kings in Israel: Bela son of Beor became king in 32
Edom, and his city was named Dinhabah; when he died, 33
he was succeeded by Jobab son of Zerah of Bozrah.
When Jobab died, he was succeeded by Husham of Te- 34
man. When Husham died, he was succeeded by Hadad 35

[a] *Verses 20–8: cp. 1 Chron. 1: 38–42.*
[b] *Heb. word of uncertain mng.*
[c] *So verse 21 and 1 Chron. 1: 41; Heb. Dishan.*
[d] *Verses 31–43: cp. 1 Chron. 1: 43–54.*

son of Bedad, who defeated Midian in Moabite country.
36 His city was named Avith. When Hadad died, he was
37 succeeded by Samlah of Masrekah. When Samlah died,
he was succeeded by Saul of Rehoboth on the River.
38 When Saul died, he was succeeded by Baal-hanan son of
39 Akbor. When Baal-hanan died, he was succeeded by
Hadar.*[a]* His city was named Pau; his wife's name was
Mehetabel daughter of Matred a woman of Me-zahab.*[b]*
40   These are the names of the chiefs descended from Esau,
according to their families, their places, by name: chief
41 Timna, chief Alvah, chief Jetheth, chief Oholibamah,
42 chief Elah, chief Pinon, chief Kenaz, chief Teman, chief
43 Mibzar, chief Magdiel, and chief Iram: all chiefs of Edom
according to their settlements in the land which they
possessed. (Esau is the father of the Edomites.)

✴   In 25: 12–18 the descendants of Ishmael were listed before
the story of the promise continued with Isaac; so here, before
we journey into the future with Jacob's son Joseph, the narrative deals with the descendants of Isaac's other son Esau.
As is made clear by the repeated emphasis upon Esau as
Edom (verses 1, 19) or as the father of the Edomites (verse 9),
we are dealing with lists which preserve traditions about the
Edomites (see the notes on 25: 22–6). That Esau–Edom was
the brother of Jacob–Israel stresses the close racial kinship
between the two peoples. What sources of information were
available to P in compiling this section we do not know, but
the material seems to come from more than one tradition,
since, within the chapter, there are no less than seven lists,
overlapping at many points, but in certain respects independent of one another.

Much of the information in these lists is repeated in 1 Chron.

[a] *Or* Hadad; *cp. 1 Chron. 1: 50.*
[b] *Or* daughter of Mezahab.

1: 35–54. Some of the names in the lists occur only here in the Old Testament, others flit in and out of the Old Testament in other contexts. For a detailed analysis and discussion of the names a larger commentary should be consulted.

1–5. List one, headed 'This is the table of the descendants of Esau' (for this title see the note on 25: 12), lists Esau's three wives and the children borne by them.

2. The extremely complex nature of the traditions can be seen in the fact that of Esau's wives listed here, only one, Basemath, appears among his wives listed in 26: 34. In 26: 34 she is described as the 'daughter of Elon the Hittite', while here it is Adah who is the *daughter of Elon the Hittite. Anah son of Zibeon the Horite:* the Hebrew text, both here and in verse 14, reads 'daughter' instead of *son* (see the N.E.B. footnote). Again, the Hebrew 'Hivite' should probably be changed to *Horite*, particularly in the light of verses 20–1 where Zibeon appears among 'the sons of Seir the Horite' (see the N.E.B. footnote).

6–8 contain brief information about Esau's settlement in the hill-country of Seir, appended to the first list.

6. *went to the district of Seir:* this, the reading of the Peshitta text (see the N.E.B. footnote), is one way of making more precise the Hebrew text which reads 'to a country'. The Septuagint provides another solution by reading 'went from the land of Canaan'.

7. The statement that Jacob and Esau parted to live in different regions, because *the land where they were staying could not support them because of their herds* seems to ignore the story of the rivalry between the brothers (cp. Abraham and Lot, 13: 5–12).

9–14. List two, headed similarly to list one *This is the table of the descendants of Esau*, lists the same sons of Esau and adds to the first two of them the names of Esau's grandsons.

15–19. List three contains the same names as list two, but introduces them as 'These are the chiefs descended from Esau'.

15. *These are the chiefs descended from Esau:* the word trans-

lated *chiefs* could equally well be rendered 'clans' or 'groups', and this would make good sense in lists which are concerned with the various sub-sections of the Edomites.

20–8. List four contains the sons of Seir, the original Horite inhabitants of the region in which the Edomites settled.

24. *mules:* the meaning of the Hebrew word translated *mules* is very uncertain (see the N.E.B. footnote). Although *mules* is the traditional Jewish interpretation, the versions render it in many different ways. A simple reordering of letters in the Hebrew would give 'water' which would make sense in context. Why this brief anecdote about Anah was remembered, we don't know.

26. *Dishon:* the Hebrew text, accidentally but not surprisingly, has confused Dishon with the very similar name Dishan, which occurs in verses 28 and 30 (see the N.E.B. footnote).

29–30. List five repeats the sons of Seir, but introduces them as *These are the chiefs descended from the Horites.*

31–9. List six lists 'the kings who ruled over Edom before there were kings in Israel' – for the significance of this for our understanding of the date of the composition of Genesis, see p. 10-11. As well as implying that the Edomites reached a reasonably stable form of nationhood before Israel, this list is interesting since it implies that Edomite kingship was elective. No dynastic principle is involved; son never succeeds father. Each successive king is identified by reference to the town from which he comes.

39. *Hadar:* the parallel passage in Chronicles, as well as the Peshitta and Septuagint, read, probably correctly, Hadad (see the N.E.B. footnote). *Matred a woman of Me-zahab:* or, with the N.E.B. footnote, 'a daughter of Mezahab'. It would be equally possible to argue that the Hebrew has the same mistake here as in verses 2 and 14, and that the text ought to be 'Matred son of Mezahab'.

40–3. List seven, headed 'These are the names of the chiefs descended from Esau', partly overlaps with lists two and three

– the names Teman and Kenaz being common to the three lists – but is otherwise radically different. One of the names which appears here as the name of a chief, Oholibamah, appears in lists one to three as the name of one of Esau's wives.

43. The final note in brackets – (*Esau is the father of the Edomites*) – affirms a precise connection with the later people. It thus underlines for Edom what the previous chapters have made clear for Israel – the relationship between people and ancestor. *

Joseph in Egypt

* The rest of the book of Genesis – with the exception of chapters 38, part of 46, and 49 – is taken up with the story of Joseph. It is no mere accident that for most people this is the most familiar section of the book. It is a masterpiece of story-telling: a fascinating, well-constructed narrative, filled with psychological insight and suspense, and climaxing in a moving dénouement. The pampered son of a doting father dreams of greatness. Jealousy and anger drive his brothers to sell him into Egyptian slavery. In Egypt, through many a twist, the tale becomes one of 'from rags to riches'. Joseph becomes Pharaoh's chief minister. When the brothers, in desperate straits, come begging for food in Egypt they fail to recognize the high official who roughly questions them, and puts their sincerity and family loyalty to the test. Eventually Joseph reveals his identity to his astonished brothers. They are reconciled, and old Jacob reunited to the son whose untimely death he had long mourned.

There is one major difference between this story of Joseph and the stories about the other patriarchs in Genesis. The narrative material in Genesis 12–36 consists, in the main, of brief incidents loosely and sometimes crudely strung together. We can hear them as tales on the lips of tribal bards, tales handed down by word of mouth across many centuries, before achieving their present literary form. The same cannot be said of the story of Joseph. It has all the marks of a short novel, self-consciously written as such. Hand in hand with this go other differences:

(i) within chapter 35 there are no fewer than four aetiologies, explanations as to why a place was called Bethel or El-bethel (verses 7, 15), why there was an oak-tree in the neighbourhood called the Oak of Weeping (verse 8), why Jacob's youngest son was called Benjamin (verse 18), why there was a stone called the Pillar of Rachel's Grave (verse 20). This is typical of chapters 12–36 as a whole. In particular there are many cult legends, explaining the origin of worship at certain religious centres (e.g. 35: 7). Within the whole story of Joseph there are only three aetiologies: 41: 51–2; 47: 13–26 (see the note on pp. 286–7) and 50: 11, none of them cult legends;

(ii) within chapters 12–36 the attitude to the world outside the close-knit tribal group tends to be hostile; intermarriage with the local inhabitants is discouraged. Joseph mingles freely with the Egyptians, becomes Pharaoh's right-hand man, and marries an Egyptian girl, the daughter of an Egyptian priest (41: 45); all this without any word of disapproval or even comment;

(iii) within chapters 12–36 God repeatedly appears to the patriarchs. He speaks directly to them at crisis points in their life. What he says controls what they do. We enter a different world in the story of Joseph. Here God does not speak. The one apparent exception to this, in 46: 1–7, merely underlines this point since it is so evidently a throwback to the material in 12–36 and not an integral part of the Joseph story. This is not to say that the ethos of the Joseph story is secular rather than religious: far from it. Brooding over the entire story is the sense of a higher providence, whose presence is indicated by passing comments, e.g. 39: 5, 21–3; 45: 5–9; but this providence does not personally intrude into the narrative, and the events unfold as the inevitable consequence of human passions, ambition, jealousy, anger and lust. The religious language of the Joseph story is markedly different from that found in the earlier chapters.

All this – and obvious historical discrepancies between the Joseph story and the rest of Genesis, which we shall note as they arise – suggest that the Joseph story comes from a different milieu from the rest of Genesis, and from a man who expresses his religious convictions in a different way from that found in the traditional patriarchal stories. The cosmopolitan atmosphere of this story, the basic human themes upon which it touches, and its literary style, have suggested to some that it comes from within the wisdom tradition in Israel, a tradition which we find in books such as Proverbs, Job and Ecclesiastes with their broad human interest, their analysis of basic human motives and problems. It is difficult to be certain. Nor is it clear when the story was first written. Much here depends on how we evaluate the local Egyptian colouring, whether we think it most nearly reflects what we know of ancient Egyptian life around the middle of the second millennium B.C., or whether, as has been recently argued, it fits better into the period from roughly the middle of the seventh to the middle of the fifth centuries B.C.

The distinctiveness of the Joseph story also raises another problem. Are we to see here the same source divisions which we have claimed for other parts of Genesis? It is usually claimed that we can trace in the Joseph story elements from both the J and E sources. Sometimes Joseph's father is called Jacob (37: 1), at other times Israel (37: 12). The account in chapter 37 of how the brothers get rid of Joseph is perplexing. First Reuben springs to Joseph's defence (37: 22), then it is Judah (37: 26). To whom indeed was Joseph sold? To Ishmaelites, according to 37: 25–7; yet in verses 28 and 36 it is Midianite merchants who come along, take Joseph down to Egypt and sell him to Potiphar. In 39: 1 we find that Potiphar bought Joseph from the Ishmaelites. Is all this evidence of two sources, the one featuring Israel, Judah and the Ishmaelites, the other featuring Jacob, Reuben and the Midianites, or are other explanations possible? Must we allow for a skilful writer's love of variety or is it possible that a story naturally featuring Reuben as the eldest son, has been adapted to take account of the rise to prominence of the tribe of Judah? In spite of differences and duplications, it must be admitted that the evidence for two separate and continuous sources in the Joseph story is far from conclusive. The more we stress the literary skill and the basic unity of the entire story, the less likely the two-source theory becomes. Some of the rough edges in the story may have arisen when the story was placed in its present context to act as a link between the traditions about the patriarchs, Abraham, Isaac and Jacob, and the memory of the nation's enslavement in Egypt; and to explain how it was that, in spite of Canaan being the land of promise, the pivotal event in Israel's religious history took place outside Canaan in the land of Egypt.   ✷

JOSEPH SOLD INTO SLAVERY

37 S̲O JACOB LIVED in Canaan, the country in which
2 his father had settled. And this is the story of the descendants of Jacob.

When Joseph was a boy of seventeen, he used to accompany his brothers, the sons of Bilhah and Zilpah, his father's wives, when they were in charge of the flock; and
3 he brought their father a bad report of them. Now Israel loved Joseph more than any other of his sons, because he was a child of his old age, and he made him a long, sleeved
4 robe. When his brothers saw that their father loved him more than any of them, they hated him and could not say a kind word to him.

5   Joseph had a dream; and when he told it to his brothers,

they hated him still more. He said to them, 'Listen to this 6
dream I have had. We were in the field binding sheaves, 7
and my sheaf rose on end and stood upright, and your
sheaves gathered round and bowed low before my sheaf.'
His brothers answered him, 'Do you think you will one 8
day be a king and lord it over us?' and they hated him still
more because of his dreams and what he said. He had 9
another dream, which he told to his father and*a* his
brothers. He said, 'Listen: I have had another dream. The
sun and moon and eleven stars were bowing down to me.'
When he told it to his father and his brothers, his father 10
took him to task: 'What is this dream of yours?' he said.
'Must we come and bow low to the ground before you,
I and your mother and your brothers?' His brothers were 11
jealous of him, but his father did not forget.

Joseph's brothers went to mind their father's flocks in 12
Shechem. Israel said to him, 'Your brothers are minding 13
the flocks in Shechem; come, I will send you to them', and
he said, 'I am ready.' He said to him, 'Go and see if all is 14
well with your brothers and the sheep, and bring me back
word.' So he sent off Joseph from the vale of Hebron and
he came to Shechem. A man met him wandering in the 15
open country and asked him what he was looking for. He 16
replied, 'I am looking for my brothers. Tell me, please,
where they are minding the flocks.' The man said, 'They 17
have gone away from here; I heard them speak of going
to Dothan.' So Joseph followed his brothers and he found
them in Dothan. They saw him in the distance, and before 18
he reached them, they plotted to kill him. They said to each 19
other, 'Here comes that dreamer. Now is our chance; let 20

[a] his father and: *so Sept.; Heb. om.*

us kill him and throw him into one of these pits and say
that a wild beast has devoured him. Then we shall see
21 what will come of his dreams.' When Reuben heard, he
22 came to his rescue, urging them not to take his life. 'Let
us have no bloodshed', he said. 'Throw him into this pit
in the wilderness, but do him no bodily harm.' He meant
to save him from them so as to restore him to his father.
23 When Joseph came up to his brothers, they stripped him
24 of the long, sleeved robe which he was wearing, took him
and threw him into the pit. The pit was empty and had no
water in it.

25 Then they sat down to eat some food and, looking up,
they saw an Ishmaelite caravan coming in from Gilead on
the way down to Egypt, with camels carrying gum traga-
26 canth and balm and myrrh. Judah said to his brothers,
'What shall we gain by killing our brother and concealing
27 his death? Why not sell him to the Ishmaelites? Let us do
him no harm, for he is our brother, our own flesh and
28 blood'; and his brothers agreed with him. Meanwhile
some Midianite merchants passed by and drew Joseph up
out of the pit. They sold him for twenty pieces of silver to
29 the Ishmaelites, and they brought Joseph to Egypt. When
Reuben went back to the pit, Joseph was not there. He
30 rent his clothes and went back to his brothers and said,
'The boy is not there. Where can I go?'

31 Joseph's brothers took his robe, killed a goat and dipped
32 it in the goat's blood. Then they tore the robe, the long,
sleeved robe, brought it to their father and said, 'Look
what we have found. Do you recognize it? Is this your
33 son's robe or not?' Jacob did recognize it, and he replied,
'It is my son's robe. A wild beast has devoured him.

Joseph has been torn to pieces.' Jacob rent his clothes, put 34
on sackcloth and mourned his son for a long time. His 35
sons and daughters all tried to comfort him, but he
refused to be comforted. He said, 'I will go to my grave[a]
mourning for my son.' Thus Joseph's father wept for him.
Meanwhile the Midianites had sold Joseph in Egypt to 36
Potiphar, one of Pharaoh's eunuchs, the captain of the
guard.[b]

* The opening chapter of the Joseph story, which reaches
its climax when he is sold into slavery in Egypt, outlines the
basic plot, and lays down the inevitable lines of development
for the rest of the story – Joseph's dreams of greatness, the
brothers' hatred, the father's grief, the dreams apparently
frustrated by slavery. It remains to be seen how the dreams
can possibly be fulfilled, how the slave can rise to prominence,
what the future relationship between Joseph and his brothers
will be, and how the father's grief can be assuaged.

1–2. Here the P editor draws our attention back from
Esau, whose descendants he has listed in chapter 36, to
Jacob, with whose family the future lies.

2. *And this is the story of the descendants of Jacob: And this is
the story of* is the same phrase translated in chapter 36 as
'This is the table of'. The N.E.B. translation assumes that as
in 2: 4 (see *Genesis 1–11*, pp. 26–8) the phrase occurs here as
a summary of what precedes, not as the heading to a formal
family tree, and at the same time acts as a link to the narrative
which follows. The Joseph story, strictly speaking, begins
with the words *When Joseph was a boy of seventeen, he used
to accompany* . . . : literally 'he was a lad with the sons of Bilhah'.
The N.E.B. rendering takes the word 'lad' in the sense
of 'assistant' or 'servant'; cp. Exod. 33: 11 where Joshua is
described as Moses' young assistant. *he brought their father a bad*

[a] my grave: *Heb.* Sheol.   [b] *Or* executioner.

report of them: there is no need to assume that Joseph's character here as a tale-bearer is a sign of a different version of the story from that in which Jacob's evident favouritism rouses the brothers' jealousy. The two could go hand in hand.

3. Jacob reflects in his dealings with his family the same kind of partiality which Rebecca, his mother, had shown, with bitter consequences; and it leads to apparent tragedy. *a child of his old age:* hardly consistent with 30: 22–4 where Joseph is simply the youngest of the sons born to Jacob in his prime, while he is still living with Laban. It would be natural to think of Joseph here as still the youngest son. What then of Benjamin who in 44: 20 is described as 'a young son born in his (i.e. Jacob's) old age'? *a long, sleeved robe:* the traditional 'coat of many colours' comes from the Septuagint version. The meaning of the Hebrew phrase is uncertain. It must denote some kind of ostentatious garment such as would not normally be worn by a working man. The only other place in the Old Testament where the phrase occurs is in 2 Sam. 13: 18–19 where it is 'the usual dress of unmarried princesses'.

5–11. The significance of dreams is well attested in the ancient world. There is extant an Egyptian manual for the interpretation of dreams which dates from around 1300 B.C.; see *A.N.E.T.* (see p. 317), p. 475). Joseph's dreams are different from dreams elsewhere in the patriarchal narratives since God nowhere appears in his dreams: contrast 28: 12–15. Nor do Joseph's dreams contain any obscure symbolism. Their meaning is instantly plain not only to Joseph, but to his brothers and to his parents. The brothers' sheaves bowing down to Joseph's sheaf, the sun, moon and eleven stars (father, mother and eleven brothers) bowing down to Joseph, admit of only one interpretation. It is noteworthy that throughout the Joseph story dreams come in pairs; compare dreams of the butler and the baker in 40: 1–19, and Pharaoh's two dreams in 41. This may be a deliberate literary stylism or it could be intended to confirm the significance of the dreams. One dream might be misleading; two dreams of similar import could hardly be (cp. the note on 41: 25–32).

9. *which he told to his father and his brothers:* the Septuagint addition 'his father and' (see the N.E.B. footnote) lines this verse up with the reference to father and brothers in verse 10. There is, however, a certain amount of Septuagint evidence for the omission of 'brothers' in verse 10. It may be that the original text talked of a two-stage process, the dreams being first told to the brothers, then to the father, who rebuked him.

10. *I and your mother:* this suggests that Rachel is still alive, and ignores the account of her death in 35: 16–20.

11. *but his father did not forget:* literally, 'kept the matter' (i.e. in his mind; cp. Luke 2: 19). The brothers see in Joseph's dreams only a threat to themselves. Jacob detects a divine revelation of the future which lies with Joseph.

12–17. Jacob unwittingly provides the brothers with an opportunity to vent their jealousy on Joseph, when he sends Joseph to visit the brothers who are tending the flocks at Shechem. Although nothing in the previous chapter has prepared us for Jacob being in the vale of Hebron in southern Canaan, Hebron appears frequently in the patriarchal narratives, particularly in the J tradition from 13: 18 onwards (see the note on 13: 18). It is a considerable journey from Hebron to Shechem in the central highlands, and Dothan is some 15 miles (24 km) further north of Shechem. The very distance separating Hebron from Dothan helps to explain how the brothers could easily dispose of Joseph, unknown to their father.

13. *I am ready:* literally, 'behold me'; see the note on 22: 1.

18–30. For the variation between Reuben and Judah, Ishmaelites and Midianites in this section, see the notes preceding this chapter (p. 213). The brothers' action – 'they plotted to kill him' (verse 18) – is motivated by more than jealousy. The twofold dream foreshadows a future which they can only regard with foreboding. The only way to prevent that future is to liquidate Joseph. Reuben, the eldest brother, acts with responsibility and compassion, aware of the shattering effect Joseph's death would have on their father. His 'Let us have no bloodshed' (verse 22) probably reflects what is later said more explicitly by Judah. Revenge upon those outside the family circle could be ruthless and swift (see chapter 34), but to kill a brother, 'our own flesh and blood' (verse 27), was a deed which a man would hesitate to perpetrate.

19. *Here comes that dreamer:* literally 'lord (*ba'al*) of dreams', one who has the gift of dreaming. The expression as used here is probably intended to convey contempt or sarcasm; it may equally suggest acknowledgement of Joseph's special mastery of dreams as pointing to the future.

22. *Throw him into this pit in the wilderness:* the pit was a man-made hole or cistern for collecting water during the rainy season. The fact that it was dry (see verse 24) indicates that the events are supposed to have happened well on into the dry season of late summer or autumn.

25. *an Ishmaelite caravan coming in from Gilead on the way down to Egypt:* from early times there was a flourishing trade with Egypt in various aromatic substances, used mainly for medicinal purposes. The traditional caravan routes led south from Damascus through Gilead whence they crossed the Jordan and cut west, past the district of Dothan, to the coastal plain, and then down to Egypt (see map p. xiv). *gum tragacanth and balm and myrrh:* these are all sticky, resinous substances produced by aromatic plants. The medicinal properties of balm and its association with Gilead are referred to by Jeremiah:

> 'Is there no balm in Gilead,
>   no physician there?' (Jer. 8: 22)

camels: see notes on 12: 16 and 24: 10.

28. *twenty pieces of silver:* this, though we do not know its value, was the going rate for a male slave between five and twenty years of age, according to Lev. 27: 5.

29. *He rent his clothes:* one of the customary public expressions of mourning in Israel. Jacob reacts similarly in verse 34, and takes the next step of 'putting on sackcloth'.

31–3. The brothers' action in tearing Joseph's ostentatious coat and dipping it in the blood of a goat has its background in the custom we noted at 31: 39. If a shepherd could bring back part of the mangled corpse of an animal savaged by a wild beast, he was free from all legal responsibility for criminal neglect. In returning Joseph's blood-stained coat to their father, the brothers are saying 'We cannot be held responsible for his death, we did what we could to protect him.' On recognizing the coat Jacob immediately fixes the blame where alone it can lie: *A wild beast has devoured him* (verse 33).

35. *His sons and daughters:* since only one daughter, Dinah, has been mentioned, *daughters* may mean 'daughters-in-law' as it does in Ruth 1: 12. '*I will go to my grave*': in Hebrew 'Sheol' (see the N.E.B. footnote) is the name of the vague, shadowy underworld to which a ghostlike double of a man goes after death. It is always spoken of in the Old Testament with a sense of shudder, as a place of darkness and gloom, of no real life, in which it was for long believed that men were cut off from any contact with God (cp. Isa. 38: 18–19). There is no theorizing about Sheol in the Joseph story. Wherever the word occurs, the N.E.B. has rightly seen that it is no more than a synonym for death or the grave (cp. 42: 38; 44: 29, 31).

36. The slave-trade is amply documented in Egyptian texts from many different centuries. There exist inventories of slaves, some of them with Semitic names. Warfare seems to have been the chief source of slaves; but private slave-dealing is also in evidence. *Potiphar:* the Egyptian equivalent of his name means 'the gift of Re', the sun-god. *one of Pharaoh's eunuchs:* eunuchs were employed in various capacities in royal service throughout the ancient Near East. In many instances the word translated *eunuchs* may mean no more than 'courtiers' or 'officials' (see 40: 7). *the captain of the guard:* the precise meaning of this title is unknown; nor is it clear

whether it has any exact Egyptian equivalent. The alternative
rendering 'executioner' (see the N.E.B. footnote) keeps a close
link with the idea of slaughter which is sometimes implied
in the Hebrew word translated *guard*. The function of this
official in the Joseph story, however, and instances of the
same phrase elsewhere in the Old Testament (cp. 2 Kings
25: 8; Dan. 2: 14) favour the more general title *captain of
the guard* (cp. 40: 1). *

JUDAH AND TAMAR

38 About that time Judah left his brothers and went south
and pitched his tent in company with an Adullamite
2 named Hirah. There he saw Bathshua the daughter of a
3 Canaanite*a* and married her. He slept with her, and she
4 conceived and bore a son, whom she*b* called Er. She con-
5 ceived again and bore a son whom she called Onan. Once
more she conceived and bore a son whom she called
Shelah, and she*c* ceased to bear children*d* when she had
6 given birth to him. Judah found a wife for his eldest son
7 Er; her name was Tamar. But Judah's eldest son Er was
wicked in the LORD's sight, and the LORD took his life.
8 Then Judah told Onan to sleep with his brother's wife, to
do his duty as the husband's brother and raise up issue for
9 his brother. But Onan knew that this issue would not be
his; so whenever he slept with his brother's wife, he spilled
his seed on the ground so as not to raise up issue for his
10 brother. What he did was wicked in the LORD's sight, and
11 the LORD took his life. Judah said to his daughter-in-law

[a] *Lit.* saw the daughter of a Canaanite whose name was Shua (*cp.
verse 12*).
[b] *So some MSS.; others* he.   [c] *So Sept.; Heb.* and he shall be.
[d] ceased...children: *or* was at Kezib.

Tamar, 'Remain as a widow in your father's house until my son Shelah grows up'; for he was afraid that he too would die like his brothers. So Tamar went and stayed in her father's house.

Time passed, and Judah's wife Bathshua died. When he 12 had finished mourning, he and his friend Hirah the Adullamite went up to Timnath at sheep-shearing. When 13 Tamar was told that her father-in-law was on his way to shear his sheep at Timnath, she took off her widow's 14 weeds, veiled her face, perfumed herself and sat where the road forks in two directions on the way to Timnath. She did this because she knew that Shelah had grown up and she had not been given to him as a wife. When Judah saw 15 her, he thought she was a prostitute, although she had veiled her face. He turned to her where she sat by the 16 roadside and said, 'Let me lie with you', not knowing that she was his daughter-in-law. She said, 'What will you give me to lie with me?' He answered, 'I will send you a 17 kid from my flock', but she said, 'Will you give me a pledge until you send it?' He asked what pledge he 18 should give her, and she replied, 'Your seal and its cord, and the staff which you hold in your hand.' So he gave them to her and lay with her, and she conceived. She 19 then rose and went home, took off her veil and resumed her widow's weeds. Judah sent the kid by his friend the 20 Adullamite in order to recover the pledge from the woman, but he could not find her. He asked the men of 21 that place, 'Where is that temple-prostitute, the one who was sitting where the road forks?', but they answered, 'There is no temple-prostitute here.' So he went back to 22 Judah and told him that he had not found her and that the

men of the place had said there was no such prostitute
23 there. Judah said, 'Let her keep my pledge, or we shall get
a bad name. I did send a kid, but you could not find her'.
24 About three months later Judah was told that his
daughter-in-law Tamar had behaved like a common
prostitute and through her wanton conduct was with
child. Judah said, 'Bring her out so that she may be
25 burnt.' But when she was brought out, she sent to her
father-in-law and said, 'The father of my child is the man
to whom these things belong. See if you recognize whose
they are, the engraving on the seal, the pattern of the
26 cord, and the staff.' Judah recognized them and said, 'She
is more in the right than I am, because I did not give her
to my son Shelah.' He did not have intercourse with her
27 again. When her time was come, there were twins in her
28 womb, and while she was in labour one of them put out
a hand. The midwife took a scarlet thread and fastened it
29 round the wrist, saying, 'This one appeared first.' No
sooner had he drawn back his hand, than his brother
came out and the midwife said, 'What! you have broken
30 out first!' So he was named Perez.[a] Soon afterwards his
brother was born with the scarlet thread on his wrist, and
he was named Zerah.[b]

＊ The Joseph story is interrupted by an incident involving
Judah and Tamar. It has always been something of a puzzle
as to why this incident was inserted into the Joseph story, and
why at this particular point. There were two strong reasons
for preserving traditions about Judah: first, the tribe of Judah
occupied a prominent position in later Hebrew history; and,
secondly, from the tribe of Judah came David, first king of

[a] *That is* Breaking out.   [b] *That is* Redness.

the united Hebrew kingdom and, for centuries, the ideal of
kingship. According to Ruth 4: 18–22 Perez, one of the
twins born to Tamar in this story, was the direct ancestor of
David. But why insert it at this particular point where it so
obviously interrupts the flow of the Joseph story? Given the
decision to preserve this story about Judah there were two
problems:

(i) Judah in this story appears as a mature man, father of
a grown-up family. There is nothing to prepare us for this
before the Joseph story begins. If Joseph is only seventeen at
the beginning of the story we would expect Judah to be still
comparatively young, much younger than this chapter
implies. If this makes it awkward to place this story about
Judah before the Joseph story, why not add it at the end?
But by that time Joseph and all his brothers are settled in
Egypt, while this story tells of something which happened to
Judah while he was still in Canaan. A suitable point at which
to insert the story, therefore, is when Joseph has just been
taken from Canaan to Egypt, but his brothers still remain in
Canaan.

(ii) We have noted that one of the things which distinguishes the Joseph story from the earlier patriarchal traditions
is its cosmopolitan atmosphere, its openness to those outside
the tribal group. This is also true of the Judah and Tamar
story. The tribe of Judah seems to have come to prominence
partly by incorporating into itself various Canaanite elements.
Judah marries a Canaanite wife; Tamar, his daughter-in-law,
is almost certainly likewise Canaanite. These Canaanite women
were part of King David's pedigree, just as at a later stage
Ruth, the Moabitess, was to make her contribution to that
pedigree.

The Judah and Tamar incident turns upon the custom of the
'levirate marriage', a custom found in one form or another
in ancient Israel and in many other cultures in the ancient
Near East. Although it is not possible to produce a completely
coherent picture from the various references in the Old Testa-

ment to the levirate marriage – regulations about it are to
be found in Deut. 25: 5–10, and it plays its part in the story
of Ruth – its main thrust is clear. Levirate marriage was
designed to ensure that in the case of a man dying childless
his name and his family should continue. It was the responsibility of the dead man's brother to marry his widow and
'to do his duty as the husband's brother and raise up issue for
his brother' (verse 8). The first child of this union was
legally considered the child of the deceased. The word
levirate comes from *levir*, the Latin equivalent of the Hebrew
word for 'brother-in-law'. According to the story, Tamar,
wife of Judah's eldest son Er, was widowed and childless.
Onan, his brother, fails to fulfil his responsibilities in terms of
the levirate marriage, and he too dies. We may note that the
story makes use of the motif of the wife whose successive
husbands die, a motif used for example in Tobit 3 and 6–8.
Judah, no doubt regarding Tamar as something of a *femme
fatale*, finds an excuse for failing to give her his youngest
son Shelah. Tamar takes a courageous and desperate step to
obtain her rights. Disguising herself as a prostitute she
inveigles her father-in-law into making her pregnant. When
Judah, as head of the family, sits in judgement upon his
adulterous daughter-in-law, she reveals and proves that he
is the father of the child in her womb. Judah acknowledges
that in the light of accepted custom she was justified in her
action. Twins are born, one of them a direct ancestor of
David.

1–11. These verses provide us with the necessary background information, which prepares the way for the action
which begins at verse 12.

1. The incident is linked to the previous chapter by a very
vague time reference: *About that time*. The story is set in the
southern Shephelah, the rolling hill-country between the
Judaean hills and the coastal plain. *an Adullamite named Hirah:*
Adullam lies in the hills some 9 miles (14½ km) north-west
of Hebron (see map p. xiv). A cave near Adullam became

David's headquarters when he was a refugee hunted by Saul (1 Sam. 22: 1). Hirah as a name appears only here in the Old Testament.

2. *Bathshua:* means 'the daughter of Shua'. The N.E.B., assuming reasonably that in verse 12 Bathshua is a proper name, anticipates the name here in a phrase which may be more literally rendered as in the N.E.B. footnote. Alternatively we may assume, as the Revised Standard Version does, that the lady is left unnamed in the narrative and that verse 12 simply refers to the 'daughter of Shua' (cp. 1 Chron. 2: 3).

3. *a son, whom she called Er:* in the light of the following verses, where in each case the child is named by the mother, it is better to read *she* instead of 'he' at this point (see the N.E.B. footnote).

5. *and she ceased to bear children:* this rendering, however suitable in context, seems unnecessary. Following the Septuagint in reading 'she' for Hebrew 'and he shall be' (see the N.E.B. footnote) we may translate 'and she was at Kezib when she gave birth...', Kezib being a variant form of the place-name Achzib, which is listed along with Adullam among the towns in the Shephelah in Josh. 15: 44.

6. *her name was Tamar: Tamar* means 'a date-palm', a symbol of fruitfulness, and hence an appropriate name for a girl. David had both a daughter and a grand-daughter with the same name (2 Sam. 13; 14: 27). The story centres around Tamar; here troubles begin with the death of her first husband, Er.

7. Although the language used *Er was wicked in the LORD's sight* is similar to that used of Onan in verse 10, we must not assume that their offence was the same. What Er did we do not know, nor is it important for the story. Since evil and tragedy are causally related for much of the Old Testament (see the notes on 18: 16–33), it is natural to attribute the tragic death of a young husband to his being *wicked in the LORD's sight.*

8–10. Onan formally accepts his duty in terms of the levirate marriage, but deliberately frustrates its intention by withdrawing in the act of intercourse and spilling his semen on the ground. Such an action, done apparently out of selfishness – the fruit of the union would not have been his – could only be regarded with abhorrence. It is, therefore, condemned as being *wicked in the LORD's sight*, a verdict which refers not to the sexual deviation, but to this means of deliberately nullifying the purpose of the levirate marriage. He is punished accordingly. His name has given us in English the word 'onanism', which normally refers to masturbation.

11. Judah now stalls. Two of his sons are dead. He uses Shelah's youthfulness as an excuse for not giving him to Tamar who, like Sarah in the book of Tobit (cp. 3: 7–9), is turning out to be a somewhat deadly partner. Tamar remains a childless widow, and returns to *her father's house*.

12. Judah, now himself widowed, fulfils the customary period of mourning and goes to join his friend at the *sheepshearing*, with its accompanying festivities (see the note on 31: 19). *Timnath:* or Timnah, listed in Josh. 15: 57 as one of the Judaean cities in the hill-country. Modern Khirbet Tibneh, some 16 miles (nearly 26 km) south-west of Jerusalem, has been identified as the site of Timnah, but there may have been more than one settlement of this name in Old Testament times.

14. Tamar, realizing that Judah is deliberately withholding Shelah from her, acts with resolution. To conceal her identity from her father-in-law, she dispensed with her *widow's weeds*, *veiled her face* and waylaid him as he travelled to Timnah. *where the road forks in two directions:* most translations see in this phrase a place-name. Thus The Revised Standard Version has 'at the entrance to Enaim'. Enam is one of the towns in the Shephelah listed in Josh. 15: 34, but there is no reference otherwise to a place named Enaim, which could mean 'Twin Springs' or 'Two Eyes'. Taking 'eye' idiomatically to mean direction, the N.E.B. eliminates an unnecessary place-name.

15. *although she had veiled her face:* better 'since she had covered her face'. It was not the covering of her face (see the note on 24: 65) that made Judah mistake her for *a prostitute*; it was the fact of a woman making herself publicly available at the roadside. The covering merely prevented Judah recognizing his own daughter-in-law.

16–19. Tamar plays her cards skilfully. A kid from the flock is agreed to be a fair price for services rendered, but until it can be sent Tamar demands as a pledge Judah's *seal and its cord* and *the staff* he carries (verse 18). Cylindrical seals, engraved with a particular design or name, were in use in Mesopotamia before 3000 B.C. They were carried, suspended from the neck by a cord. When rolled on soft clay, they left an impression which was the recognized legal equivalent of a personal signature. From Mesopotamia they spread throughout the ancient Near East. Although we know that in certain Babylonian business transactions a staff changed hands to clinch the deal, the staff referred to here is probably no more than the staff Judah normally carried, immediately to be recognized as his by its design or ornamentation. Having conceived a child by Judah, Tamar returned to her father's house to await the course of events.

20–3. Judah tries in vain to find the woman, give her the promised kid, and retrieve his personal pledge. Although in verse 15 Judah takes the woman to be a common prostitute, Hebrew *zonah*, she is referred to in verses 21 and 22 by another word, Hebrew *qedeshah*, literally 'a holy woman', a woman functioning in the cult of the gods and goddesses of fertility, a *temple-prostitute*. In Canaanite society, intercourse with such a temple-girl was not only socially acceptable, but an act of deep religious significance. Judah's Canaanite friends seem to assume that he had been dealing with such a woman. To Hebrew readers of the story it would make little difference. Such temple prostitution is condemned in the law (Deut. 23: 17–18), and is dismissed by the prophets as sheer immorality (e.g. Hos. 4: 13–14).

23. Judah seems to be somewhat concerned about his

dignity. *we shall get a bad name:* this translation introduces too much of a moral note into the proceedings. It would be better rendered 'or we shall become a laughing-stock'. Having tried in vain to keep his side of the bargain, he is prepared to cut his losses. To be involved with a prostitute is one thing; but to continue to scour the countryside in search of an elusive woman, could only end up by making him look ridiculous in the eyes of the community.

24. Tamar, now with child, is called before Judah, head of the clan, on a charge of prostitution. He pronounces sentence: *'Bring her out so that she may be burnt.'* In the law, death by burning is the penalty reserved for a priest's daughter convicted of prostitution (Lev. 21: 9); in all other cases the penalty is death by stoning (Deut. 22: 20–4).

25. As the penalty is about to be enforced, Tamar plays her trump card. She produces *the seal, the cord* and *the staff* as tokens of paternity.

26. *She is more in the right than I am:* in this response Judah is not passing any moral judgement. The Hebrew word for 'righteous', here translated 'in the right' is being used in a strictly legal sense (cp. the notes on 18: 16ff.). In the light of accepted social custom and the duty of levirate marriage, Tamar's actions are justified, Judah's are not. She is the innocent party, he the guilty.

27–30. The story ends with the birth of Tamar's twins. It probably enshrines the memory of rivalry between two groups within the clan of Judah, the Perez group and the Zerah group. Cp. the story of the birth rivalry of Rebecca's twins in 25: 22–6. Since status in the family depends on who is born first, the midwife twines a scarlet thread round the hand which first appears. The other twin, however, is delivered first. This is the twin from whose family line David was to come (1 Chron. 2: 5–15); so we have another example of preference belonging to the younger (cp. also 48: 8–20).

29. By a piece of popular etymologizing the name Perez is taken to mean 'Breaking out' (see the N.E.B. footnote).

and to reflect the midwife's cry '*What! you have broken out first!*'

30. The name Zerah is then taken to mean 'Redness' (see the N.E.B. footnote) and to refer to *the scarlet thread on his wrist.* ✳

JOSEPH AND AN UNFAITHFUL WIFE

When Joseph was taken down to Egypt, he was bought **39** by Potiphar, one of Pharaoh's eunuchs, the captain of the guard, an Egyptian. Potiphar bought him from the Ishmaelites who had brought him there. The LORD was 2 with Joseph and he prospered. He lived in the house of his Egyptian master, who saw that the LORD was with him 3 and was giving him success in all that he undertook. Thus 4 Joseph found favour with his master, and he became his personal servant. Indeed, his master put him in charge of his household and entrusted him with all that he had. From the time that he put him in charge of his household 5 and all his property, the LORD blessed the Egyptian's household for Joseph's sake. The blessing of the LORD was on all that was his in house and field. He left everything 6 he possessed in Joseph's care, and concerned himself with nothing but the food he ate.

Now Joseph was handsome and good-looking, and a 7 time came when his master's wife took notice of him and said, 'Come and lie with me.' But he refused and said to 8 her, 'Think of my master. He does not know as much as I do about his own house, and he has entrusted me with all he has. He has given me authority in this house second 9 only to his own, and has withheld nothing from me except you, because you are his wife. How can I do anything so

Joseph in Egypt

10 wicked, and sin against God?' She kept asking Joseph day after day, but he refused to lie with her and be in her com-
11 pany. One day he came into the house as usual to do his work, when none of the men of the household were there
12 indoors. She caught him by his cloak, saying, 'Come and lie with me', but he left the cloak in her hands and ran out
13 of the house. When she saw that he had left his cloak in
14 her hands and had run out of the house, she called out to the men of the household, 'Look at this! My husband has brought in a Hebrew to make a mockery of us. He came
15 in here to lie with me, but I gave a loud scream. When he heard me scream and call out, he left his cloak in my
16 hand and ran off.' She kept his cloak with her until his
17 master came home, and then she repeated her tale. She said, 'That Hebrew slave whom you brought in to make
18 a mockery of me, has been here with me. But when I screamed for help and called out, he left his cloak in my
19 hands and ran off.' When Joseph's master heard his wife's story of what his slave had done to her, he was furious.
20 He took Joseph and put him in the Round Tower, where the king's prisoners were kept; and there he stayed in the
21 Round Tower. But the LORD was with Joseph and kept faith with him, so that he won the favour of the governor
22 of the Round Tower. He put Joseph in charge of all the
23 prisoners in the tower and of all their work.[a] He ceased to concern himself with anything entrusted to Joseph, because the LORD was with Joseph and gave him success in everything.

[a] *So Sept.; Heb. adds* he was doing.

✴ The Joseph story now resumes. In many ways, however, in theme, style and language, chapter 39 stands on its own in the Joseph story. The name Potiphar appears only in verse 1. Elsewhere the story refers to an Egyptian (verses 2, 5) or to Joseph's 'master' (verses 4, 7, 8, 19). It could be that the phrase 'Potiphar, one of Pharoah's eunuchs, the captain of the guard' has been introduced into the beginning of the story to provide a link with the end of chapter 37. A more natural continuation of chapter 37 is to be found in chapter 40 (cp. p. 238). The story of Joseph and Potiphar's wife is, moreover, the only incident in the Joseph story which refers to Yahweh, the LORD; elsewhere it is always 'God'. On four occasions the LORD is mentioned, and in each case it is to draw attention to the providence which is silently, but surely shaping the unfolding drama. At the beginning Joseph the slave rises to a position of trust in his master's household because 'the LORD was with him' (verses 2 and 3). The household prospers because 'the LORD blessed' it (verse 5). At the end, even in prison, 'the LORD was with Joseph and kept faith with him' (verse 21); and again Joseph succeeds 'because the LORD was with Joseph' (verse 23).

Central to this section, verses 7–18, is the tale of how Joseph spurns the amorous advances of his master's wife. In frustrated revenge she denounces him to her husband for attempted rape. Joseph is imprisoned. This tale has many parallels throughout the ancient Near East and beyond (cp. T. H. Gaster: *Myth, Legend and Custom in the Old Testament* (see p. 317), pp. 217–18) presumably because it is a recurring human situation, one version of the eternal triangle theme. There is a thirteenth-century B.C. Egyptian version called 'The Tale of Two Brothers', Anpu (Anubis) and Bata. Anpu's wife, failing in an attempt to seduce Bata, falsely accuses him before Anpu of attempting to rape her. When Bata eventually proves his innocence, the erring wife is killed (cp. *A.N.E.T.* (see p. 317), pp. 23–5). In many respects the Egyptian version is very different from the Genesis story. It has religious and mythological features which are not present in the Joseph story. There is no need to assume any direct relationship between the two. The Genesis story could almost have been told to illustrate the dangers, to which the book of Proverbs repeatedly draws attention, of getting involved with a 'loose woman' or 'the wife of another man' (e.g. Prov. 6: 23–35; 7: 6–23).

2. *he prospered:* the same Hebrew word is translated 'success' in verse 3. The slave's success story, his being put in charge of the household is attributed to one fact, a fact of which his master is said to be aware (verse 3): *The LORD was with Joseph.*

5. *the LORD blessed the Egyptian's household for Joseph's sake:* no man is an island in the Old Testament; for good and for ill, for blessing and for curse, his life is bound up with those whose lives he touches (see the notes on 18: 16ff.). So the success which the LORD brought to Joseph is reflected in the success which comes to his master's household.

6. His master entrusts Joseph with everything *but the food he ate.* This exception is probably rooted in certain food taboos. Later in the Joseph story, where Joseph is entertaining his brothers, the narrative notes that the Egyptians were served separately 'for Egyptians hold it an abomination to eat with Hebrews' (43: 32).

7. *Joseph was handsome and good-looking:* see the note on 29: 17 where the same Hebrew words, translated differently, are applied to Rachel, to describe her attractiveness.

8–9. Joseph refuses his master's wife's advances on two grounds: first, it would be a violation of the trust that had been placed in him; and secondly, it would be a sin against God. It is characteristic of much of the thinking of the Old Testament to emphasize this twofold dimension in human actions, the way they impinge on other people and the way they relate to God.

10–18. Her infatuation persists. When she cannot have Joseph's love, she turns to revenge. She uses a cloak she had seized as proof of attempted rape. She denounces him first to the men of the household, the other slaves, and then to her husband.

12. *She caught him by his cloak:* the cloak is the long shirt or undergarment, which was usually tied at the waist. We are probably intended to picture Joseph escaping from her clutches and running naked *out of the house* into the inner courtyard as he fled to the safety of the slaves' quarters.

14. *My husband has brought in a Hebrew:* for the Old Testament use of the word *Hebrew* (cp. 'Hebrew slave' in verse 17) see the note on 14: 13. *to make a mockery of us:* here, and in verse 17, this phrase could equally well be translated 'to make love to us'. For this meaning of a Hebrew word elsewhere translated 'laughing' see the note on 26: 8.

18. *when I screamed for help:* according to Deut. 22: 24, such a scream for help would be legal proof of a woman's innocence in a case of rape. She had tried to resist and summon help.

20. There have been many attempted explanations of his master's apparent leniency towards Joseph, including the suggestion that he half suspected his wife's infidelity. Normally, both in Israel and in Egypt, such attempted rape of a married woman would have been a capital offence. There is always a danger in trying to read motives into a biblical story. The demands of the story make it impossible that Joseph should die at this point, so he ends up in prison. The meaning of the phrase here rendered *the Round Tower,* which the N.E.B. assumes is a technical expression, is uncertain. There is no obvious Egyptian parallel to it.

21. *kept faith with him:* see the note on 24: 12. Joseph's success story is repeated in prison. Just as he had 'found favour with his master' (verse 4), so now *he won the favour of the governor;* just as his master had entrusted everything in the household to him, so now he achieves a similar position of responsibility in prison.

22. *in the tower:* i.e. in the Round Tower; the Hebrew

expression is the same as that in the preceding verses. *and of all
their work:* although the N.E.B. follows the shorter Septuagint
text (see the N.E.B. footnote), it would be equally possible
to retain the longer Hebrew text and translate 'he was responsible for carrying out everything that was done there'.   ✶

JOSEPH INTERPRETS DREAMS

40 It happened later that the king's butler and his baker
2 offended their master the king of Egypt. Pharaoh was
angry with these two eunuchs, the chief butler and the
3 chief baker, and he put them in custody in the house of
the captain of the guard, in the Round Tower where
4 Joseph was imprisoned. The captain of the guard appointed Joseph as their attendant, and he waited on them.
5 One night, when they had been in prison for some time,
they both had dreams, each needing its own interpretation—the king of Egypt's butler and his baker who were
6 imprisoned in the Round Tower. When Joseph came to
them in the morning, he saw that they looked dejected.
7 So he asked these eunuchs, who were in custody with him
in his master's house, why they were so downcast that
8 day. They replied, 'We have each had a dream and there
is no one to interpret it for us.' Joseph said to them, 'Does
not interpretation belong to God? Tell me your dreams.'
9 So the chief butler told Joseph his dream: 'In my dream',
10 he said, 'there was a vine in front of me. On the vine
there were three branches, and as soon as it budded, it
11 blossomed and its clusters ripened into grapes. Now I had
Pharaoh's cup in my hand, and I plucked the grapes,
crushed them into Pharaoh's cup and put the cup into
12 Pharaoh's hand.' Joseph said to him, 'This is the interpre-

tation. The three branches are three days: within three 13
days Pharaoh will raise you[a] and restore you to your post,
and then you will put the cup into Pharaoh's hand as you
used to do when you were his butler. But when things go 14
well with you, if you think of me, keep faith with me and
bring my case to Pharaoh's notice and help me to get out
of this house. By force I was carried off[b] from the land of 15
the Hebrews, and I have done nothing here to deserve
being put in this dungeon.'

When the chief baker saw that Joseph had given a 16
favourable interpretation, he said to him, 'I too had a
dream, and in my dream there were three baskets of white
bread on my head. In the top basket there was every kind 17
of food which the baker prepares for Pharaoh, and the
birds were eating out of the top basket on my head.'
Joseph answered, 'This is the interpretation. The three 18
baskets are three days: within three days Pharaoh will 19
raise you[c] and hang you up on a tree, and the birds of the
air will eat your flesh.'

The third day was Pharaoh's birthday and he gave a feast 20
for all his servants. He raised[d] the chief butler and the chief
baker in the presence of his court. He restored the chief 21
butler to his post, and the butler put the cup into Pharaoh's
hand; but he hanged the chief baker. All went as Joseph 22
had said in interpreting the dreams for them. Even so the 23
chief butler did not remember Joseph, but forgot him.

✻   The story of Joseph's interpretation of the dreams of
Pharaoh's butler and baker is joined somewhat uneasily to

[a] *Lit*. lift up your head.   [b] *Or* stolen.
[c] *Lit*. lift up your head; *so Vulg.; Heb. adds* from off you.
[d] *Lit*. lifted up the heads of.

the account of his involvement with Potiphar's wife. The end of chapter 39 sees Joseph in the hands of the governor of the Round Tower and in charge of all the other prisoners; now he is in custody in the house of 'the captain of the guard', a description used of Potiphar at the end of chapter 37, and he is appointed as attendant on two of the prisoners. Apart from the reference to the Round Tower, chapter 40 would be the natural continuation of chapter 37. The captain of the guard uses his Hebrew slave as the personal servant of two important state officials who have fallen from grace. The slave's gift of being able to interpret their dreams correctly becomes the springboard of his rise to power.

1. *It happened later:* for this vague time link see the note on 15: 1. *the king's butler: butler* is perhaps a misleading translation, since it has in English a much wider connotation than the underlying Hebrew word which would be more accurately rendered 'cupbearer'. Both the butler and the baker were important court officials; they are described in verse 2 as 'the chief butler and the chief baker'. There is no need to look for specific Egyptian equivalents for these titles. All royal courts had such officials. When Solomon entertained the Queen of Sheba the narrative refers to 'the food on his table' and to his 'cupbearers' (1 Kings 10: 5). The Assyrian officer who represents the king in Judah is given the title Rab-shakeh (see 2 Kings 18: 17, N.E.B. footnote) which means 'chief cupbearer'. Neither such a title, nor that of 'chief baker', is to be regarded literally; an honorific position, perhaps originally connected with a specific function, has come to be used in a general sense (cp. also Nehemiah as cup-bearer (Neh. 2: 1) and such terms as Lord Chamberlain). *offended their master:* no explanation as to how they had offended is given. None is needed. In a despotic régime a royal whim may consign an official to disgrace. Joseph is there, according to 39: 9 because he had refused to 'sin' or offend – the same Hebrew word is used in both passages – against God.

6–8. The butler and the baker look *dejected* because, had they been free, they could have consulted professional dream interpreters. Joseph lays claim to a gift which, he declares, can only come from God, who is the source of all true interpretation. There is implicit here a declaration of the superiority of Israel's God over all the skills of Egypt. Just as Moses and Aaron, through God's power, were to outdo all the wise men, sorcerers and magicians of Egypt (see Exod. 7–8), so Joseph, through God's gift, can outdo all the Egyptian interpreters of dreams.

9–13. The chief butler has a dream of a vine and grapes and wine, suited to the title of his office. The detail which demands clarification is the significance of the *three branches* (verse 10). Joseph interprets this to mean that within three days the butler will be restored to his post. *Pharaoh will raise you* (verse 13): this is the first of three occurrences in this chapter of a phrase which literally means 'lift up the head' (see the N.E.B. footnote). Each time it has a different meaning. In verse 13 it means Pharaoh 'will pardon you' or 'will be gracious to you'. In verse 19 it has an ominous meaning, Pharaoh 'will hang you', lifting up your head in a rather different way. In verse 20 it means 'restored to a position of responsibility'. Since the narrative deliberately plays upon the ambiguity of this expression, the N.E.B. rightly translates it neutrally as 'raise' in all three cases.

14. The same Hebrew verb commonly translated 'remember', lies behind the translations *think of me* and *bring my case to Pharaoh's notice*, the latter being a good example of the legal use of this verb.

15. *in this dungeon:* not the usual word for prison; the same word is translated 'pit' in 37: 22. Joseph's comment that he had been *carried off* or 'stolen' (see the N.E.B. footnote) *from the land of the Hebrews* seems to presuppose a rather different version of the story from that found in chapter 37.

16–19. The chief baker's dream is likewise apt to his title. The ominous feature is that the bread he carries never reaches

Pharaoh; it is eaten by the birds. The number three again
signifies three days; the birds pecking the bread signify th
birds who will peck the flesh of the unfortunate baker.

16. *white bread:* the Hebrew word translated *white brea*
could also be linked with the Hebrew word for 'hole'. In
this case we should see here a reference to perforated o
wicker baskets instead of white bread.

19. *will raise you:* see note on verse 13. The Hebrew tex
adds after *will raise you* (literally 'lift your head') the word
'from off you' (see the N.E.B. footnote). This destroys th
deliberate ambiguity in the expression and was probably
added by a scribe to make the meaning explicit. *hang yoi
up on a tree:* this does not necessarily imply death by hanging
The reference could be to the public exposure of the body
of a criminal executed in some other way.

20. By the fourth century B.C. *Pharaoh's birthday* wa
lavishly celebrated in Egypt, and was the occasion for granting
an amnesty to certain types of criminals. How much older
this custom was we do not know.

23. The closing comment that the chief butler, when
restored to Pharaoh's favour *did not remember Joseph, bu
forgot him* serves to keep the element of suspense in the story
alive. We are left asking ' What happens next?'. ✱

JOSEPH BECOMES CHIEF MINISTER OF EGYPT

41 Nearly two years later Pharaoh had a dream: he was
2 standing by the Nile, and there came up from the river
seven cows, sleek and fat, and they grazed on the reeds.
3 After them seven other cows came up from the river,
gaunt and lean, and stood on the river-bank beside the first
4 cows. The cows that were gaunt and lean devoured the
5 cows that were sleek and fat. Then Pharaoh woke up. He
fell asleep again and had a second dream: he saw seven

ars of corn, full and ripe, growing on one stalk. Growing 6
up after them were seven other ears, thin and shrivelled by
the east wind. The thin ears swallowed up the ears that 7
were full and ripe. Then Pharaoh woke up and knew that
it was a dream. When morning came, Pharaoh was 8
troubled in mind; so he summoned all the magicians and
sages of Egypt. He told them his dreams,*a* but there was
no one who could interpret them for him. Then Pharaoh's 9
chief butler spoke up and said, 'It is time for me to recall
my faults. Once Pharaoh was angry with his servants, and 10
he imprisoned me and the chief baker in the house of the
captain of the guard. One night we both had dreams, each 11
needing its own interpretation. We had with us a young 12
Hebrew, a slave of the captain of the guard, and we told
him our dreams and he interpreted them for us, giving
each man's dream its own interpretation. Each dream came 13
true as it had been interpreted to us: I was restored to my
position, and he was hanged.'

Pharaoh thereupon sent for Joseph, and they hurriedly 14
brought him out of the dungeon. He shaved and changed
his clothes, and came in to Pharaoh. Pharaoh said to him, 15
'I have had a dream, and no one can interpret it to me.
I have heard it said that you can understand and interpret
dreams.' Joseph answered, 'Not I, but God, will answer 16
for Pharaoh's welfare.' Then Pharaoh said to Joseph, 'In 17
my dream I was standing on the bank of the Nile, and 18
there came up from the river seven cows, fat and sleek,
and they grazed on the reeds. After them seven other cows 19
came up that were poor, very gaunt and lean; I have never
seen such gaunt creatures in all Egypt. These lean, gaunt 20

[a] *So Sam.; Heb.* dream.

21 cows devoured the first cows, the fat ones. They wer
swallowed up, but no one could have guessed that the
were in the bellies of the others, which looked as gaunt
22 before. Then I woke up. After I had fallen asleep again
I saw in a dream seven ears of corn, full and ripe, growin
23 on one stalk. Growing up after them were seven othe
24 ears, shrivelled, thin, and blighted by the east wind. Th
thin ears swallowed up the seven ripe ears. When I tol
all this to the magicians, no one could explain it to me
25 Joseph said to Pharaoh, 'Pharaoh's dreams are on
26 dream. God has told Pharaoh what he is going to do. Th
seven good cows are seven years, and the seven good ear
27 of corn are seven years. It is all one dream. The seven lea
and gaunt cows that came up after them are seven year
and the empty ears of corn blighted by the east wind wi
28 be seven years of famine. It is as I have said to Pharaoh
29 God has let Pharaoh see what he is going to do. There ar
to be seven years of great plenty throughout the land
30 After them will come seven years of famine; all the year
of plenty in Egypt will be forgotten, and the famine wi
31 ruin the country. The good years will not be remembere
in the land because of the famine that follows; for it wi
32 be very severe. The doubling of Pharaoh's dream mean
that God is already resolved to do this, and he will ver
33 soon put it into effect. Pharaoh should now look for
shrewd and intelligent man, and put him in charge of th
34 country. This is what Pharaoh should do: appoint con
trollers over the land, and take one fifth of the produce o
35 Egypt during the seven years of plenty. They shoul
collect all this food produced in the good years that ar

[a] After...again: *so Sept.; Heb. om.*

coming and put the corn under Pharaoh's control in store
in the cities, and keep it under guard. This food will be a 36
reserve for the country against the seven years of famine
which will come upon Egypt. Thus the country will not
be devastated by the famine.'

The plan pleased Pharaoh and all his courtiers, and he 37, 38
said to them, 'Can we find a man like this man, one who
has the spirit of a god*a* in him?' He said to Joseph, 'Since 39
a god*b* has made all this known to you, there is no one so
shrewd and intelligent as you. You shall be in charge of 40
my household, and all my people will depend on your
every word. Only my royal throne shall make me greater
than you.' Pharaoh said to Joseph, 'I hereby give you 41
authority over the whole land of Egypt.' He took off his 42
signet-ring and put it on Joseph's finger, he had him
dressed in fine linen, and hung a gold chain round his
neck. He mounted him in his viceroy's chariot and men 43
cried 'Make way!'*c* before him. Thus Pharaoh made him
ruler over all Egypt and said to him, 'I am the Pharaoh. 44
Without your consent no man shall lift hand or foot
throughout Egypt.' Pharaoh named him Zaphenath- 45
paneah, and he gave him as wife Asenath the daughter of
Potiphera priest of On. And Joseph's authority extended
over the whole of Egypt.

Joseph was thirty years old when he entered the service 46
of Pharaoh king of Egypt. When he took his leave of the
king, he made a tour of inspection through the country.
During the seven years of plenty there were abundant 47
harvests, and Joseph gathered all the food produced in 48

[a] Or of God.
[b] Or God.   [c] *Egyptian word of uncertain mng.*

Egypt during those years and stored it in the cities, putting
49 in each the food from the surrounding country. He stored
the grain in huge quantities; it was like the sand of the
sea, so much that he stopped measuring: it was beyond all
measure.

50   Before the years of famine came, two sons were born to
Joseph by Asenath the daughter of Potiphera priest of On.
51 He named the elder Manasseh,*a* 'for', he said, 'God has
caused me to forget all my troubles and my father's
52 family.' He named the second Ephraim,*b* 'for', he said,
'God has made me fruitful in the land of my hardships.'
53 When the seven years of plenty in Egypt came to an end,
54 seven years of famine began, as Joseph had foretold. There
was famine in every country, but throughout Egypt there
55 was bread. So when the famine spread through all Egypt,
the people appealed to Pharaoh for bread, and he ordered
56 them to go to Joseph and do as he told them. In every
region there was famine, and Joseph opened all the
granaries and sold corn to the Egyptians, for the famine
57 was severe. The whole world came to Egypt to buy corn
from Joseph, so severe was the famine everywhere.

* From being a humble slave interpreting the dreams of
two of Pharaoh's discredited officials, Joseph becomes the
chief minister of all Egypt. His rise to power is as swift as it
is unexpected. Pharaoh is troubled by dreams which none
of his magicians or sages can interpret. The chief butler
recalls the Hebrew slave he had forgotten. Joseph is whisked
from prison to palace. Stressing again his total dependence
upon God, he provides an interpretation which makes sense
to Pharaoh. But Joseph in this narrative is no mere interpreter

[a] *That is* Causing to forget.   [b] *That is* Fruit.

of dreams, he also functions as a wise counsellor, a skilful politician giving Pharaoh shrewd advice to enable him to cope with the coming crisis. Pharaoh in return gives Joseph the authority and power, as ruler over Egypt, to implement his plans. Joseph becomes fully Egyptianized, with an Egyptian name, and married to an Egyptian wife, a priest's daughter, who presents him with two sons, probably twins (see 48: 8–20) though the term is not used.

1–8. Pharaoh, like Joseph in chapter 37, has two dreams similar in import; seven 'gaunt and lean' cows devouring seven 'sleek and fat' cows, seven 'thin and shrivelled' ears of corn swallowing up seven 'full and ripe' ears.

8. For the significance of the failure of Pharaoh's magicians and sages, see the note on 40: 6–8. *dreams*: since Pharaoh had two dreams it is better to follow the Samaritan text here and read the plural rather than the singular 'dream' which is the reading of the Hebrew text (see the N.E.B. footnote).

9–13. The chief butler belatedly recalls Joseph's gift of interpreting dreams, and how, in his experience, the interpretation has been vindicated by events.

9. *It is time for me to recall my faults*: since his faults consist entirely of his ungrateful forgetfulness of Joseph, the plural *faults* is probably used here in an abstract sense. The word translated *faults* is the same as that previously translated 'sin' or 'offence' (see the note on 40: 1).

14. *He shaved and changed his clothes*: there is probably more to this than mere courtesy or protocol. It marks the metamorphosis of Joseph. The life of the slave is now at an end; the new life of prestige and power is about to begin; cp. Deut. 21: 10–14 where an attractive woman, taken captive in war, 'shall shave her head, pare her nails, and discard the clothes which she had when captured', and, after a suitable period, begins a new life as the wife of her captor.

16. *'Not I, but God, will answer for Pharaoh's welfare'*: it is hard to see what is meant in context by this translation of a highly idiomatic Hebrew expression containing the word

shalom, 'peace, welfare'. It makes better sense to translate
'Not I, but God, will give Pharaoh the right answer (or
interpretation)'.

17–24. Pharaoh vividly recounts his dreams, with the
addition of a few personal comments, e.g. in verses 19 and 21

22. *After I had fallen asleep again:* this, the reading of the
Septuagint text (see the N.E.B. footnote), fits in with verse
where we are told that after Pharaoh woke up from his first
dream 'He fell asleep again.' The Hebrew text, which launches
Pharaoh straight into the account of his second dream after
the words 'I woke up', is perhaps more graphic.

25–32. Joseph's interpretation of Pharaoh's dreams depends
upon three premisses:

(i) the two dreams are in fact one dream as far as their
meaning is concerned;

(ii) the number seven indicates a period of time, 'seven
years', just as the three branches of 40: 12 signified three days.

(iii) the good cows devoured by the gaunt cows, the good
ears disappearing into the blighted ears, signify abundance
giving way to famine.

The doubling of the dream is also taken to be an indication
of the certainty and the imminence of what the dreams por-
tray.

27. *seven years of famine:* a seven-year period of drought
occurs in both Canaanite and Babylonian literature. A second
century B.C. Egyptian document, a forgery purporting to
tell of events about 2600 B.C., also speaks of 'seven years of
famine'; proof that even in Egypt, dependent upon the
annual rise and fall of the Nile, such a situation was at least
not unthinkable.

33–6. Joseph caps his interpretation with practical advice
as to how to deal with the situation portrayed in the dreams –
a commonsense scheme to store, during the years of plenty
food for distribution during the years of famine.

33. *a shrewd and intelligent man:* the Hebrew word translated *intelligent* does not refer merely to intellectual ability

t often describes a person who possesses certain practical
kills, as here.

37–45. Joseph is chosen as the obvious man to implement
he plan he has suggested.

38. *one who has the spirit of a god in him:* on the lips of
Pharaoh it is better to translate *spirit of a god*, rather than
'spirit of God' (see the N.E.B. footnote). A Hebrew reader
would naturally see a reference to the one true God, whose
providence was at work in all that happened to Joseph, and
whose spirit was the source of all the skills Joseph possessed.
For the spirit of God as the source of all that is outstanding
in human life see *Genesis 1–11*, p. 16.

40. *You shall be in charge of my household:* the wheel has
turned full circle. The Hebrew slave who was once in charge
of Potiphar's household, has now come, through imprison-
ment, to be in charge of Pharaoh's household.

42. The symbols of authority are now given to Joseph.
The *signet-ring* would incorporate Pharaoh's own personal
seal, and thus anything stamped with it would have Pharaoh's
authority. In ancient Egypt, as far back as the third millennium B.C. one of the vizier's titles was 'seal-bearer of the
king'. *dressed in fine linen:* given a robe symbolic of his status
and office. *a gold chain round his neck:* such gold chains were
commonly worn by high Egyptian officials. They were often
bestowed by Pharaoh as a reward for services rendered.

43. *his viceroy's chariot:* literally 'the chariot of the second'
'Hebrew *mishneh* – i.e. 'second (to the king)'). Earlier translations assume that the word 'second' refers to another
chariot, i.e. in his second chariot. The N.E.B. translation
is preferable. '*Make way!*': the Hebrew text reads *Abrek*, an
Egyptian word of uncertain meaning (see the N.E.B. footnote). It has been interpreted to mean 'Attention!'

45. *Pharaoh named him Zephenath-paneah:* just as Jacob's
new name Israel indicated his new character and destiny, so
Joseph's new Egyptian name points to his new, wholly
Egyptianized life. The name *Zaphenath-paneah* means in

Egyptian 'God speaks, and he lives'. His wife Asenath als
bears a common Egyptian name meaning 'belonging to th
goddess Neith'. *daughter of Potiphera priest of On: Potipher*
is a longer, variant form of 'Potiphar', though this Potipher
is obviously a different person from Potiphar, the captain o
the guard, being a priest of On. On was an ancient and famou
religious centre east of the Nile in the Delta region. It wa
dedicated to the worship of the solar disk, the sun-god. I
hellenistic times it was called Heliopolis, 'Sun City'.

46. *Joseph was thirty years old when he entered the servic
of Pharaoh:* this seems to be one of the precise chronologica
notes which the P editors add to the text. When last any refer
ence was made to Joseph's age he was a boy of seventee
(37: 2). The narrative hardly gives the impression tha
thirteen years have elapsed between 37: 2 and 41: 40.

48. *gathered all the food:* rather, 'gathered any food' o
'any crops'. It is not intended that all the food produced i
the years of plenty was stored (cp. verse 34).

50-2. The birth of Joseph's two sons, Manasseh an
Ephraim. Both have good Hebrew names, and both name
are provided with explanations related to Joseph's experience
Both names are the names of tribes who later were part o
the federation of Israel. *Manasseh* is taken to mean 'Causin
to forget' (see the N.E.B. footnote). It is linked to the Hebrew
verb 'to forget', since God, through the transformation o
Joseph's fortunes, has made him forget the bitter past. *all m
troubles and my father's family:* i.e. all the troubles whic
sprang from family friction. As the next chapter clearl
shows, Joseph was far from forgetting his father's family
Ephraim is taken to mean 'Fruit' (see the N.E.B. footnote)
and is a play on the Hebrew verb translated *made me fruitfu*
By packing him off to Egypt as a slave, Joseph's brothers ha
attempted to ensure that his dreams of greatness would neve
come to fruition; but the very *hardships* to which they ha
submitted him were to be the pathway to that greatness.

53-7. Egypt successfully survives the *seven years of famine* thanks to Joseph's foresight and planning. But not only Egypt, *The whole world* is caught up in the famine. Peoples from surrounding countries come to Egypt in search of scarce food. The stage is set for a further meeting and a reconciliation between Joseph and his brothers. ✶

FAMILY RECONCILIATION

✶ With Joseph's elevation to power in Egypt, one theme in his dreams has been fulfilled; but there is another. What is to be his relationship to the brothers who tried to liquidate him? Will they recognize his greatness? The story would obviously be incomplete lacking reconciliation with his brothers, and his father's grief turned into unhoped-for joy. Such is the theme of chapters 42–5, a theme developed with marvellous delicacy of touch and continuing suspense until, after two visits to Egypt and four somewhat testy interviews with the Egyptian chief minister, the brothers to their astonishment hear him say, 'I am Joseph; can my father be still alive?' (45: 3). The compelling and moving simplicity of the narrative, however, should not blind us to the fact that, in its present form, it contains within itself some odd contradictions and inconsistencies, which have been taken as proof of the documentary hypothesis, but may perhaps admit of other explanations (see pp. 213–14). In the first visit to Egypt, undertaken at Jacob's request (chapter 42), Reuben plays a leading role (cp. verses 22 and 37). This visit ends with Simeon left behind in Egypt as a hostage to guarantee that the brothers will return, bringing with them young Benjamin. In the lead up to the second visit, however, Judah plays the role of spokesman for the brothers. It is particularly odd that, at the beginning of chapter 43 in the discussion between Judah and his father – here called Israel – about the necessity for a further visit to Egypt, nothing is said about Simeon. This version of the story seems to know nothing of the Simeon hostage incident; the laconic words at the end of 43: 23

'Then he brought Simeon out to them', read like an attempt to tie together the different stories. Further, the accusation of spying made against the brothers by Joseph in chapter 42, and faithfully reported to Jacob, is entirely omitted by Judah when he recalls the interview with Joseph in 43: 3–7, nor does Judah mention it in his speech in 44: 18–23. It is tempting to conclude, therefore, that in basic outline the Joseph story has room for only one visit by the brothers to Egypt, and that this visit appears in two different forms, one in chapter 42, the other in chapters 43–4. Even chapter 42 has its own inner problems. In verse 27 we are told that, during the journey home, the brothers stopped for the night. One of the brothers opened his sack and found 'his silver at the top of the pack'. This seems to be totally ignored in verse 35 which makes all the brothers empty their sacks when they get home and 'each of them found his silver inside'. And when we turn to 43: 21 we find that all the brothers open their packs and find the silver during the journey home. Even if we assume two versions of this section of the Joseph story, in broad outline and in basic theme they are the same. Famine drives the brothers to Egypt in search of food. There they meet the governor, Joseph. He recognizes them, but they, not surprisingly, fail to recognize him. After putting their family loyalty to a searching test, Joseph reveals his identity and reconciliation takes place. ✳

THE FIRST VISIT

42 When Jacob saw that there was corn in Egypt, he said to
2 his sons, 'Why do you stand staring at each other? I have heard that there is corn in Egypt. Go down and buy some so that we may keep ourselves alive and not starve.'
3 So Joseph's brothers, ten of them, went down to buy
4 grain from Egypt, but Jacob did not let Joseph's brother Benjamin go with them, for fear that he might come to harm.

So the sons of Israel came down with everyone else to 5
buy corn, because of the famine in Canaan. Now Joseph 6
was governor of all Egypt, and it was he who sold the
corn to all the people of the land. Joseph's brothers came
and bowed to the ground before him, and when he saw 7
his brothers, he recognized them but pretended not to
know them and spoke harshly to them. 'Where do you
come from?' he asked. 'From Canaan,' they answered,
'to buy food.' Although Joseph had recognized his 8
brothers, they did not recognize him. He remembered 9
also the dreams he had had about them; so he said to
them, 'You are spies; you have come to spy out the weak
points in our defences.' They answered, 'No, sir: your 10
servants have come to buy food. We are all sons of one 11
man. Your humble servants are honest men, we are not
spies.' 'No,' he insisted, 'it is to spy out our weaknesses 12
that you have come.' They answered him, 'Sir, there are 13
twelve of us, all brothers, sons of one man in Canaan.
The youngest is still with our father, and one has disappeared.' But Joseph said again to them, 'No, as I said 14
before, you are spies. This is how you shall be put to the 15
proof: unless your youngest brother comes here, by the
life of Pharaoh, you shall not leave this place. Send one of 16
your number to bring your brother; the rest will be kept
in prison. Thus your story will be tested, and we shall see
whether you are telling the truth. If not, then, by the life
of Pharaoh, you must be spies.' So he kept them in prison 17
for three days.

On the third day Joseph said to the brothers, 'Do what 18
I say and your lives will be spared; for I am a God-
fearing man: if you are honest men, your brother there 19
shall be kept in prison, and the rest of you shall take corn

20 for your hungry households and bring your youngest brother to me; thus your words will be proved true, and you will not die.'[a]

21 They said to one another, 'No doubt we deserve to be punished because of our brother, whose suffering we saw; for when he pleaded with us we refused to listen.

22 That is why these sufferings have come upon us.' But Reuben said, 'Did I not tell you not to do the boy a wrong? But you would not listen, and his blood is on our

23 heads, and we must pay.' They did not know that Joseph

24 understood, because he had used an interpreter. Joseph turned away from them and wept. Then, turning back, he played a trick on them. First he took Simeon and bound

25 him before their eyes; then he gave orders to fill their bags with grain, to return each man's silver, putting it in his sack, and to give them supplies for the journey. All this

26 was done; and they loaded the corn on to their asses and

27 went away. When they stopped for the night, one of them opened his sack to give fodder to his ass, and there

28 he saw his silver at the top of the pack. He said to his brothers, 'My silver has been returned to me, and here it is in my pack.' Bewildered and trembling, they said to each other, 'What is this that God has done to us?'

29 When they came to their father Jacob in Canaan, they

30 told him all that had happened to them. They said, 'The man who is lord of the country spoke harshly to us and

31 made out that we were spies. We said to him, "We are

32 honest men, we are not spies. There are twelve of us, all brothers, sons of one father. One has disappeared, and the

33 youngest is with our father in Canaan." This man, the

[a] *Prob. rdg.; Heb. adds* and they did so.

lord of the country, said to us, "This is how I shall find
out if you are honest men. Leave one of your brothers
with me, take food*ª* for your hungry households and go.
Bring your youngest brother to me, and I shall know that 34
you are not spies, but honest men. Then I will restore your
brother to you, and you can move about the country
freely."' But on emptying their sacks, each of them 35
found his silver inside, and when they and their father saw
the bundles of silver, they were afraid. Their father Jacob 36
said to them, 'You have robbed me of my children. Joseph
has disappeared; Simeon has disappeared; and now you
are taking Benjamin. Everything is against me.' Reuben 37
said to his father, 'You may kill both my sons if I do not
bring him back to you. Put him in my charge, and I shall
bring him back.' But Jacob said, 'My son shall not go with 38
you, for his brother is dead and he alone is left. If he comes
to any harm on the journey, you will bring down my
grey hairs in sorrow to the grave.'*ᵇ*

✻ 1–2. For Egypt as a natural granary in a time of famine,
see the note on 12: 10.

1. *Why do you stand staring at each other?*: i.e. 'remain
idle'. The Greek translators may have had a different text
suggesting 'delay'.

4. Benjamin is Joseph's only full brother, the only other
son of Rachel, Jacob's favourite wife. Benjamin presumably
now occupies what once was Joseph's place in his father's
affections. Jacob keeps him at home *for fear that he might come
to harm*. Jacob has a long memory. Once Joseph had gone to
be with his brothers, and had disappeared. Something equally
tragic might happen to Benjamin.

[a] *So Sept.; Heb. om.*   [b] *Heb.* Sheol.

6. It is perhaps straining credulity to believe that the *governor of all Egypt* would deal personally with all who sought to buy food, but the story demands that Joseph and his brothers should meet, and this provides a reasonable context. The description of Joseph as *governor* occurs only here, and uses a word which is found elsewhere in the Old Testament only in books of a fairly late date, such as Ecclesiastes and Esther. *Joseph's brothers came and bowed to the ground before him:* unwittingly they are fulfilling the dreams Joseph had recounted to them in 37: 5-11. This Joseph recognizes; see verse 9.

7-17. Ancient Egypt seems often to have looked at the world outside her borders with suspicion and hostility. Its north-eastern frontier facing Canaan was heavily fortified. Since it was subject to attack by northern invaders, a charge of spying was serious. The dialogue is terse and vivid. 'Where do you come from?' 'Canaan.' The answer to this harsh opening question immediately leads to the accusation 'you have come to spy' (verse 9). In spite of protestations of innocence, the charge is repeated: 'it is to spy...that you have come' (verse 12). A further attempt to explain is roughly brushed aside: 'as I said before, you are spies' (verse 14).

9. *the weak points in our defences:* literally 'the nakedness of the land' (Authorized Version): what you would not want potential enemies to see. In verse 12 the same Hebrew expression is translated 'our weaknesses'.

10-11. *your servants... Your humble servants:* see the note on 18: 3. In both cases the Hebrew here simply reads 'your servants', a deferential equivalent to 'we' when addressing a superior.

13. *one has disappeared:* or 'is gone', a matter-of-fact statement, with the brothers neither admitting nor denying any responsibility for what happened to the one who disappeared.

15-20. Joseph puts the onus of proof on the brothers. They are guilty of spying unless or until they can prove the contrary. The only way to do so is to send for the youngest

son who, they claim, has been left behind with their father in
Canaan. Joseph's demand is at first harsh. All shall stay in
prison in Egypt, except one who must go home and bring
this brother. Then the harshness is modified. One brother is
to be left as a hostage, the others may return home and bring
back the youngest brother. Joseph seems to be preparing the
way for a reunion of all the brothers. Only Benjamin is
missing; he must be brought to Egypt. But, at the same time,
he is testing the brothers. Once again they will return to their
father minus one of their number. Will this recall to their
conscience an old crime? How will they react this time? With
a callousness similar to that they once displayed in the case of
Joseph, or have they learned anything from the bitter experience of seeing their father suffer?

15. *by the life of Pharaoh:* or 'as Pharaoh lives', an oath
formula. Just as a true worshipper of the LORD would swear
an oath with the words 'as the LORD lives' (cp. 1 Kings
17: 1: N.E.B. 'by the life of the LORD'), so one of Pharaoh's
servants swears a solemn oath with the words 'as Pharaoh
lives'.

18. *for I am a God-fearing man:* since Joseph is here speaking
as an Egyptian, perhaps we should translate 'for I fear (or
'reverence') the gods'. He is admitting an authority higher
than himself. They must trust him, in this light, to act
responsibly. He wishes to test them to see if they will do
likewise.

20. The omission at the end of this verse of the words in
the Hebrew text 'and they did so' (see the N.E.B. footnote) is
unnecessary. While 'and they did so' is a literal translation,
the words could also mean 'so they agreed'. This makes
excellent sense in context.

21–2. Joseph's plan works. The shadow of a guilty past
falls heavily upon the brothers. Unaware that Joseph can
understand what they are saying, they indulge in mutual
recrimination. Reuben, who in 37: 21–2 had tried to act as
Joseph's protector, reminds them pointedly of the blood

guilt which must be upon them. *we deserve to be punished:* or
'we are suffering the consequences' of the way in which we
treated our brother. The underlying Hebrew word denotes,
in legal contexts, either guilt or the consequences of guilt.

24. *Joseph turned away from them and wept:* whatever Joseph
intended, it was not revenge. With difficulty he conceals his
true feelings from the brothers. Several times in the narrative
Joseph weeps. When first he sees Benjamin 'he went into the
inner room and wept' (43: 30). The reconciliation scene is
marked by Joseph giving vent to long-concealed emotions
and weeping (45: 1–2, 15). *he played a trick on them:* Hebrew
'he spoke to them'. The N.E.B. interpretation is unnecessary.
After *wept* we could translate 'When he was able to speak to
them again, he picked out Simeon.' *Simeon:* the next eldest
son after Reuben.

25–8. By putting the money back in their packs Joseph is
giving the screw another turn. The brothers' visit to Egypt
had turned out to be an alarming experience – imprisoned
on a charge of spying, forced to leave Simeon as a hostage,
now the money they had paid for corn reappearing in a sack
of corn they were carrying home. It was all the more ominous
because there was no obvious explanation. On the apparent
contradiction between verses 27 and 35, see above p. 250.

28. *Bewildered:* we could retain something of the Hebrew
idiom by translating 'their hearts sank'. '*What is this that
God has done to us?*': since the money in the sack is to them
a total mystery, they can only conclude that they must be
at the mercy of some higher fate or providence, the workings
of which they cannot understand.

33. *take food for your hungry households:* the Hebrew is
literally 'take the hunger of your households', which may be
a cryptic way of saying 'take something to satisfy your hungry
folk at home'. Some of the versions, including the Septuagint
(see the N.E.B. footnote), correctly interpret the meaning by
inserting the word *food*.

34. *you can move about the country freely:* or 'you can trade

in the country'; the verb translated *move about* frequently refers to travelling merchants.

35. *bundles of silver:* or 'bags of money'.

36–8. Jacob's reply is brief and poignant. Joseph gone, Simeon gone, now they want to take Benjamin. His answer, in spite of Reuben's eloquent and unselfish plea, can only be 'No.' He is already old; further grief would kill him.

38. *to the grave:* see the note on 37: 35.   ✳

THE SECOND VISIT TO JOSEPH

The famine was still severe in the country. When they had **43** 1, 2 used up the corn they had brought from Egypt, their father said to them, 'Go back and buy a little more corn for us to eat.' But Judah replied, 'The man plainly warned 3 us that we must not go into his presence unless our brother was with us. If you let our brother go with us, we will go 4 down and buy food for you. But if you will not let him, 5 we will not go; for the man said to us, "You shall not come into my presence, unless your brother is with you."' Israel said, 'Why have you treated me so badly? Why did 6 you tell the man that you had yet another brother?' They 7 answered, 'He questioned us closely about ourselves and our family: "Is your father still alive?" he asked, "Have you a brother?", and we answered his questions. How could we possibly know that he would tell us to bring our brother to Egypt?' Judah said to his father Israel, 'Send 8 the boy with me; then we can start at once. By doing this we shall save our lives, ours, yours, and our dependants', and none of us will starve. I will go surety for him and you 9 may hold me responsible. If I do not bring him back and restore him to you, you shall hold me guilty all my life. If 10 we had not wasted all this time, by now we could have gone back twice over.'

11 Their father Israel said to them, 'If it must be so, then do this: take in your baggage, as a gift for the man, some of the produce for which our country is famous: a little balsam, a little honey, gum tragacanth, myrrh, pistachio 12 nuts, and almonds. Take double the amount of silver and restore what was returned to you in your packs; perhaps it 13 was a mistake. Take your brother with you and go 14 straight back to the man. May God Almighty make him kindly disposed to you, and may he send back the one[a] whom you left behind, and Benjamin too. As for me, if 15 I am bereaved, then I am bereaved.' So they took the gift and double the amount of silver, and with Benjamin they started at once for Egypt, where they presented themselves to Joseph.

16 When Joseph saw Benjamin with them, he said to his steward, 'Bring these men indoors, kill a beast and make 17 dinner ready, for they will eat with me at noon.' He did as Joseph told him and brought the men into the house. 18 When they came in they were afraid, for they thought, 'We have been brought in here because of that affair of the silver which was replaced in our packs the first time. He means to trump up some charge against us and 19 victimize us, seize our asses and make us his slaves.' So they approached Joseph's steward and spoke to him at the 20 door of the house. They said, 'Please listen, my lord. 21 After our first visit to buy food, when we reached the place where we were to spend the night, we opened our packs and each of us found his silver in full weight at the

[a] *So Sam.; Heb.* other.

top of his pack. We have brought it back with us, and 22
have added other silver to buy food. We do not know who
put the silver in our packs.' He answered, 'Set your minds 23
at rest; do not be afraid. It was your God, the God of your
father,*a* who hid treasure for you in your packs. I did
receive the silver.' Then he brought Simeon out to them.

The steward brought them into Joseph's house and 24
gave them water to wash their feet, and provided fodder
for their asses. They had their gifts ready when Joseph 25
arrived at noon, for they had heard that they were to eat
there. When Joseph came into the house, they presented 26
him with the gifts which they had brought, bowing to the
ground before him. He asked them how they were and 27
said, 'Is your father well, the old man of whom you
spoke? Is he still alive?' They answered, 'Yes, my lord, 28
our father is still alive and well.' And they bowed low and
prostrated themselves. Joseph looked and saw his own 29
mother's son, his brother Benjamin, and asked, 'Is this
your youngest brother, of whom you told me?', and to
Benjamin he said, 'May God be gracious to you, my
son!' Joseph was overcome; his feelings for his brother 30
mastered him, and he was near to tears. So he went into
the inner room and wept. Then he washed his face and 31
came out; and, holding back his feelings, he ordered the
meal to be served. They served him by himself, and the 32
brothers by themselves, and the Egyptians who were at
dinner were also served separately; for Egyptians hold it
an abomination to eat with Hebrews. The brothers were 33
seated in his presence, the eldest first according to his age
and so on down to the youngest: they looked at one

[a] *Or, with Sam.,* fathers.

34 another in astonishment. Joseph sent them each a portion from what was before him, but Benjamin's was five times larger than any of the other portions. Thus they drank with him and all grew merry.

1–10. A second visit is necessitated by continuing famine. When Jacob suggests it, Judah counters by warning his father that they dare not return to Egypt without Benjamin. The account which Judah gives of the first interview with 'the man' in Egypt, differs in several respects from that described in 42: 7–17, and recounted in 42: 32–4. In addition to the fact that nothing is said about the charge of spying, Joseph, according to chapter 42, had not, as Judah avers, questioned them closely about their family. They had volunteered the information to counter the charge of spying. But Judah's version concentrates upon what is now the key factor in the story – Benjamin. Will Jacob allow him to go to Egypt? What will happen to him when he gets there? Why indeed is 'the man' so interested in him? The father's dilemma is harsh; either death by starvation or the risk of losing Benjamin, as he had once lost the only other son of his favourite wife Rachel.

6. *Why have you treated me so badly?*: rather, 'Why have you put me in this difficult situation?' or 'brought this trouble upon me?'; the immediate difficulty or trouble springing from the fact that the brothers had told of Benjamin's existence.

9. *I will go surety for him and you may hold me responsible*: Judah's offer is neither as passionate nor as eloquent as Reuben's in 42: 37, but it is a clear acceptance of responsibility for Benjamin's safety. This was the man who, according to 37: 26–7, took the initiative in selling Joseph to the Ishmaelites, and joined with his brothers in disclaiming all responsibility for what had happened.

10. *If we had not wasted all this time*: 'dillydallied' would

e a good English equivalent of the Hebrew word translated
asted all this time. The same word in 19: 16 is translated
lingered'.

11–15. Israel accepts the inevitable. He tries to ensure that
: will have a favourable outcome. Gifts must be sent to the
Egyptian official. Favours could hardly be expected from any
uch high-ranking official without appropriate gifts. The
rothers must also take double the amount of money they
leed to buy grain. On the most favourable interpretation,
he money found in their sacks must have been a mistake.
t must be repaid.

11. *some of the produce for which our country is famous:* the gifts
offered would thus serve to authenticate the brothers' claim
hat they came from Canaan. *balsam...gum tragacanth,*
myrrh: see the note on 37: 25; *honey* was also used for medi-
inal purposes. *pistachio nuts:* long considered a delicacy in
he Near East.

12. *perhaps it was a mistake:* putting the most hopeful
nterpretation on the 'money in the sacks' incident, an
ncident which the brothers had already interpreted rather
lifferently; see 42: 28.

14. *God Almighty:* see the note on 17: 1. *the one whom you*
left behind: this is a paraphrase based on the Samaritan text
see the N.E.B. footnote). It hardly seems necessary. The
Hebrew text reads 'so that he may release to you your other
rother (i.e. Simeon) and Benjamin'. Since Benjamin is not
n an Egyptian prison we must assume that the word 'release'
or *send back* is used in a slightly different sense when applied
o the two brothers. *if I am bereaved, then I am bereaved:* into
hese words is poured all the impotent resignation which
grips Israel.

16–23. This section, involving the steward, who is depicted
as being privy to Joseph's intentions, serves to underline the
ncreasing unease and bewilderment of the brothers. The
econd visit begins ominously. The brothers' worst fears
seem confirmed when they are taken by the steward to his

master's house. They are going to be victimized for th
unfortunate affair of the silver in the sacks. Anxiously the
take the steward aside, protest their mystification and inno
cence, and offer to return the money. The steward's reply ,
reassuring: 'I did receive the silver', but hardly enlightening
It is as if he were saying, 'Yes, you are right: there is a highe
fate at work here. You cannot understand it, but you mu:
believe that it is friendly.' As a token that all may yet be wel
Simeon is restored to them.

18. *seize our asses and make us his slaves:* there is a patheti
undertone to these words; as if the governor of all Egyp
would have any personal interest in confiscating the asses o
a few starving Canaanites, and in making them his slave:
But the brothers cannot see beyond their own little world
and it seems so evidently threatened.

21. *in full weight:* literally 'in its weight', i.e. of correc
weight, the value of the silver depending upon its weight.

23. *Set your minds at rest:* this is a good rendering of a phras
containing the Hebrew word *shalom*, which older Englis
versions (e.g. the Authorized Version) render baldly 'peace'
your God, the God of your father: see p. 12; whether we rea
the singular *father* or, with the Samaritan text (see the N.E.B
footnote), the plural 'fathers' makes no difference to th
meaning.

24-30. The interview between Joseph and the brother
proceeds with formal correctness. The brothers offer thei
gifts. Joseph politely inquires after their health, and asks abou
their father, 'the old man of whom you spoke' (verse 27)
Identifying Benjamin, he expresses to him good wishes. I
is as if Joseph is playing a game with them, a game of calcu
lated politeness. It is a game he finds hard to sustain. The sigh
of Benjamin, the full brother whom he had not seen for many
years, is too much for him. He has to retire to give vent to
his feelings. The time for revealing his identity to the brother
has not yet come. They have one final test to endure.

28. *Yes, my lord, our father is still alive and well:* as most othe

English versions indicate, the Hebrew text does not read *my lord*, but makes the brothers introduce their father as 'your servant'. For this self-depreciatory way of addressing a superior, see the note on 42: 10. The N.E.B. change hardly seems necessary. Translate 'Your humble servant, our father, is still alive and well.'

29. '*May God be gracious to you, my son!*': like our English expression 'God bless you', this may be taken at the level of conventional politeness, or it may mean much more. It is the struggle between these two levels which leads Joseph to the point of breakdown.

30. *Joseph was overcome:* literally, 'Joseph hurried', which may be a very compressed way of saying 'Joseph hurried to leave the room.' It is difficult to see how the N.E.B. justifies *overcome. his feelings for his brother mastered him:* more literally, 'his compassion for his brother was hot'. The same idiom is found in 1 Kings 3: 26 where it describes a mother 'moved with love' for her child. *and wept:* see the note on 42: 24.

31–4. The emotional intensity of the narrative is broken, as it turns to describe, with a touch of humour, the banquet which follows. It is a banquet of surprises. The brothers find themselves seated at table in order of precedence according to their age – how could the Egyptian governor have known? Benjamin is singled out for special favour – why? But if the brothers had any deep qualms, they were soon to be drowned in the pleasure of wine.

32. As a high official Joseph eats separately. The other Egyptians present and the brothers are likewise segregated, *for Egyptians hold it an abomination to eat with Hebrews* (see the note on 39: 6). The word translated *abomination* often refers to something which is abhorrent or detestable on religious grounds.

34. A choice *portion* sent personally by the host to an honoured guest, is an age-old and still-practised custom in the Near East. Benjamin is specially favoured since his portion *was five times larger than any of the other portions* (contrast

the threatened doom on Benjamin in chapter 44). *and*
grew merry: literally 'and they became drunk with him
The events of the next day were to have an immediate
sobering effect on the brothers.   ✳

BENJAMIN IN DANGER

44 Joseph gave his steward this order: 'Fill the men's pack
with as much food as they can carry and put each man'

2 silver at the top of his pack. And put my goblet, my silve
goblet, at the top of the youngest brother's pack with th

3 silver for the corn.' He did as Joseph said. At daybreak th
brothers were allowed to take their asses and go on thei

4 journey; but before they had gone very far from the city
Joseph said to his steward, 'Go after those men at once
and when you catch up with them, say, "Why have you

5 repaid good with evil? Why have you stolen the silve
goblet?*a* It is the one from which my lord drinks, an
which he uses for divination. You have done a wicke

6 thing."' When he caught up with them, he repeated a

7 this to them, but they replied, 'My lord, how can you say
such things? No, sir, God forbid that we should do any

8 such thing! You remember the silver we found at the top
of our packs? We brought it back to you from Canaan
Why should we steal silver or gold from your master'

9 house? If any one of us is found with the goblet, he shal
die; and, what is more, my lord, we will all become you

10 slaves.' He said, 'Very well, then; I accept what you say.
The man in whose possession it is found shall be my slave,

11 but the rest of you shall go free.' Each man quickly

12 lowered his pack to the ground and opened it. The

[a] Why...goblet?: *so Sept.; Heb. om.*

steward searched them, beginning with the eldest and finishing with the youngest, and the goblet was found in Benjamin's pack.

At this they rent their clothes; then each man loaded his 13 ass and they returned to the city. Joseph was still in the 14 house when Judah and his brothers came in. They threw themselves on the ground before him, and Joseph said, 15 'What have you done? You might have known that a man like myself would practise divination.' Judah said, 16 'What shall we say, my lord? What can we say to prove our innocence? God has found out our sin. Here we are, my lord, ready to be made your slaves, we ourselves as well as the one who was found with the goblet.' Joseph 17 answered, 'God forbid that I should do such a thing! The one who was found with the goblet shall become my slave, but the rest of you can go home to your father in peace.'

Then Judah went up to him and said, 'Please listen, my 18 lord. Let me say a word to your lordship, I beg. Do not be angry with me, for you are as great as Pharaoh. You, 19 my lord, asked us whether we had a father or a brother. We answered, "We have an aged father, and he has a 20 young son born in his old age; this boy's full brother is dead and he alone is left of his mother's children,[a] he alone, and his father loves him." Your lordship answered, 21 "Bring him down to me so that I may set eyes on him." We told you, my lord, that the boy could not leave his 22 father, and that his father would die if he left him. But 23 you answered, "Unless your youngest brother comes here with you, you shall not enter my presence again." We went back to your servant our father, and told him 24

[a] Or, *with one form of Sept.*, to his father.

25 what your lordship had said. When our father told us to
26 go and buy food, we answered, "We cannot go down; for without our youngest brother we cannot enter the man's presence; but if our brother is with us, we will go."
27 Our father, my lord, then said to us, "You know that my
28 wife bore me two sons. One left me, and I said, 'He must have been torn to pieces.' I have not seen him to this day.
29 If you take this one from me as well, and he comes to any harm, then you will bring down my grey hairs in trouble
30 to the grave."[a] Now, my lord, when I return to my father without the boy—and remember, his life is bound
31 up with the boy's—what will happen is this: he will see that the boy is not with us[b] and will die, and your servants will have brought down our father's grey hairs in
32 sorrow to the grave.[a] Indeed, my lord, it was I who went surety for the boy to my father. I said, "If I do not bring him back to you, then you shall hold me guilty all my
33 life." Now, my lord, let me remain in place of the boy as your lordship's slave, and let him go with his brothers.
34 How can I return to my father without the boy? I could not bear to see the misery which my father would suffer.'

✳ 1–12. The trap is sprung. At daybreak the brothers set off for home, but they do not get very far. Their money has again been put back into their sacks, but in addition Joseph's silver goblet has been planted in Benjamin's sack. Not far from the city they are overtaken by an irate steward. How dare they steal his master's goblet! The missing goblet is found in Benjamin's sack and he must remain in Egypt as a slave; the others are free to return home. How will they react?

[a] *Heb.* Sheol.   [b] with us: *so Sam.; Heb. om.*

2. *my goblet, my silver goblet:* as verse 5 makes clear, the
gnificance of the silver goblet lies not in its intrinsic value,
ut in the fact that it had a sacred function; it was used for
vining. Mechanical means of attempting to read the future
ere commonplace in the ancient world. Divination by means
f liquids seems to have been particularly popular in Mesopot-
nia. Mix a drop of oil with water or drop a small object
to water in a cup, and see the future in the resultant patterns.
he penalty for the theft of a goblet used for such a sacred
urpose would normally be death.

5. The Septuagint addition at the beginning of this verse,
Vhy have you stolen the silver goblet? (see the N.E.B. footnote),
arifies the meaning though it is not strictly necessary.
)seph and his steward would presumably know what the *it*
to which they are referring. *he uses for divination:* again,
ithout comment, the narrative attributes to Joseph a prac-
ce which is rigorously forbidden in later Israel. Israel is not
) tolerate in her midst 'augur or soothsayer or diviner or
)rcerer' (Deut. 18: 10).

9. The brothers are so sure of their innocence – based on
1eir past record of returning the silver found in their sacks –
1at they themselves propose the extreme penalty. He who
as absconded with the goblet *shall die*, the rest will *all become
)ur slaves*.

10. The steward modifies the penalty. Joseph has no inter-
st in harming Benjamin; he wishes to place the brothers in
situation roughly parallel to that in which they dealt with
im. Will they be prepared to leave Benjamin behind as
slave in Egypt, and return, minus their youngest brother,
) their father?

13. *they rent their clothes:* see the note on 37: 29.

16. *our sin:* literally 'the sin (or guilt) of your servants';
.milarly in verse 18 'me' is literally 'your servant', and in
erse 19 'us' is 'his servants' (see the note on 43: 28). Judah,
)eaking on behalf of the others, now expresses his total
ewilderment. They are in the hands of a fate they cannot

understand, and against which they cannot argue. They can only accept the verdict of guilty: *God has found out our sin.*

17. In context, *in peace* must mean something like 'unharmed' or 'safe and sound'.

18–34. Judah's long and masterly speech prepares the way for reconciliation. It would be unwise to read too much into the ways in which Judah's account of the first interview with Joseph differs from that found in 42: 7–17. The interest in the story has shifted. Everything now focusses on Benjamin and the shattering effect upon his father if anything should happen to this 'young son, born in his old age' (verse 20). Judah's speech hinges on two main points. The first, greatly daring, is a criticism of the all-powerful Egyptian, and an appeal to him to reconsider his decision. The moving description of Benjamin's place in his father's affections; the extreme hesitation with which Jacob had yielded to the demand to take Benjamin to Egypt; the fatal effect of Benjamin's non-return on an old man to whom life had already dealt a bitter blow in the disappearance of his favourite son Joseph – all this is designed to show the Egyptian lord that his demand to keep Benjamin is, in the circumstances, unreasonable, cruelly unreasonable. Judah, however, recognizes that the demand of justice must be met; so, secondly, he offers to take Benjamin's place, to remain in Egypt as a slave, while the others return home. Only so could he be true to the promise he had made to his father, to go surety for Benjamin's safe return. Break that promise and he could never face his father again. No more need be said. Judah's words show how completely the brothers have changed, and it is a measure of that change that his speech evokes our sympathy. It remains now for the Egyptian lord to reveal his true identity, and for the family to be reunited.

18. *for you are as great as Pharaoh*: as far as the brothers are concerned, this official is the equal of Pharaoh, in so far as he has absolute power to decide their fate.

20. It would be unwise to follow one form of the Septua-

gint text and eliminate from this verse the reference to *his mother's children* (see the N.E.B. footnote). As verse 27 makes clear, the particular hurt in the situation is that Joseph and Benjamin were the sole children of Rachel, Jacob's favourite wife. This is also the justification for the N.E.B. rendering the word 'brother' as *full brother* in this context.

27. *Our father, my lord:* see the note on 43: 28.

28. For the first time the brothers reveal to Joseph something of the deep and long-lasting hurt that the report of his death had inflicted on their father. *One left me:* or 'one went out from me'. Perhaps the sense of finality and resignation implied in these simple words would be better conveyed in English by 'One was taken from me.'

29. *to the grave:* see the note on 37: 35.

31. *the boy is not with us: with us*, the reading of the Samaritan text (see the N.E.B. footnote) is not strictly necessary. The Hebrew could be rendered 'the boy is missing'.

34. The transformation of Judah is complete. The man who once returned to his father without Joseph, no longer has the heart to return to his father *without the boy*, Benjamin.   ✶

JOSEPH REVEALS HIS IDENTITY

Joseph could no longer control his feelings in front of his **45** attendants, and he called out, 'Let everyone leave my presence.' So there was nobody present when Joseph made himself known to his brothers, but so loudly did he 2 weep that the Egyptians and Pharaoh's household heard him. Joseph said to his brothers, 'I am Joseph; can my 3 father be still alive?' His brothers were so dumbfounded at finding themselves face to face with Joseph that they could not answer. Then Joseph said to his brothers, 'Come 4 closer', and so they came close. He said, 'I am your brother Joseph whom you sold into Egypt. Now do not 5 be distressed or take it amiss that you sold me into slavery here; it was God who sent me ahead of you to save men's

6 lives. For there have now been two years of famine in the country, and there will be another five years with neither

7 ploughing nor harvest. God sent me ahead of you to ensure that you will have descendants on earth, and to preserve

8 you all, a great band of survivors. So it was not you who sent me here, but God, and he has made me a father[a] to Pharaoh, and lord over all his household and ruler of all

9 Egypt. Make haste and go back to my father and give him this message from his son Joseph: "God has made me lord

10 of all Egypt. Come down to me; do not delay. You shall live in the land of Goshen and be near me, you, your sons and your grandsons, your flocks and herds and all that

11 you have. I will take care of you there, you and your household and all that you have, and see that you are not reduced to poverty; there are still five years of famine to

12 come." You can see for yourselves, and so can my brother Benjamin, that it is Joseph himself who is speaking to you.

13 Tell my father of all the honour which I enjoy in Egypt, tell him all you have seen, and make haste to bring him

14 down here.' Then he threw his arms round his brother Benjamin and wept, and Benjamin too embraced him

15 weeping. He kissed all his brothers and wept over them, and afterwards his brothers talked with him.

16　When the report that Joseph's brothers had come reached Pharaoh's house, he and all his courtiers were

17 pleased. Pharaoh said to Joseph, 'Say to your brothers: "This is what you are to do. Load your beasts and go to

18 Canaan. Fetch your father and your households and bring

[a] *Or* counsellor.

them to me. I will give you the best that there is in Egypt, and you shall enjoy the fat of the land." You shall also tell 19 them:[a] "Take wagons from Egypt for your dependants and your wives and fetch your father and come. Have no 20 regrets at leaving your possessions, for all the best that there is in Egypt is yours."' The sons of Israel did as they 21 were told, and Joseph gave them wagons, according to Pharaoh's orders, and food for the journey. He provided 22 each of them with a change of clothing, but to Benjamin he gave three hundred pieces of silver and five changes of clothing. Moreover he sent his father ten asses carrying the 23 best that there was in Egypt, and ten she-asses loaded with grain, bread, and provisions for his journey. So he dis- 24 missed his brothers, telling them not to quarrel among themselves on the road, and they set out. Thus they went 25 up from Egypt and came to their father Jacob in Canaan. There they gave him the news that Joseph was still alive 26 and that he was ruler of all Egypt. He was stunned and could not believe it, but they told him all that Joseph had 27 said; and when he saw the wagons which Joseph had sent to take him away, his spirit revived. Israel said, 'It is 28 enough. Joseph my son is still alive; I will go and see him before I die.'

* 1–15. It is almost superfluous to comment on this reconciliation scene. So much in the story that the brothers could not understand has been leading to this moment. The high Egyptian official, whose actions have puzzled them, is revealed as none other than the brother they had once sold into slavery.

1. *Joseph could no longer control his feelings:* the third and final time this happens. Whereas, on the two previous occasions (42: 24; 43: 30), Joseph had to take steps to conceal

[a] *So Sept.; Heb.* You are commanded.

his true feelings from his brothers, now he asks his Egyptian *attendants* to withdraw, so that in the privacy of a family gathering he may reveal his identity.

3. *can my father be still alive?*: for Joseph an all-important question. True, the brothers had repeatedly claimed to have an aged father, but Joseph wishes to be reassured that the father, who was already old when Joseph was sold into slavery, is in fact still alive. *His brothers were so dumbfounded*: the idea of confusion or dismay is often present in the Hebrew word translated *dumbfounded*. To see again a long-lost brother is surprise enough, but to see again the brother they had once sold into slavery now in a position of power in Egypt, must have added an uneasy edge to their surprise. Joseph's first concern, therefore, is to reassure them.

5. *it was God who sent me ahead of you to save men's lives*: without minimizing the brothers' part in what had happened (*you sold me into slavery here*), Joseph, four times over – see verses 7, 8 and 9 – emphasizes that God had been working in and through what the brothers had done, and working with a constructive purpose.

6. *neither ploughing nor harvest*: the famine had already such a tight grip on the country, that all agricultural work, even *ploughing* had been given up as futile.

7. *descendants on earth...a great band of survivors*: the N.E.B. translation assumes that the reference is purely to physical survival; but the word translated *descendants* can also be rendered 'remnant'. The idea of a remnant and survivors who will live through tragedy and the judgement of God to become the nucleus of a continuing religious community, the people of God, is found elsewhere in the Old Testament – see the story of Noah, Gen. 6–8, and Isa. 37: 32. Joseph's presence in Egypt is thus God's way of ensuring that the pilgrimage of faith, which began with the promises God made to Abraham, will not come to a premature end.

8. *a father to Pharaoh*: among the many grandiose titles which the Egyptian vizier, Ptah-hotep (about 2450 B.C.)

pplied to himself was that of 'father to God', i.e. the god-
ing, see *A.N.E.T.* (see p. 317), p. 412. The title may well
idicate a man who regards himself as chief counsellor to
haraoh (see the N.E.B. footnote). *lord over all his household:*
robably a title equivalent to Lord Chamberlain.

9. *give him this message from his son Joseph:* literally 'thus
ys your son Joseph'. For this characteristic formula intro-
ucing a message or letter see the note on 32: 4.

10. *You shall live in the land of Goshen:* Goshen is the district
t the eastern end of the Wadi Tumilat, east of the Nile
etween Port Said and Suez (see map p. xiii). If the phrase *be
ear me* implies that the Egyptian capital was at this period in
ie Nile delta, then this would be one reason for setting the
:ory of Joseph in the period when Egypt was ruled by
siatic foreigners, known as the Hyksos, about 1770–1550
.c. They, unlike earlier native Egyptian dynasties, established
ieir capital at Avaris in the Delta region. That groups of
:ibesmen were admitted into the district of Goshen in times
f famine is confirmed by a report from an Egyptian frontier
fficial in this district, written towards the end of the thirteenth
entury B.C.: '[We] have finished letting the Bedouin tribes
f Edom pass the fortress... to the pools of Per-Atum...to
.eep them alive and to keep their cattle alive' (*A.N.E.T.*
;ee p. 317), p. 259).

11. Jacob's going to Egypt is carefully motivated. It is at
oseph's urgent request, and in a situation of extreme and
ontinuing famine, that he is to contemplate going. Only
uch factors could justify his leaving Canaan, the land pro-
nised to Abraham and his descendants (see 12: 10). Joseph's
equest is backed up in verses 16–20 by Pharaoh's command.

14. The outward expression of emotion is always much
nore open and intense in the East than in Western society.
t would not, in any way, be considered unmanly or inappro-
riate for Joseph and Benjamin to be *weeping.*

15. *and afterwards his brothers talked with him:* tantalizingly,
'et typically, the narrative does not tell us what they talked

about. But if the chronological data in the narrative are to be trusted, they had almost twenty years of news to share.

16–28. It is Pharaoh who now commands the brothers to bring their father and families to settle in Egypt, and to enjoy 'the best that there is in Egypt' (verse 18) – ironically, for their descendants Egypt was to become 'the land of slavery' (Exod. 20: 2), and another Pharoah refuses to let them leave, thus setting the scene for the key event in Israel's religious history, the exodus.

19. *You shall also tell them:* since the *You* in the Hebrew text is singular, the Hebrew 'You are commanded' (see the N.E.B. footnote) can only refer to Joseph being commanded by Pharaoh. But in context this makes no sense. The Septuagint reading, *You shall also tell them*, literally 'you command them' gives the required meaning.

22. *a change of clothing:* Revised Standard Version, 'festal garments'. Although the meaning of the Hebrew word is not certain, it probably indicates expensive garments which would be worn in place of ordinary clothes on important occasions. Joseph makes no pretence of concealing his particular affection for his full brother Benjamin. He receives *three hundred pieces of silver and five changes of clothing*, just as at the banquet he had received five portions.

23. Jacob had sent the brothers to Egypt with a small, but appropriate, gift for the high official of 'the produce for which our country is famous' (43: 11): he receives in return *ten asses* laden with *the best that there was in Egypt*.

24. *telling them not to quarrel among themselves on the road:* the time for recrimination is over, the past is buried. Any attempt to assign blame for the errors of the past must therefore be scotched. This may also be the reason why, when the brothers tell Jacob about Joseph, they make no confession of their guilt, nor does Jacob have any word of censure to say to them.

26–7. The news that his long-lost son, Joseph, is not only alive, but ruler of all Egypt, is almost too much for Jacob

He was stunned, literally, 'his heart fainted', or as we should say 'he almost died of shock'. It is only when he sees the tangible evidence of Joseph's concern, *the wagons which Joseph had sent to take him* down to Egypt, that *his spirit revived*, that is, his vigour and vitality returned.

28. *It is enough*: Jacob's sole remaining ambition, an ambition he never expected to see fulfilled, can now be satisfied: *I will go and see him* (i.e. Joseph) *before I die.* ✷

JACOB SETS OUT FOR EGYPT

So Israel set out with all that he had and came to Beer- **46** sheba where he offered sacrifices to the God of his father Isaac. God said to Israel in a vision by night, 'Jacob, 2 Jacob', and he answered, 'I am here.' God said, 'I am 3 God, the God of your father. Do not be afraid to go down to Egypt, for there I will make you a great nation. I will 4 go down with you to Egypt, and I myself will bring you back again without fail; and Joseph shall close your eyes.' So Jacob set out from Beersheba. Israel's sons conveyed 5 their father Jacob, their dependants, and their wives in the wagons which Pharaoh had sent to carry them.

✷ Joseph has requested, Pharaoh has commanded, but more than human motivation is needed to justify Jacob leaving the promised land to go to Egypt. In a previous situation of famine, Isaac had been specifically warned by God not to go down to Egypt (26: 1–6). There is, therefore, inserted at this point into the Joseph story a brief episode – probably a blend of J and E material – which links us with the way in which the other patriarchal traditions are presented: God appears to Jacob in a night vision.

1. *So Israel set out*: the assumption seems to be that Israel's point of departure is Hebron, where he was at the beginning

of the Joseph story (37: 14). *to Beersheba where he offered sacrifices to the God of his father Isaac:* compare 26: 23-4 where the LORD appears to Isaac at Beersheba, and thus guarantees its importance and sanctity as a place of worship.

2. *Jacob, Jacob...I am here:* see the note on 22: 1.

3. *I am God, the God of your father:* see the notes on 26: 24; 32: 9-12. *I will make you a great nation:* part of the promise made to Abraham at the moment when he left his home country to journey to Canaan (12: 2). It is repeated now to Jacob at the moment of his leaving Canaan, as if to say that this leaving of Canaan is part of God's purposes, and in no way a negation of the promise made to Abraham.

4. *I will go down with you to Egypt:* recalling God's promise to Jacob, 'I will be with you', as Jacob once fearfully set out for Paddan-aram (28: 15). *I myself will bring you back again without fail:* although 50: 12-13 describes how Jacob's sons bring his body back to Canaan for burial in the family grave, it is likely that in the mind of the narrator Jacob/Israel is not merely an individual, but the nation which lived on bearing his name. These words, therefore, point forward to the exodus and the subsequent settlement of the tribes in Canaan. *and Joseph shall close your eyes:* a reference to the widespread custom of closing the eyes of the dead. It implies that there will be no further separation from his favourite son Joseph, who will be there even at the end to ensure that everything is done appropriately. *

JACOB'S FAMILY

6 They took the herds and the stock which they had acquired in Canaan and came to Egypt, Jacob and all
7 his descendants with him, his sons and their sons, his daughters and his sons' daughters: he brought all his descendants to Egypt.

These are the names of the Israelites who entered 8[a]
Egypt: Jacob and his sons, as follows: Reuben, Jacob's
eldest son. The sons of Reuben: Enoch, Pallu, Hezron and 9
Carmi. The sons of Simeon: Jemuel, Jamin, Ohad, 10
Jachin, Zohar, and Saul, who was the son of a Canaanite
woman. The sons of Levi: Gershon, Kohath and Merari. 11
The sons of Judah: Er, Onan, Shelah, Perez and Zerah; of 12
these Er and Onan died in Canaan. The sons of Perez were
Hezron and Hamul.[b] The sons of Issachar: Tola, Pua, Iob 13
and Shimron. The sons of Zebulun: Sered, Elon and 14
Jahleel. These are the sons of Leah whom she bore to 15
Jacob in Paddan-aram, and there was also his daughter
Dinah. His sons and daughters numbered thirty-three in
all.

The sons of Gad: Ziphion, Haggi, Shuni, Ezbon, Eri, 16
Arodi and Areli. The sons of Asher: Imnah, Ishvah, Ishvi, 17
Beriah, and their sister Serah. The sons of Beriah: Heber
and Malchiel. These are the descendants of Zilpah whom 18
Laban gave to his daughter Leah; sixteen in all, born to
Jacob.

The sons of Jacob's wife Rachel: Joseph and Benjamin. 19
Manasseh and Ephraim were born to Joseph in Egypt. 20
Asenath daughter of Potiphera priest of On bore them to
him. The sons of Benjamin: Bela, Becher and Ashbel; and 21
the sons of Bela:[c] Gera, Naaman, Ehi, Rosh, Muppim,
Huppim and Ard. These are the descendants of Rachel; 22
fourteen in all, born to Jacob.

[a] *Verses 8–25: cp. Exod. 6: 14–16; Num. 26: 5–50; 1 Chron. 4: 1, 24;*
5: 3; 6: 1; 7: 1, 6, 13, 30; 8: 1–5.
[b] *Or, with Sam.*, Hamuel.
[c] and the sons of Bela: *so Sept. (cp. 1 Chron. 8: 3); Heb. om.*

23, 24   The son[a] of Dan: Hushim. The sons of Naphtali:
25   Jahzeel, Guni, Jezer and Shillem. These are the descendants of Bilhah whom Laban gave to his daughter Rachel;
seven in all, born to Jacob.

26   The persons belonging to Jacob who came to Egypt, all
his direct descendants, not counting the wives of his sons,
27   were sixty-six in all. Two sons were born to Joseph in
Egypt. Thus the house of Jacob numbered seventy[b] when
it entered Egypt.

✳   After a brief introduction (verses 6–7), the P tradition
presents a list of the names of the family of Jacob at the time
when they entered Egypt. Such lists are used for two purposes: first, to summarize what is known about the peoples
descended from characters who are not central to the main
theme of Genesis – thus we have the lists of the sons of
Ishmael (25: 12–18) and the sons of Esau (chapter 36) – and,
secondly, to mark significant transition points in the life of
Israel. Thus the list of the descendants of Shem (11: 10–32)
leads into the call of Abraham, and the beginning of the
patriarchal pilgrimage, while here Jacob's sons are listed at a
point which is to mark the opening of a new chapter in that
story, the entry into Egypt. Num. 26: 5–50 gives us basically
the same list, with added detail, on the other side of the exodus,
a list of 'the Israelites who came out of Egypt' (Num. 26: 4).
In addition to Num. 26: 5–50, the information given here is
embedded in more detailed material in 1 Chron. 4: 1–8: 5, and
partly repeated in Exod. 6: 14–16, which lists the sons of
Reuben, Simeon and Levi. For a detailed discussion of the
relationship between these lists, and the often minor variations
in the form of the names listed, a larger commentary should
be consulted.

[a] Prob. rdg.; Heb. sons.   [b] Or, with Sept., seventy-five.

There are, however, several more general points about this list worth noting:

(i) The list has obviously been inserted into the narrative at this point; verse 28 being the natural continuation of verse 5.

(ii) The list does not exactly coincide with what is referred to in verse 7 as Jacob's 'sons and their sons, his daughters and his sons' daughters'. Only one daughter, Dinah, is listed (verse 15), and one grand-daughter, Serah (verse 17).

(iii) The number 'seventy' (verse 27) is firmly fixed in Old Testament tradition as the number of the Israelites who settled in Egypt. Thus Deut. 10: 22: 'When your forefathers went down into Egypt, they were only seventy strong' (cp. Exod. 1: 5). This number is carefully adhered to in the present list; thirty-three descendants of Leah, sixteen from Zilpah, fourteen from Rachel, and seven from Bilhah, seventy in all. There are, however, difficulties in this. Although thirty-three sons, grandsons, and great-grandsons descended from Leah are listed in verses 8–15, two of them, Er and Onan, 'died in Canaan' (verse 12). The total thirty-three, as an element in the number seventy, can only be maintained by including the daughter, Dinah, and Jacob himself. But it hardly makes sense to include Jacob himself in a number which claims to represent his 'sons and daughters' (verse 15). Likewise, in verse 26 it is claimed that Jacob's direct descendants who came to Egypt were sixty-six in all. To get this number we are obviously expected to deduct from seventy, Joseph already in Egypt, his two sons born there, and again presumably Jacob. Thus Jacob again features in the number seventy, in direct contradiction to Exod. 1: 5 where the seventy more naturally refer to 'all direct descendants of Jacob'.

(iv) There are several points where the Septuagint text differs from the Hebrew, not only in giving variant forms of names, but in more substantial matters. Let us take two examples:

(a) In verse 21 the N.E.B. translation, minus the words 'and the sons of Bela' (see the N.E.B. footnote), fairly repre-

Joseph in Egypt

sents the Hebrew text. It thus attributes to Benjamin ten sons. I Chron. 8: 1–3, however, lists only five sons of Benjamin, only two of whom, Bela and Ashbel, have names similar to those given here. It then lists 'the sons of Bela', and includes among them Gera who is here listed as one of the sons of Benjamin. This is the justification for following the Septuagint text here: this reduces Benjamin's sons to three, adds the phrase 'and the sons of Bela', and then lists six grandsons and one great-grandson, Arad, son of Gera. Both the Hebrew and the Septuagint texts, however, imply that, at the time of entry into Egypt, Benjamin is a mature family man, which is hardly the impression given in the Joseph story where he is usually described as 'the boy' (43: 8; 44: 20) and it is assumed that he is still young. It hardly helps to discover another, different tradition about the sons of Benjamin in Num. 26: 38–41.

(b) In verse 27 where the Hebrew gives the standard number 'seventy', the Septuagint reads 'seventy-five'. The Septuagint number is the result of adding to verse 20 the names of five sons and grandsons of Ephraim and Manasseh, derived in the main from Num. 26: 28–37. It is this number, seventy-five, which is followed in Stephen's speech in Acts 7: 14. The whole question of lists of this kind and of their different forms is very complex; variations in such lists are common in the Bible and are also normal in other societies, ancient and modern, where interests in family lines reflect various concerns, political and social.

13. *Hamul:* the Samaritan-text form of this name, 'Hamuel', differs only slightly from the Hebrew. The corresponding passage in Num. 26: 21 reads 'Hamul'.

23. *The son of Dan:* in view of the fact that only one son, Hushim, is listed, it is preferable to change the Hebrew 'sons' to the singular *son:* 'sons' being an error which has crept into the text by analogy, since all the previous sections begin 'the sons of'. ✳

280

THE INTERVIEW WITH PHARAOH

Judah was sent ahead that he might appear[a] before Joseph 28
in Goshen, and so they entered Goshen. Joseph had his 29
chariot made ready and went up to meet his father Israel
in Goshen. When they met, he threw his arms round him
and wept, and embraced him for a long time, weeping.
Israel said to Joseph, 'I have seen your face again, and you 30
are still alive. Now I am ready to die.' Joseph said to his 31
brothers and to his father's household, 'I will go and tell
Pharaoh; I will say to him, "My brothers and my father's
household who were in Canaan have come to me."'
Now his brothers were shepherds, men with their own 32
flocks and herds, and they had brought them with them,
their flocks and herds and all that they possessed. So 33
Joseph said, 'When Pharaoh summons you and asks you
what your occupation is, you must say, "My lord, we 34
have been herdsmen all our lives, as our fathers were before us." You must say this if you are to settle in the land
of Goshen, because all shepherds are an abomination to
the Egyptians.'

Joseph came and told Pharaoh, 'My father and my **47**
brothers have arrived from Canaan, with their flocks and
their cattle and all that they have, and they are now in
Goshen.' Then he chose five of his brothers and presented 2
them to Pharaoh, who asked them what their occupation 3
was, and they answered, 'My lord, we are shepherds, we
and our fathers before us, and we have come to stay in this 4
land; for there is no pasture in Canaan for our sheep,
because the famine there is so severe. We beg you, my

[a] *So Sam.; Heb.* guide.

5 lord, to let us settle now in Goshen.' Pharaoh said to
Joseph, 'So your father and your brothers have come to
6 you. The land of Egypt is yours; settle them in the best
part of it. Let them live in Goshen, and if you know of any
capable men among them, make them chief herdsmen
over my cattle.'

7 Then Joseph brought his father in and presented him to
8 Pharaoh, and Jacob gave Pharaoh his blessing. Pharaoh
9 asked Jacob his age, and he answered, 'The years of my
earthly sojourn are one hundred and thirty; hard years
they have been and few, not equal to the years that my
10 fathers lived in their time.' Jacob then blessed Pharaoh and
11 went out from his presence. So Joseph settled his father
and his brothers, and gave them lands in Egypt, in the best
part of the country, in the district of Rameses, as Pharaoh
12 had ordered. He supported his father, his brothers, and all
his father's household with all the food they needed.[a]

✻ This section, which follows naturally from 46: 5, continues the J narrative of Jacob's journey to Egypt. It includes
a brief, but moving, account of Jacob's reunion with Joseph
(46: 29–30), and then seeks to explain through the medium of
an interview between five of Jacob's sons and Pharaoh why it
was that Jacob and his family settled in the region of Goshen.
There follows in 47: 7–12 a meeting between the aged patriarch
Jacob and Pharaoh. With its emphasis upon Jacob blessing
Pharaoh, and a subsequent settlement not in Goshen but 'in
the district of Rameses' (verse 11), this represents the P
account of Jacob's coming to Egypt.

28. As in chapter 43, Judah fulfils the link role between Jacob
and Joseph. He is sent ahead *that he might appear before Joseph
in Goshen.* This is the reading of the Samaritan text (see the

[a] *Lit.* with food to a drop.

N.E.B. footnote). The Hebrew text may be understood differently; Judah is sent to 'guide' Joseph, to show Joseph the way to the rendezvous with Jacob in Goshen.

29-30. The account of the meeting of father and son is effective in its restraint. We are given no hint as to what Joseph said to Jacob. The whole emphasis is upon this being the long-desired moment of fulfilment for Jacob.

30. *Now I am ready to die:* 47: 28, from the P source, assumes that he survives for another seventeen years, but it is natural to think that in the J source Jacob died soon after he met Joseph.

46: 31 – 47: 6. The interview with Pharaoh is stage-managed by Joseph. The brothers are carefully primed on what to say to ensure that Pharaoh will permit them to settle in Goshen. Settlement in such a sensitive frontier district was only likely on the assumption that they would be less acceptable elsewhere, nearer the great city centres of Egyptian life.

34. *My lord:* see the note on 43: 28. *herdsmen:* the Hebrew expression here is the same as that translated in verse 32 as 'men with their own flocks and herds'; perhaps 'keepers of livestock' would be better in both cases. *all shepherds are an abomination to the Egyptians:* there is no extant ancient Egyptian evidence to confirm this comment. It is not difficult, however, to imagine that the somewhat uncouth herdsmen coming in from the desert steppe would be regarded with a certain amount of contempt by the inhabitants of the Nile valley, accustomed to a very different way of life and a complex, highly developed civilization.

47: 2. *five of his brothers:* it is curious how the number five echoes across the Joseph story – 'one fifth of the produce of Egypt' (41: 34), 'five changes of clothing' (45: 22), Benjamin's portion 'five times larger' (43: 34), 'one fifth of the crop' to be given to Pharaoh (47: 24). Attempts have been made to link this to the significance of five in the Egyptian calendar or to certain Egyptian religious practices, but this is pure speculation.

5-6. These verses are awkward in context. The Septuagint reorders them in a way which makes much more sense. It reads, 'Pharaoh said to Joseph, "They may live in Goshen, and if you know of any capable men among them, make them chief over my herds."' This sentence provides a neat conclusion to the section 46: 28 – 47: 4. The Septuagint then continues, 'And Jacob and his sons came to Egypt to Joseph, and Pharaoh the king of Egypt heard it and said to Joseph, 'Your father and brothers have come to you. The land of Egypt is yours; settle them in the best part of it.' This makes a good introduction to verses 7–12, which say nothing of Goshen, but talk about 'the best part of the country, in the district of Rameses' (verse 11).

7. *Jacob gave Pharaoh his blessing:* this could mean no more than a formal greeting; just as in verse 10 'Jacob then blessed Pharaoh' might simply mean Jacob said goodbye to Pharaoh. In context, however, more is probably intended. The aged patriarch has something to bestow upon Pharaoh, which Pharaoh cannot give to him. Pharaoh may rule Egypt, but Jacob is the inheritor of God's promises and the fullness of life which goes with them.

9. *The years of my earthly sojourn are one hundred and thirty:* a purely factual statement. It is doubtful whether we should read too much into the word translated *earthly sojourn:* the same Hebrew word is used at the end of the verse and translated *lived.* Jacob is not moralizing about the brevity or transitoriness of human life. Abraham lived 175 years (25: 7), Isaac 180 (35: 28). Jacob, with his 130 years has therefore had comparatively few. They have also been *hard* or bad years, a fact to which Jacob's own shortcomings had contributed not a little.

11. *in the district of Rameses:* if the Joseph story is to be set in the Hyksos period, then this statement is an anachronism, since the Delta region did not have the name *Rameses* attached to it until the time of Rameses II in the thirteenth century B.C. (cp. Exod. 1: 11).

12. *with all the food they needed:* literally, 'with food to a drop' (see the N.E.B. footnote). The word interpreted as 'drop' can also mean 'descendants' or 'little children': hence the Revised Standard Version 'according to the number of

their dependants'. Perhaps we could render 'down to the very youngest'. ✻

JOSEPH'S LAND REFORMS

There was no bread in the whole country, so very severe 13 was the famine, and Egypt and Canaan were laid low by it. Joseph collected all the silver in Egypt and Canaan in 14 return for the corn which the people bought, and deposited it in Pharaoh's treasury. When all the silver in 15 Egypt and Canaan had been used up, the Egyptians came to Joseph and said, 'Give us bread, or we shall die before your eyes. Our silver is all spent.' Joseph said, 'If your 16 silver is spent, give me your herds and I will give you bread in return.' So they brought their herds to Joseph, 17 who gave them bread in exchange for their horses, their flocks of sheep and herds of cattle, and their asses. He maintained them that year with bread in exchange for their herds. The year came to an end, and the following 18 year they came to him again and said, 'My lord, we cannot conceal it from you: our silver is all gone and our herds of cattle are yours. Nothing is left for your lordship but our bodies and our lands. Why should we perish 19 before your eyes, we and our land as well? Take us and our land in payment for bread, and we and our land alike will be in bondage to Pharaoh. Give us seed-corn to keep us alive, or we shall die and our land will become desert.' So Joseph bought all the land in Egypt for Pharaoh, 20 because the Egyptians sold all their fields, so severe was the famine; the land became Pharaoh's. As for the people, 21 Pharaoh set them to work as slaves[a] from one end of the

[a] *So Sam.; Heb.* gathered them into the cities.

22 territory of Egypt to the other. But Joseph did not buy
the land which belonged to the priests; they had a fixed
allowance from Pharaoh and lived on this, so that they
had no need to sell their land.

23   Joseph said to the people, 'Listen; I have today bought
you and your land for Pharaoh. Here is seed-corn for
24 you. Sow the land, and give one fifth of the crop to
Pharaoh. Four fifths shall be yours to provide seed for
your fields and food for yourselves, your households, and
25 your dependants.' The people said, 'You have saved our
lives. If it please your lordship, we will be Pharaoh's
26 slaves.' Joseph established it as a law in Egypt that one fifth
should belong to Pharaoh, and this is still in force. It was
only the priests' land that did not pass into Pharaoh's
hands.

* The Hebrews seem to have been very interested in the way
in which life in Egypt was in many respects different from the
life to which they were accustomed. In particular the auto-
cratic power of Pharaoh was the subject of speculation. All
land – so it was believed – belonged to Pharaoh. The Egyptians were little better than landless serfs, subject to heavy
taxation, the only exception to this being the priesthood.
Such was the situation which existed in his day, claims the J
narrator: it was 'still in force' (verse 26). And the reason for it
was Joseph! The steps Joseph took during the years of famine
were directly responsible for the Egyptian land system. To
begin with Joseph sold grain for money (verses 14–15); then,
when money was exhausted, the people traded in their livestock in exchange for food (verses 16–17). Ultimately, their
livestock gone, the people were forced to sell their land and
themselves to purchase seed corn (verses 18–19). From then on,
with the exception of the priests, all were serfs who annually
gave one fifth of their crops to Pharaoh (verses 23–5).

It is doubtful whether there is any point in trying to glean from Egyptian sources the date of the introduction into Egypt of such a system of land tenure, and thus find evidence for dating the Joseph story. Did the writer have any detailed knowledge of Egyptian land tenure, or was he just basing his story on general impressions? In theory all land in Egypt seems to have belonged to Pharaoh from time immemorial. That, however, never seems to have excluded private ownership of land; nor is there any evidence for a period when the entire population, with the exception of the priests, were serfs. Many Egyptians in all periods were serfs, and no doubt to a Hebrew lacking detailed knowledge of Egyptian life, all of them may have seemed to be so. But why trace this system of land tenure back to Joseph? It could be that to the writer this is but another illustration of Joseph's wisdom and political skill. It is also possible, however, that he is taking an ironic delight in tracing to Joseph a system which made slaves of the Egyptians, in the land in which the Hebrews themselves were to be slaves.

13. The words *and Canaan* do not make much sense either here or in verses 14 and 15. The passage is concerned solely with conditions in Egypt where Jacob's family is now settled. The words *and Canaan* were probably added to stress the link with the rest of the Joseph story, the plot of which depends upon famine affecting not only Egypt but also the surrounding countries, including Canaan.

18. *The year came to an end, and the following year:* we are not told which years in the seven-year period these are; nor should we try to manufacture chronology in an account which is vividly portraying the increasing pressures on the Egyptians.

21. *Pharaoh set them to work as slaves:* the subject of this sentence could equally well be Joseph. The Hebrew text does not state that Joseph – or Pharaoh at Joseph's instigation - set them to work as slaves; that is the reading of the Samaritan and Septuagint texts. The Hebrew says 'he gathered them into the cities' (see the N.E.B. footnote), as if to suggest that the

people were forced to move from the countryside into the cities where the granaries were. This involves redistribution of population and the dispossession of the farmers. Either way their status is lowered. Could there be here an analogy to prophetic criticism of those 'who add house to house and join field to field' (Isa. 5: 8)?

22. The priesthood in Egypt often wielded immense power, political as well as religious, since the Egyptian state was a theocracy with the living Pharaoh the incarnation of the supreme god. The priests, particularly at important religious centres such as Heliopolis and Thebes, had to be handled circumspectly by Pharaoh. Several Egyptian royal decrees, granting the temples immunity from civil obligations, have survived; see *A.N.E.T.* (see p. 317), p. 212. This verse implies that the priests were in receipt of *a fixed allowance* from Pharaoh, a sort of tax-free bounty, which enabled them to buy the necessary food, without resorting to selling their land.

24. *one fifth of the crop to Pharaoh:* not an exorbitant demand for an eastern autocrat to make. According to 1 Macc. 10: 30 King Demetrius tried to win the favour of the Jews by exempting them from a tax system which demanded one third of their grain and one half of their fruit.

25. A Hebrew reader could hardly fail to ponder upon the irony in this verse. The Egyptians come willingly to be slaves, because *You* (Joseph) *have saved our lives* or 'kept us alive'. The Hebrews were to be saved, and find new life, when their God, the LORD, delivered them from slavery in Egypt.   *

JACOB PREPARES FOR DEATH

27 Thus Israel settled in Egypt, in Goshen; there they acquired land, and were fruitful and increased greatly.
28 Jacob stayed in Egypt for seventeen years and lived to be
29 a hundred and forty-seven years old. When the time of

his[a] death drew near, he summoned his son Joseph and said to him, 'If I may now claim this favour from you, put your hand under my thigh and swear by the LORD[b] that you will deal loyally and truly with me and not bury me in Egypt. When I die like my forefathers, you shall 30 carry me from Egypt and bury me in their grave.' He answered, 'I will do as you say'; but Jacob said, 'Swear it.' 31 So he swore the oath, and Israel sank down over the end of the bed.[c]

The time came when Joseph was told that his father **48** was ill, so he took with him his two sons, Manasseh and Ephraim. Jacob heard that his son Joseph was coming to 2 him, and he[d] summoned his strength and sat up on the bed. Jacob said to Joseph, 'God Almighty appeared to me 3 at Luz in Canaan and blessed me. He said to me, "I will 4 make you fruitful and increase your descendants until they become a host of nations. I will give this land to your descendants after you as a perpetual possession." Now, 5 your two sons, who were born to you in Egypt before I came here, shall be counted as my sons; Ephraim and Manasseh shall be mine as Reuben and Simeon are. Any 6 children born to you after them shall be counted as yours, but in respect of their tribal territory they shall be reckoned under their elder brothers' names. As I was 7 coming from Paddan-aram[e] I was bereaved of Rachel your mother[f] on the way, in Canaan, whilst there was still

[a] *Heb.* Israel's.
[b] and...LORD: *prob. rdg., cp. Pesh.; Heb. om.*
[c] *Or, with Sept.,* top of his staff (*cp. Heb.* 11: 21).
[d] *Heb.* Israel. [e] *So Sam.; Heb.* Paddan.
[f] your mother: *so Sam.; Heb. om.*

some distance to go to Ephrath,*a* and I buried her there by the road to Ephrath,*a* that is Bethlehem.'

8   When Israel saw Joseph's sons, he said, 'Who are these?' Joseph replied to his father, 'They are my sons whom God has given me here.' Israel said, 'Bring them to me, I beg you, so that I may take them on my knees.'*b*

10 Now Israel's eyes were dim with age, and he could not see; so Joseph brought the boys close to his father, and he

11 kissed them and embraced them. He said to Joseph, 'I had not expected to see your face again, and now God has

12 granted me to see your sons also.' Joseph took them from

13 his father's knees and bowed to the ground. Then he took the two of them, Ephraim on his right at Israel's left and Manasseh on his left at Israel's right, and brought them

14 close to him. Israel stretched out his right hand and laid it on Ephraim's head, although he was the younger, and, crossing his hands, laid his left hand on Manasseh's head;

15 but Manasseh was the elder. He blessed Joseph and said:

'The God in whose presence my forefathers lived,
  my forefathers Abraham and Isaac,
    the God who has been my shepherd all my life
      until this day,

16   the angel who ransomed me from all misfortune,
      may he bless these boys;
    they shall be called by my name,
      and by that of my forefathers, Abraham and Isaac;
    may they grow into a great people on earth.'

17 When Joseph saw that his father was laying his right hand

[a] *Or, with Sam. (cp. 35: 16, 19)*, Ephrathah.
[b] *Or* may bless them.

on Ephraim's head, he was displeased; so he took hold of
his father's hand to move it from Ephraim's head to
Manasseh's. He said, 'That is not right, my father. This is 18
the elder; lay your right hand on his head.' But his father 19
refused; he said, 'I know, my son, I know. He too shall
become a people; he too shall become great, but his
younger brother shall be greater than he, and his descendants shall be a whole nation in themselves.' That 20
day he blessed them and said:

> 'When a blessing is pronounced in Israel,
>   men shall use your names[a] and say,
> God make you like Ephraim and Manasseh',

thus setting Ephraim before Manasseh. Then Israel said to 21
Joseph, 'I am dying. God will be with you and will bring
you back to the land of your fathers. I give you one ridge 22
of land[b] more than your brothers: I took it from the
Amorites with my sword and my bow.'

* Jacob is approaching death. Just as Abraham and Isaac
were concerned to ensure that what they had received from
God – symbolized by the words 'promise' and 'blessing' –
should be handed on into the future, so Jacob takes steps to
pass the blessing on to Joseph and Joseph's sons. The overlaps
and the breaks in continuity within this section are most easily
explained on the assumption that all three sources J, E and P
had their own accounts of the close of Jacob's life. Thus 47:
29–30 read like a death-bed scene, introduced by the words
'When the time of Israel's death drew near' (see the N.E.B.
footnote). The version of 48: 1–2 is similar, and introduced by

[a] *So Sept.; Heb. has the singular.*
[b] ridge of land: *Heb.* shechem, *meaning* shoulder.

a reference to Jacob's last illness; it features Joseph's two sons, Manasseh and Ephraim, and finds its logical continuation in 48: 8 and the subsequent blessing pronounced upon Manasseh and Ephraim. This is interrupted, however, by 48: 3–6 which speak of the coming new status of Joseph's sons, this time introducing them in the order Ephraim and Manasseh. Notice also the curious and apparently unmotivated constant change between the names Israel and Jacob, e.g. Israel in 47: 27, Jacob in 47: 28, Israel in 47: 29 (see the N.E.B. footnote), Jacob and Israel in 47: 31, Jacob and Israel (see the N.E.B. footnote) in 48: 2.

It is usual to attribute to the P source 47: 27–8 and 48: 3–7; to the J source 47: 29–31; and to the E source 48: 1–2; and in 48: 8–22 to see a now indissoluble blend of material from J and E.

28. It is characteristic of the P source that it delights in chronological information, Jacob living to the age of *a hundred and forty-seven years*. This assumes that he lived in Egypt for seventeen years (cp. 47: 9). The J source depicts him as 'ready to die' (46: 30) once he meets Joseph, and this finds its natural continuation in verse 29.

29. For the significance of a solemn oath sworn with *hand under...thigh* see the note on 24: 2. *and swear by the LORD:* these words, found in the Peshitta text (see the N.E.B. footnote), bring out the meaning, but are not strictly necessary. The solemn, binding, religious character of the vow is indicated by the hand under the *thigh*, and by the words that immediately follow: *deal loyally and truly with me* (see the note on 20: 13).

30. Jacob wishes to be buried with his *forefathers*, Abraham, Isaac and their wives, in the family grave at Machpelah (see chapter 23). His return to Canaan in death is also intended to symbolize that, although his family may have to live temporarily in Egypt, their true home is Canaan, the promised land. The fulfilment of Jacob's request is described in 50: 1–13.

31. Joseph's assent, '*I will do as you say*' is not in itself

enough. He must solemnly swear *the oath*. The words of such
an oath are charged with power which, in the event of any
violation of the oath, will have terrifying consequences.
Israel sank down over the end of the bed: these words have long
been something of a puzzle. The Septuagint, by changing the
vowels in the Hebrew word, reads 'staff' instead of *bed* (see
the N.E.B. footnote), and thus depicts Israel as 'leaning on the
top of his staff'. This is how the passage is cited in the New
Testament in Heb. 11: 21. The real difficulty, however, is in
the verb *sank down*. Normally in the Old Testament it implies
an attitude of worship. It is not clear what is intended here: is
it an attitude expressing Israel's gratitude for Joseph's vow, or
does it indicate a reverent gesture in acknowledgement that
a religious act has taken place in the swearing of the oath?

48: 1. The introduction of Joseph's two sons, Manasseh and
Ephraim, in the correct order of precedence by birth, prepares
the way for the strange reversal of their positions, the precedence given to Ephraim over Manasseh, according to the
blessing Jacob gives them in 48: 14–19.

3–5. These verses recall and paraphrase the promise made
to Jacob on his return from Paddan-aram (see the notes on
35: 1–15). The new element is Joseph's two sons, Ephraim and
Manasseh, elevated to full status as Jacob's own sons. This
reflects something of the complex history of the twelve-tribe
federation which made up the people of Israel. The number
twelve remains more or less constant, but the names vary.
Gen. 35: 22–6 and 49 list the twelve sons of Jacob; in Num.
1: 5–15, however, one of them, Levi, has disappeared (see
Num. 1: 47–53) and the Joseph group is divided into two,
Ephraim and Manasseh. The political reality of the later tribal
situation is thus traced back to the dying actions of Jacob/Israel,
the eponymous ancestor of the nation.

6. The new status is to apply only to Ephraim and Manas-
seh, not to any other children Joseph may have. Curiously, the
Old Testament is silent about any other children born to
Joseph.

7. This brief note about the death and burial of Rachel (see 35: 16–20) is poorly related to its context, particularly if, with the Hebrew text, we do not read the words *your mother* (see the N.E.B. footnote). It has been suggested that the elevation of the two grandsons of Jacob's favourite wife Rachel, is intended to compensate for the fact that Rachel died leaving only two sons, and thus maintaining only a minority stake in the future twelve-tribe nation. This is how the Good News Bible paraphrases this verse, but it is doubtful whether this can be read into it. It is reasonable enough that somewhere in the context of Jacob's last days the death and burial of Rachel should be recalled. She alone of the leading figures in the patriarchal narratives was not buried in the family grave at Machpelah. She was, however, like all the others, buried in Canaan on the way to Ephrath (see the N.E.B. footnote and the note on 35: 16). What is not clear is why it appears at this point in Jacob's speech to Joseph. *Paddan-aram:* the Hebrew reading 'Paddan' is an abbreviated form, which the Samaritan text gives in its more usual form *Paddan-aram* (see the N.E.B. footnote).

8–22. The impression given in this account of Jacob's death-bed blessing of his grandsons, Ephraim and Manasseh, is that they are young boys, who sit on their grandfather's knee, and have to be lifted down by their father. This is inconsistent with P's statement in 47: 28 that Jacob lived in Egypt for seventeen years. In that case both Ephraim and Manasseh would have been at least twenty at Jacob's death (cp. 41: 50). Central to this incident is a theme which we have come across more than once in Genesis. However men act, and whatever they plan, God often furthers his purposes in strange ways and through unexpected people. Joseph carefully places his eldest son Manasseh on Jacob's right, so that he may be blessed by the more powerful and more auspicious right hand; Ephraim the younger is placed on the left. But the blind old man, sitting up in bed, uncannily crosses his hands, so that his right hand rest on Ephraim and his left on Manasseh. Joseph protests, only to be told that the old man is well aware of what he is doing. Ephraim is destined for a future greater than that of Manasseh. Did Jacob recall the time when another blind old man was tricked into giving his blessing to a younger son (see chapter 27)?

8. *When Israel saw Joseph's sons:* this is not necessarily inconsistent with verse 10 which speaks of Israel's eyes being 'dim with age, and he could not see': *saw* may merely mean 'noticed'. Israel could have been aware of their presence, and yet not able to see them clearly.

9. *so that I may take them on my knees:* most other English translations render 'so that I may bless them' (see the N.E.B. footnote). The words 'bless' and 'knee', however, are closely related in Hebrew. The justification for giving an unusual, technical meaning to the verb here lies in verse 12 which speaks of Joseph taking the boys off their grandfather's knees. To place a child on one's knees was to acknowledge paternity (see the note on 30: 3). In this case it indicates Jacob's solemn adoption of the Egyptian sons of Joseph, thus guaranteeing their status in his family (cp. verses 3–6).

13. *on his right...on his left:* see the note on 35: 18.

15–16. *He blessed Joseph and said:* the Septuagint text reads 'He blessed them' (i.e. Ephraim and Manasseh). This fits in better with the context and with the content of the blessing in verses 15–16, which is directed to 'these boys' (verse 16), rather than to Joseph. On the other hand, verse 20 contains a blessing on Ephraim and Manasseh. The Hebrew text, by addressing the first blessing to Joseph, avoids a double blessing on his children. If we follow the Hebrew text, as the N.E.B. does, then the blessing Joseph receives lies solely in the future of his sons.

This first blessing appears in poetic, almost hymn-like form; notice the balanced lines beginning *The God in whose presence ...the God who...the angel who...* It has three interrelated elements:

(i) it recalls the past: *The God in whose presence my fore-*

fathers lived – for the meaning of this expression see the note on
17: 1;

(ii) it speaks of what has been Jacob's personal experience,
describing God's relationship to him in two metaphors: God
as *my shepherd*, one of the common titles for a king in the
ancient Near East, but here probably emphasizing the guidance and protection Jacob has known (cp. Ps. 23); and God or
the angel (see the note on 16: 7) as the one *who ransomed me*, or
'who has acted as my *go'el*'. The Hebrew word *go'el* denotes
the nearest male next-of-kin, one of whose responsibilities was
the levirate marriage (see chapter 38) and another to buy back
the freedom of a brother who had fallen into slavery for debt
(cp. Lev. 25: 25–8). The word *go'el* was destined for a great
religious future when Old Testament writers used it to describe what God had done in delivering, redeeming, his
people out of slavery in Egypt (cp. e.g. Exod. 6: 6; Isa. 41: 14).
ransomed me from all misfortune may equally well be translated
'delivered me from all harm', and could refer to a wide
variety of situations in which God's liberating presence was
experienced;

(iii) it points to the future, and the coming from Joseph's
sons of *a great people on earth*, in fulfilment of the promises made
to Abraham and Isaac.
In this weaving together of past, present and future to form the
tapestry of God's purposes, this blessing is characteristic of
much of the religious thinking we find in the Old Testament.

19. *I know, my son, I know*: Jacob is well aware of correct
protocol; the elder son ought to have prior status, but Jacob
believes he is serving a higher purpose, a purpose in which the
younger brother shall be greater than the older – Isaac and
Ishmael, Jacob and Esau, now Ephraim and Manasseh. *his
descendants shall be a whole nation in themselves*: this anticipates
the situation in which the northern kingdom, with its capital
at Samaria, was often called Ephraim (see Hos. 5: 3; 7: 8).

20. *When a blessing is pronounced in Israel*: literally, 'in you
Israel will be blessed or will bless itself'; see the note on 12: 3.

your names: this is the reading of the Septuagint; the singular 'your name' of the Hebrew text (see the N.E.B. footnote) would have to refer to the composite name 'Ephraim and Manasseh' which others would use in asking a blessing for themselves.

21. *bring you back to the land of your fathers:* just as Jacob makes Joseph swear to take his body back to Canaan, so he expresses the same wish for Joseph. In 50: 25 Joseph, on the point of death, makes his brothers take a similar oath.

22. *I give you one ridge of land:* the word translated *ridge of land* means 'shoulder'. It is also the place-name Shechem (see the N.E.B. footnote). It is hard to see what this means unless it contains an oblique reference to the capture of Shechem (see map, p. xiv). If it does, it can hardly be the tradition about the capture of Shechem in chapter 34. Jacob did not there take Shechem *with my sword and my bow*. He expressed disapproval of the action of Simeon and Levi (34: 30). To translate *ridge of land* or 'mountain slope' (Revised Standard Version) solves no problems, since it leaves us asking, which ridge of land and to what incident does this refer. *the Amorites:* see the note on 15: 16. *

THE TESTAMENT OF JACOB

Jacob summoned his sons and said, 'Come near, and I will **49** tell you what will happen to you in days to come.

> Gather round me and listen, you sons of Jacob;   2
>   listen to Israel your father.
> Reuben, you are my first-born,   3
>   my strength and the first fruit of my vigour,
>   excelling in pride, excelling in might,
>   turbulent as a flood, you shall not excel;   4
>   because you climbed into your father's bed;
>   then you defiled his concubine's couch.

5   Simeon and Levi are brothers,
            their spades*a* became weapons of violence.

6   My soul shall not enter their council,
            my heart shall not join their company;
            for in their anger they killed men,
            wantonly they hamstrung oxen.

7   A curse be on their anger because it was fierce;
            a curse on their wrath because it was ruthless!
            I will scatter them in Jacob,
            I will disperse them in Israel.

8   Judah, your brothers shall praise you,
            your hand is on the neck of your enemies.
            Your father's sons shall do you homage.

9   Judah, you lion's whelp,
            you have returned from the kill, my son,
            and crouch and stretch like a lion;
            and, like a lion,*b* who dare rouse you*c*?

10   The sceptre shall not pass from Judah,
            nor the staff from his descendants,*d*
            so long as tribute is brought to him*e*
            and the obedience of the nations is his.

11   To the vine he tethers his ass,
            and the colt of his ass to the red vine;
            he washes his cloak in wine,
            his robes in the blood of grapes.

12   Darker than wine are his eyes,
            his teeth whiter than milk.

[a] *Heb. word of uncertain mng.*
[b] *Or* lioness.   [c] *Heb.* him.
[d] *Lit.* from between his feet.
[e] so...him; *or, as otherwise read,* until he comes to Shiloh.

Zebulun dwells by the sea-shore,   13
  his shore is a haven for ships,
  and his frontier rests on Sidon.

Issachar, a gelded*[a]* ass   14
  lying down in the cattle-pens,
  saw that a settled home was good   15
  and that the land was pleasant,
  so he bent his back to the burden
  and submitted to perpetual forced labour.

Dan—how insignificant his people,   16
  lowly as any tribe in Israel!*[b]*
  Let Dan be a viper on the road,   17
  a horned snake on the path,
  who bites the horse's fetlock
  so that the rider tumbles backwards.

  For thy salvation I wait in hope, O LORD.   18

Gad is raided by raiders,   19
  and he raids them from the rear.

Asher shall have rich food as daily fare,   20
  and provide dishes fit for a king.

Naphtali is a spreading terebinth   21
  putting forth lovely boughs.

Joseph is a fruitful tree*[c]* by a spring   22
  with branches climbing over the wall.
  The archers savagely attacked him,   23
  they shot at him and pressed him hard,
  but their bow was splintered by the Eternal   24

[a] *So Sam.; Heb.* bony.
[b] *Or* Dan shall judge his people as one of the tribes of Israel.
[c] *Or* a fruitful ben-tree.

and the sinews of their arms were torn apart[a]
by the power of the Strong One of Jacob,
by the name of the Shepherd[b] of Israel,
25   by the God of your father—so may he help you,
by God[c] Almighty—so may he bless you
with the blessings of heaven above,
the blessings of the deep that lurks below.
The blessings of breast and womb
26   and the blessings of your father are stronger
than the blessings of the everlasting pools[d]
and the bounty of the eternal hills.
They shall be on the head of Joseph,
on the brow of the prince among[e] his brothers.
27   Benjamin is a ravening wolf:
in the morning he devours the prey,
in the evening he snatches a share of the spoil.'

28   These, then, are the twelve tribes of Israel, and this is
what their father Jacob said to them, when he blessed
29 them each in turn. He gave them his last charge and said,
'I shall soon be gathered to my father's kin; bury me with
my forefathers in the cave on the plot of land which
30 belonged to Ephron the Hittite, that is the cave on the
plot of land at Machpelah east of Mamre in Canaan, the
field which Abraham bought from Ephron the Hittite for
31 a burial-place. There Abraham was buried with his wife
Sarah; there Isaac and his wife Rebecca were buried; and
32 there I buried Leah. The land and the cave on it were

[a] *Prob. rdg., cp. Sept.; Heb.* and the arms of his hands were active.
[b] *Prob. rdg.; Heb. adds* stone.
[c] *So Sam.; Heb.* with.   [d] *Or* hills.
[e] the prince among: *or* the one cursed by.

bought from the Hittites.' When Jacob had finished 33
giving his last charge to his sons, he drew his feet up on to
the bed, breathed his last, and was gathered to his father's
kin.

* This chapter begins and ends with Jacob's sons gathered
round his death-bed, listening to his words. Into this setting
there has been inserted a lengthy poem, verses 2–28, often
called 'The Blessing of Jacob' from the words of verse 28, in
which Jacob 'blessed them each in turn'. 'Blessing', however,
is hardly the appropriate word to use to describe the content of
certain sections in this poem, so let us refer to it more neutrally
as 'The Testament of Jacob'. It deals in turn with the twelve
sons of Jacob as listed in 35: 23–6, though in a slightly different
order. It is interested in them, however, not as individuals but
as tribes. 'These, then, are the twelve tribes of Israel' as verse
28 correctly states. We are dealing in this poem with a series of
very old cameos of tribal history. They vary considerably in
length, ranging all the way from the substantial sections on
Judah (verses 8–12) and Joseph (verses 22–6) to the brief two-
line statements about Gad, Asher and Naphtali (verses 19–21).
They vary in character. The section on Judah contains a
eulogy proclaiming future greatness; that on Joseph is deeply
religious and contains a noble blessing. Reuben, Simeon and
Levi, on the contrary, are roundly condemned. Other sections
express no value judgement at all, but are purely factual statements, such as Zebulun dwelling 'by the sea-shore' (verse 13).

The poem probably incorporates material of widely different date, ranging all the way from the early days of the
settlement in Canaan in the thirteenth century B.C. to the
emergence, over 200 years later, of the Davidic monarchy,
which seems to be presupposed by the section on Judah. It
invites comparison with other tribal poems in the Old Testament, such as the Song of Deborah in Judg. 5, and the
Blessing of Moses in Deut. 33: 2–29. In certain of its sections it

seems to reflect a situation earlier than that in the Blessing of
Moses; Levi in Gen. 49: 5 is still a secular tribe, cursed for its
military ferocity, whereas in the Blessing of Moses Levi is
praised for what later became its distinctive place in the life of
Israel, its priestly role (Deut. 33: 8–11). The poem has been
inserted here to stress that the tribes who made up Israel were
no random collection of disparate groups. Their history, far
from being haphazard, was the outworking of a purpose
expressed in the power-charged, dying words of their
eponymous ancestor Jacob/Israel. Much of the material in the
poem is concerned with what we would call secular and
political issues, but we must remember that for Israel all of its
life was set within the framework of God's purposes.

Since the poem contains very old material, the text at times
is uncertain. In some sections a wide variety of interpretations
is possible. For example, verse 21 on Naphtali reads in the
Revised Standard Version:

> 'Naphtali is a hind let loose,
>   that bears comely fawns.'

The N.E.B. reads:

> 'Naphtali is a spreading terebinth
>   putting forth lovely boughs.'

3–4. *Reuben:* Old Testament tradition never questions Reuben's status as Jacob's *first-born*. The tribe of Reuben, however, remained a comparatively insignificant Transjordan
group that did not display the gifts of leadership that ought to
have gone with such a status. Judg. 5: 15 describes it as being
'split into factions', and unable to help the other tribes in the
hour of crisis. Deut. 33: 6 depicts it as a group threatened with
extinction.

4. *turbulent as a flood:* the verdict here is, proud and un-
stable. *you climbed into your father's bed:* see the note on 35: 22.
his concubine's couch: this translation involves changing the
vowels of the traditional Hebrew text which reads 'he

mounted my couch'. The change to 'he' from 'you' is awkward. The Septuagint, followed by the N.E.B., takes the easy way out by changing to 'you'. A slightly different alteration to the final word would enable the line to be translated 'then you defiled my couch to my sorrow'.

5–7. *Simeon and Levi:* the verdict is severe, a curse which implies the dispersion and disintegration of these two groups. Simeon and Levi play no part in the developing political history of Israel. In Deut. 33 there is no mention of Simeon, while Levi has become a priestly caste. In what is said about Simeon and Levi there is a reference back to the savage role they played in the sack of Shechem (chapter 34). *their spades:* this translation of a word of which the meaning is very uncertain (see the N.E.B. footnote) assumes that it is related to the Hebrew word meaning 'to dig'. 'Swords' (Revised Standard Version) or 'knives' have also been suggested. Most of the early versions seem to have been guessing. With a slight change the whole line could be rendered: 'they determined upon violent destruction'.

6. *my heart*, literally, 'my liver', involves changing the vowels of a Hebrew word traditionally understood as 'my honour' or 'my glory'. Since the liver is closely associated with strong emotions in Hebrew psychology, *heart* is a good English equivalent. The traditional text might be defended, however, as meaning 'my being'; 'honour' or 'glory' (literally, 'weight'), indicating the essence of a person. *they hamstrung oxen:* by cutting the tendons in the legs. Such an act is not mentioned in chapter 34, where it is only claimed that they seized the livestock. In war, seizure of livestock is legitimate, senseless mutilation is not.

7. *I will scatter them in Jacob:* it is clear from this statement that although this section on Simeon and Levi is embedded in 'the Testament of Jacob', it cannot be Jacob who is here speaking in the first person. The section is best taken as a prophetic oracle, with God's messenger speaking in God's name. The verdict is therefore God's verdict.

8–12. *Judah:* this long and highly eulogistic section on Judah contrasts sharply with the brief reference in the Blessing of Moses (Deut. 33 : 7), where Judah seems to be very much on the fringe of the Israelite federation. Here Judah is acclaimed as the acknowledged head of the tribal federation, successful and powerful, establishing a dynasty which will usher in an age of paradisal bounty. It touches upon themes which are developed at length in some of the royal psalms (e.g. Pss. 72 and 89). It presupposes the establishment of the Davidic monarchy and the state of Judah.

8. *your brothers shall praise you:* a play on the name Judah, since the verb 'to praise' in Hebrew contains the three letters in 'Judah'.

9. *you lion's whelp:* lions were common in the ancient Near East. As symbols of power and ferocity they are associated with various gods and goddesses. Amos 1 : 2 says 'The LORD roars from Zion'; *lion's whelp* is therefore a good description of the overmastering power and strength of Judah. Possibly on the basis of this passage, the future king or Messiah is referred to as 'the Lion from the tribe of Judah' (Rev. 5 : 5). *like a lion:* or 'lioness' (see the N.E.B. footnote). It is probable that the word used here refers to a different species or breed of lions. It is doubtful whether 'lioness' is correct. English is poorly supplied with words for different species or stages of a lion's life: Job 4 : 10–11 uses five different words. *who dare rouse you:* there is no need to change the Hebrew 'him' (see the N.E.B. footnote) to *you.* The lion simile is continued in this phrase; Judah is like a lion who ought not to be meddled with.

10. *The sceptre* and *the staff* symbolize authority, the authority either of a tribal chieftain or a king. *from his descendants:* the literal meaning, 'from between his feet' (see the N.E.B. footnote), may be defended in terms of the picture of a chief or king occupying his seat of authority, with the symbols of that authority lying on the ground at his feet. The translation *from his descendants* assumes, as do certain of the versions, that the phrase 'between his feet' is a euphemism for

procreation; cp. Deut. 28: 57 where the literal Hebrew, 'which comes from between her feet', is translated by the N.E.B.: 'the afterbirth which she expels'. *so long as tribute is brought to him*: the meaning of the text here has been endlessly discussed, and it is doubtful whether there can be any certainty. There are broadly three approaches:

(i) the text contains a reference to the place-name Shiloh. Thus we may translate 'until he comes to Shiloh' (see the N.E.B. footnote). But what then is the point of the reference to Shiloh? According to Josh. 18 it was at Shiloh, destined to be one of the important religious centres in the early period of the settlement in Canaan, that the land of Canaan was divided out among the tribes. The text might then mean that Judah was to be the acknowledged military leader until the battle to secure the settlement was over. Nowhere, however, in Joshua or Judges is there any hint that Judah did play such a decisive role. It would also be possible to translate 'until Shiloh comes', but in this case we do not know who Shiloh was, nor is there any real justification for the later view that Shiloh was one of the titles of the coming king or Messiah;

(ii) with many of the versions translate 'until he comes to whom it belongs' (Revised Standard Version), the 'it' in this case referring to rule or dominion. This could be taken as a cryptic prophecy of the emergence of the Davidic dynasty in Judah or of the coming of the Messiah;

(iii) the N.E.B. rendering, *so long as tribute is brought to him*, involves a redivision of words, but makes good sense in context and continues the thought expressed in the first half of the verse. Judah's power will last so long as others are prepared to recognize it and continue to pay the tribute that vassals ought to pay to their overlord.

11. This gives a picture of paradise on earth, nature limitless in her bounty, *the vine* so common that asses are tethered to it, *wine* so abundant that people wash their clothes in it (cp. Amos 9: 13–14).

12. *Darker than wine . . . whiter than milk:* vigorous vitality

and health, deep, dark eyes, shining white teeth. The Revised Standard Version translation

> 'his eyes shall be red with wine
> and his teeth white with milk'

is equally valid, and continues the picture of nature's bounty; people able to have their fill of the good things of life, be they wine or milk.

13. *Zebulun:* a brief notice of Zebulun's maritime position. In Deut. 33: 18–19 Zebulun and Issachar are both associated with the sea. This fact was worth noting, for the Hebrews on the whole were not a maritime people. The Zebulun group, like many another, seems to have moved at different times in its history, Josh. 19: 10–16 locating the tribe inland in Galilee. *sea-shore . . . shore:* a good attempt to preserve something of the flavour of the original, with its twofold occurrence of a Hebrew word which, when first used, means *shore* and, if the text is correct, secondly means something like *haven*.

14–15. *Issachar:* is castigated for exchanging robust independence for the self-satisfied serfdom of life in the Canaanite-dominated fertile valleys. Issachar is caustically described as a docile, if well-fed, beast of burden. The tribe was evidently not always so docile; it is warmly commended in Judg. 5: 15 for fighting alongside the other tribes against the Canaanites.

14. *gelded ass:* this follows the Samaritan text (see the N.E.B. footnote). The Hebrew text might be rendered 'rawboned'. *lying down in the cattle-pens:* thus domesticated and well-cared for. The meaning of the word translated *cattle-pens*, however, is disputed. Another possible translation is 'crouching between the saddle-bags', a vivid description of a beast of burden.

16–17. *Dan:* The tribe of Dan migrated from the south to occupy territory in the north of Canaan (see Judg. 18). It was always a fairly small tribe, small but deadly against its enemies, says this section, as deadly as a snake that can unseat a horse-

man. *how insignificant his people:* this translation assumes giving
to a word which usually means 'judge' a meaning not
clearly found elsewhere in the Old Testament, but with a
parallel in Arabic. The emphasis upon Dan being insignificant
fits in well with verse 17. There seems little reason, however,
to depart from the more traditional translation, 'Dan shall
judge his people' (see the N.E.B. footnote) a rendering which
involves the same kind of play on the name Dan as in 30: 6
(see the note). The verb translated 'judge', can also mean
'plead for', the meaning being that Dan, one of the smallest
tribes, pleads for status as part of the tribal federation.

18. The relationship between this verse and the preceding
verses is uncertain. It may be an insertion by a pious scribe,
sparked off by the thought of the small causing the downfall
of the mighty. When Israel was crushed, as she often was, by
powerful enemies, a man of faith could draw hope from knowing Israel's future was in God's hands: *For thy salvation I wait
in hope, O LORD.* In just such a situation the author of
Isa. 40–55 declares, 'those who look to the LORD will win new
strength' (Isa. 40: 31), where the verb translated 'look to' is
the same as that here translated *wait in hope.*

19. *Gad:* a Transjordan tribe exposed to raiders coming in
from the desert, and capable, in such border conflicts, of
giving as good as it got. Deut. 33: 20 compares Gad to a lion.
The entire statement about Gad plays upon the letters 'g'
and 'd' which are basic to the Hebrew verb translated *raided.*
A different popular explanation of the name *Gad* is given in
30: 11 (see the note).

20. *Asher:* settled along the fertile coast north of Mt
Carmel. It was in close proximity to the Phoenician merchant
cities, and therefore became rich and prosperous, enjoying the
kind of food *fit for a king* (cp. Deut. 33: 24).

21. *Naphtali:* closely linked geographically with Asher,
and according to Deut. 33: 23 'richly favoured'. Very
different translations of this verse are possible. The N.E.B.
by using different vowels replaces the traditional 'hind' by

terebinth, and translates as *boughs* a word which could mean 'lambs' or 'fawns'. Whether it is a spreading terebinth or a fruitful hind, the picture is one of prosperity.

22–6. *Joseph:* textually this is the most difficult section in the entire poem. It seems to be a very early snatch of tribal poetry, since it presupposes that the Joseph group has pre-eminence among the tribes. Joseph is the 'prince among his brothers' (verse 26). It is probably, therefore, earlier than the section on Judah.

22. *a fruitful tree:* while the picture of *Joseph* as *a fruitful tree* or 'ben-tree' (see the N.E.B. footnote) growing beside *a spring* and trailing over a wall, makes sense, the text is very obscure. An alternative translation draws, like many of the other tribal metaphors, upon the animal world, and gives:

> 'Joseph is a wild colt,
>   a wild colt by a spring,
>   wild asses on the hillside.'

This would stress the sturdy independence of Joseph. (A 'ben-tree' is a species of moringa, tall and erect, with very green leaves.)

23–4. The picture now changes to Joseph as a warrior, harried by enemies, but successfully countering their attacks by the power of God.

24. The text in the first half of this verse is uncertain. The N.E.B. translation assumes several alterations to the traditional Hebrew text, some of them following hints in the Septuagint. Yet the Septuagint, like many modern translations, may sometimes be doing no more than guessing. An alternative translation, closer to the Hebrew, might be:

> 'their bows remained for ever rigid
>   and their strong hands trembled'

the Strong One of Jacob: or 'the Champion of Jacob', another divine title linking God with the name of a patriarch. It occurs only here in Genesis, and elsewhere in the Old Testament only in poetic passages (e.g. Ps. 132: 2, 5). *the Shepherd:*

see the note on 48: 15. The Hebrew text reads after *Shepherd* another title for God, the 'Stone *of Israel*' (see the N.E.B. footnote). 'Rock' is a common title for God in parts of the Old Testament (e.g. Deut. 32: 15, 30, 31), but nowhere else is 'Stone' used in this way. Stone, however, is used as a symbol of strength (Job 6: 12) and could appropriately be applied to God.

25–6. These verses contain a blessing which is closely paralleled in thought and language in Deut. 33: 13–16, both passages ending with the same phrase containing a reference to the head and brow of Joseph, 'prince among his brothers'. This blessing is unusual in the patriarchal narratives since it is concerned predominantly with the bounty of nature. It may have been modelled on traditional Canaanite agricultural blessings.

25. *the God of your father:* see the notes on 26: 24; 32: 9–12. *God Almighty:* see the note on 17: 1. *God* is the reading of the Samaritan text (see the N.E.B. footnote). The Hebrew text reads simply *the Almighty*, an abbreviated form of the divine title which appears elsewhere in the patriarchal narratives as *God Almighty. the deep that lurks below:* for *the deep* see the note on 'the abyss' at Gen. 1: 2 (*Genesis 1–11*, pp. 15–16). Perhaps there are echoes here of the chaos goddess of the dark waters, but such dark powers are tamed and at the disposal of the beneficent God of Joseph.

26. *everlasting pools:* it would be better to follow the N.E.B. footnote and read 'everlasting hills' or 'mountains'. The parallel passage in Deut. 33: 15 has 'ancient mountains' and 'everlasting hills' in successive lines. *prince among his brothers:* the Hebrew word *nazir*, translated *prince* means literally 'one set apart' or consecrated. Regulations for a specially 'set apart' religious group, the Nazirites, are to be found in Num. 6: 1–8. Joseph is here 'set apart' to rule, hence *prince*. The word could also mean 'separated from' in a negative sense, hence the translation in the footnote 'the one cursed by'; but this does not make as good sense in context.

27. *Benjamin:* always a small tribe, it gave Israel its first

king in the person of Saul (1 Sam. 9: 1–2). The description of
Benjamin as *a ravening wolf* must not be taken as a condemna-
tion. It is rather a celebration of the fierce vitality and courage
of Benjamin, necessary virtues in a group which had to fight
for survival.

29–33. The P source recounts Jacob's last charge to his
sons, that they should bury him in the family grave at
Machpelah. This section is thus a parallel to 47: 29–31 from the
J source.

33. *he drew his feet up on to the bed:* this expression is found
only here in the Old Testament. It may be similar to our 'he
took to his bed'. *gathered to his father's kin:* see the note on
25: 8. ✻

THE CLOSING SCENES

50 Then Joseph threw himself upon his father, weeping and
2 kissing his face. He ordered the physicians in his service to
3 embalm his father Israel, and they did so, finishing the task
in forty days, which was the usual time for embalming.
4 The Egyptians mourned him for seventy days; and then,
when the days of mourning for Israel were over, Joseph
approached members of Pharaoh's household and said,
'If I can count on your goodwill, then speak for me to
5 Pharaoh; tell him that my father made me take an oath,
saying, "I am dying. Bury me in the grave that I bought*a*
for myself in Canaan." Ask him to let me go up and bury
6 my father, and afterwards I will return.' Pharaoh answered, 'Go and bury your father, as he has made you
7 swear to do.' So Joseph went to bury his father, accompanied by all Pharaoh's courtiers, the elders of his house-
8 hold, and all the elders of Egypt, together with all Joseph's

[a] *Or* dug.

own household, his brothers, and his father's household;
only their dependants, with the flocks and herds, were
left in Goshen. He took with him chariots and horsemen; 9
they were a very great company. When they came to 10
the threshing-floor of Atad beside the river Jordan, they
raised a loud and bitter lament; and there Joseph observed
seven days' mourning for his father. When the Canaanites 11
who lived there saw this mourning at the threshing-floor
of Atad, they said, 'How bitterly the Egyptians are
mourning!'; accordingly they named the place beside the
Jordan Abel-mizraim.*a*

Thus Jacob's sons did what he had told them to do. 12
They took him to Canaan and buried him in the cave on 13
the plot of land at Machpelah, the land which Abraham
had bought as a burial-place from Ephron the Hittite, to
the east of Mamre. Then, after he had buried his father, 14
Joseph returned to Egypt with his brothers and all who
had gone up with him.

When their father was dead Joseph's brothers were 15
afraid and said, 'What if Joseph should bear a grudge
against us and pay us out for all the harm that we did to
him?' They therefore approached*b* Joseph with these 16
words: 'In his last words to us before he died, your father
gave us this message for you: "I ask you to forgive your 17
brothers' crime and wickedness; I know they did you
harm." So now forgive our crime, we beg; for we are
servants of your father's God.' When they said this to him,
Joseph wept. His brothers also wept*c* and prostrated them- 18

[a] *That is* Mourning (*or* Meadow) of Egypt.
[b] *So some Sept. MSS.; Heb.* commanded.
[c] *Prob. rdg.; Heb.* came.

selves before him; they said, 'You see, we are your
19 slaves.' But Joseph said to them, 'Do not be afraid. Am
20 I in the place of God? You meant to do me harm; but
God meant to bring good out of it by preserving the lives
21 of many people, as we see today. Do not be afraid. I will
provide for you and your dependants.' Thus he comforted them and set their minds at rest.

22   Joseph remained in Egypt, he and his father's house-
23 hold. He lived there to be a hundred and ten years old and
saw Ephraim's children to the third generation; he also
recognized as his*a* the children of Manasseh's son Machir.
24 He said to his brothers, 'I am dying; but God will not fail
to come to your aid and take you from here to the land
which he promised on oath to Abraham, Isaac and Jacob.'
25 He made the sons of Israel take an oath, saying, 'When
God thus comes to your aid, you must take my bones
26 with you*b* from here.' So Joseph died at the age of a
hundred and ten. He was embalmed and laid in a coffin in
Egypt.

* All three sources now draw the threads together, and
each, in a different way, brings the patriarchal saga to a conclusion. The P source briefly in verses 12–13 describes how
Jacob's sons fulfil their father's dying charge to bury him 'in
the cave on the plot of land at Machpelah'. Thus in death
Jacob is laid to rest with his fathers in the promised land. The
J source, verses 1–11 and 14, also brings Jacob back to Canaan,
but the burial place is not named. Jacob in his dying words to
Joseph refers to 'the grave I bought for myself in Canaan'
(verse 5), and this can hardly be Machpelah. The mention of
two places east of Jordan may go back to a tradition that

[a] he also recognized as his: *lit.* there were born on his knees.
[b] with you: *so many MSS.; others om.*

Jacob was buried somewhere in Transjordan. This source graphically describes the lengthy embalming process, and the funeral cortège fit for a king, as Jacob takes his last journey accompanied by his sons and an Egyptian military escort. The E source, verses 15–26, is much more interested in the interplay of characters and the underlying theological significance of the story. The long dormant guilty conscience of the brothers has finally to be set at rest, not merely through Joseph's magnaminity, but through God taking the evil they intended and transforming it to serve his own gracious purposes. But the God of the past is also the God of the future. The final promise which Joseph, on his death-bed, extracts from his brothers, looks forward to the exodus and another journey to Canaan.

2. *to embalm his father:* embalming was common Egyptian practice. It was closely related to ideas about death and the possibility of a second life beyond the grave. Here it is presented as merely a convenient method of preserving Jacob's body till it could be carried back to Canaan for burial.

3. *forty days:* embalming was a lengthy and costly process, skilled work; *forty days* is probably intended to be an approximate figure. Egyptian texts vary in the length of time prescribed for embalming. The *seventy days* of mourning corresponds to Egyptian custom; it would include the period for embalming. It is certainly much longer than what was regarded as normal in Israel.

4–6. Joseph's request to Pharaoh for leave to go and bury his father is made through intermediaries. Contact with the dead would probably make him personally unfit to enter the presence of the Egyptian god-king.

5. *the grave that I bought for myself in Canaan:* if we translate *bought* or 'dug' (see the N.E.B. footnote) this statement directly contradicts 47: 30 where Jacob makes Joseph swear to bury him in the grave of his forefathers. It is arguable, however, that 'prepared' or 'made ready' is equally possible as a translation.

7–9. Jacob's impressive funeral cortège. Perhaps in this

solemn journey to Canaan there is foreshadowed another departure from Egypt, in which Pharaoh's *chariots and horsemen* play a very different role, pursuing rather than escorting, and drowning in the sea (see Exod. 15: 19).

10. *the threshing-floor of Atad:* a place east of, rather than *beside the river Jordan*. The cortège makes a détour round the southern end of the Dead Sea and travels north in Trans-jordan. The threshing-floor, usually a flat surface near the village, would be a convenient stopping-place. It is possible, however, that the full name of this place in Hebrew was *Goren ha' atad*, i.e. Briar Threshing Floor.

11. Here we are given a popular explanation of the place-name *Abel-mizraim*. The name ought to mean 'Meadow of Egypt' or 'Creek of Egypt'. The word *abel* however, sounds like the Hebrew word *ebel*, meaning mourning, hence *Abel-mizraim* was interpreted to mean 'Mourning of Egypt' (see the N.E.B. footnote). The name is said to have arisen from the way in which the Egyptians there *bitterly* mourned Jacob.

14. The J source's last comment. Joseph and his brothers *returned to Egypt*. It was there in Egypt that the next act in the drama of Israel's history was to be played.

15. *Joseph's brothers were afraid:* the Hebrew text traditionally read 'saw' instead of *were afraid*, i.e. 'When Joseph's brothers saw that their father was dead, they said' (Revised Standard Version). The translation *were afraid*, however, is more in keeping with what follows – forms of the verbs 'to see' and 'to be afraid' are often confused in Hebrew. The brothers seem to be incapable of grasping that this all-powerful brother had genuinely forgiven them. Their father dead, they expected him to settle old scores.

16–17. There is no record anywhere in the narrative of a dying request by Jacob to Joseph *to forgive your brothers' crime and wickedness*. Such a request is unlikely. Jacob must have assumed from Joseph's actions that he had forgiven. The brothers probably invent this request to steady their nerves.

16. *They therefore approached Joseph:* instead of *approached* the Hebrew text reads 'commanded' (see the N.E.B. foot-note). It could be that the Hebrew should be interpreted as 'they made known to Joseph their father's command'.

17. *we are servants of your father's God:* they appeal not merely to family ties, but to the religious tradition which dominated the family life. *Joseph wept:* see the note on 42: 24. No explanation is given here why he wept. Was it because he was upset to see the way in which the brothers still so mis-understood him that they could think him capable of such an act?

18. *His brothers also wept:* there seems little reason to depart from the traditional Hebrew text which reads, 'His brothers came . . .' They come to throw themselves upon his mercy, and again, unwittingly, fulfil the dreams with which the Joseph story begins (37: 5–11).

19–21. Joseph's reply echoes the words he used when he first revealed his identity to his brothers (45: 5). The same truth, however, is here stated in a slightly different way. It is not a question of personal forgiveness. God has given his verdict, and Joseph does not query it. He asks, *Am I in the place of God?*. God's verdict is clear. Whatever the brothers intended by what they did, God intended, or *meant*, some-thing else. They meant to destroy one man; God used what they did to preserve *the lives of many people*. Out of their evil intentions had come good. Notice the twice repeated *Do not be afraid*; such fear is groundless, though it may be seen as the inevitable expression of their inner doubts and guilt.

22. *a hundred and ten years:* the ideal life-span according to numerous Egyptian documents.

23. It was part of the Hebrew ideal of the full life that you should 'live to see your children's children' (Ps. 128: 6); so Joseph lived to see *Ephraim's children to the third generation*, and also *recognized as his* (see the note on 30: 3) the grandchildren of his other son Manasseh. *Machir:* according to Num. 32: 39–40 the tribe of Machir occupied the district of Gilead.

24–6. Joseph's dying words are of similar import to Jacob's. He dies in Egypt, but makes his brothers take a solemn oath that Egypt will not be his final resting-place.

24. *God will not fail to come to your aid:* this looks forward to the experience of enslavement in Egypt, and to the way in which God, according to the Book of Exodus, came to their aid, literally 'visited' an enslaved people to set them free, and lead them *to the land which he promised on oath to Abraham, Isaac and Jacob.* So the end recalls the beginning: and a man who left his own country in response to a call from God, came to Canaan and there heard God say 'I give this land to your descendants' (12: 7).

25. *with you:* whether we read these words, or with most Hebrew manuscripts omit them (see the N.E.B. footnote), makes no difference to the sense. Exod. 13: 19 describes the fulfilment of this oath: 'Moses took the bones of Joseph with him, because Joseph had exacted an oath from the Israelites.'

26. The closing words are in one sense words of quiet finality; Joseph *embalmed*, lying in a *coffin*, or 'sarcophagus', *in Egypt*. But this is only the end of the beginning. The scene is now set for the events which will ensure that the God of Abraham, Isaac and Jacob will become for all time 'the LORD your God, who brought you out of Egypt, out of the land of slavery' (Exod. 20: 2).   ✳

A NOTE ON FURTHER READING

Fuller and more detailed studies of the text of Genesis 12–50 will be found in the commentaries by G. von Rad, *Genesis*, S.C.M. Old Testament Library, 3rd ed. (S.C.M., 1972) and by B. Vawter, *On Genesis: A New Reading* (Geoffrey Chapman, 1977). The Anchor Bible commentary on *Genesis* (Doubleday & Co., 1966) by E. A. Speiser provides a fresh translation and an excellent introduction to the problem of the literary sources, and sets the material within its wider cultural background. There is still much of value in the older commentaries by S. R. Driver, Westminster Commentaries, 12th ed. (1926) and by J. Skinner, International Critical Commentary (1910). Among the shorter commentaries, of particular value is that by N. M. Sarna, *Understanding Genesis*, The Heritage of Biblical Israel (Schocken Books, 1964); useful also are D. Kidner, Tyndale Old Testament Commentary (Tyndale Press, 1969), C. T. Fritsch, The Layman's Bible Commentary (1963), and H. Gunkel, *The Legends of Genesis* (Schocken Books, 1968).

Comparative material drawn from a rich variety of sources is gathered together in T. H. Gaster, *Myth, Legend, and Custom in the Old Testament* (Harper & Row, 1969), which incorporates much material from J. G. Frazer, *Folklore in the Old Testament* (Macmillan & Co., 1923). The most complete and valuable collection of comparative text material is J. B. Pritchard (ed.), *Ancient Near Eastern Texts relating to the Old Testament* (*A.N.E.T.*), 3rd ed. (Princeton University Press, 1969). Briefer selections of texts with commentary will be found in *Documents from Old Testament Times*, ed. D. Winton Thomas (Nelson & Sons, 1958); and in *Near Eastern Religious Texts relating to the Old Testament*, ed. W. Beyerlin, S.C.M. Old Testament Library (S.C.M., 1978). The question of the historicity of the patriarchal traditions has been much debated in recent years; a useful summary of the problems is contained in 'The Patriarchal Traditions' in *Israelite and Judaean History*, ed. J. H. Hayes and J. M. Miller, pp. 70–148, S.C.M. Old Testament Library (S.C.M., 1977).

INDEX

319